Microsoft·
MCSE
Readiness Review

Exam 70-073
Microsoft Windows NT·
Workstation 4.0

Microsoft Press

PUBLISHED BY
Microsoft Press
A Division of Microsoft Corporation
One Microsoft Way
Redmond, Washington 98052-6399

Library of Congress Cataloging-in-Publication Data
MCSE Readiness Review—Exam 70-073: Microsoft Windows NT Workstation 4.0 /
   Jill L. Spealman.
       p. cm.
   Includes index.
   ISBN 0-7356-0537-8
   1. Electronic data processing personnel--Certification.
  2. Microsoft software--Examinations--Study guides. 3. Microsoft
Windows NT. I. Microsoft Corporation.
QA76.3.M33255 1998
005.4'469--dc21   98-39269
                                     CIP

Printed and bound in the United States of America.

3 4 5 6 7 8 9   QMQM   3 2 1 0 9

Distributed in Canada by ITP Nelson, a division of Thomson Canada Limited.

A CIP catalogue record for this book is available from the British Library.

Microsoft Press books are available through booksellers and distributors worldwide. For further
information about international editions, contact your local Microsoft Corporation office or contact
Microsoft Press International directly at fax (425) 936-7329. Visit our Web site at mspress.microsoft.com.

Program Manager: Jeff Madden
Project Editor: Michael Bolinger

Contents

Welcome to Microsoft Windows NT Workstation 4.0

Welcome to *MCSE Readiness Review—Exam 70-073: Microsoft Windows NT Workstation 4.0*. The Readiness Review series gives you a focused, timesaving way to identify the information you need to know to pass the Microsoft Certified Professional (MCP) exams. The series combines a realistic electronic assessment with a review book to help you become familiar with the types of questions you will encounter on the MCP exam. By reviewing the objectives and sample questions, you can focus on the specific skills that you need to improve before taking the exam.

This book helps you evaluate your readiness for the MCP Exam 70-073: Implementing and Supporting Microsoft Windows NT Workstation 4.0. When you pass this exam, you earn core credit toward the Microsoft Certified Systems Engineer (MCSE) certification, or the Microsoft Certified Systems Engineer + Internet certification.

Note You can find a complete list of MCP exams and their related objectives on the Microsoft Certified Professional Web site at http://www.microsoft.com/mcp.

The Readiness Review series lets you identify any areas in which you may need additional training. To help you get the training you need to successfully pass the certification exams, Microsoft Press publishes a complete line of self-paced training kits and other study materials. For comprehensive information about the topics covered in the Implementing and Supporting Microsoft Windows NT Workstation 4.0 exam, you might want to see the corresponding training kits—*Microsoft Windows NT Network Administration Training* and *Microsoft Windows NT Technical Support Training.*

Before You Begin

This MCSE Readiness Review consists of two main parts: the Readiness Review electronic assessment on the accompanying compact disc, and this Readiness Review book.

The Readiness Review Components

The electronic assessment is a practice certification exam that helps you evaluate your skills. It provides instant scoring feedback, so you can determine areas in which additional study may be helpful before you take the certification exam. Although your score on the electronic assessment does not necessarily indicate what your score will be on the certification exam, it does give you the opportunity to answer questions that are similar to those on the actual certification exam.

The Readiness Review book is organized by the exam's objectives. Each chapter of the book pertains to one of the seven primary groups of objectives on the actual exam, called the Objective Domains. Each Objective Domain lists the tested skills that you need to master to adequately answer the exam questions. Because the certification exams focus on real-world skills, the tested skills lists provide suggested practices that emphasize the practical application of the exam objectives.

Within each Objective Domain you will find the related objectives that are covered on the exam. Each objective provides you with the following:

- Key terms you must know in order to understand the objective, which can help you answer the objective's questions correctly.

- Several sample exam questions with the correct answers. The answers are accompanied by discussions as to why each answer is correct or incorrect. (These questions match the questions you find on the electronic assessment.)

- Suggestions for further reading or additional resources to help you understand the objective and increase your ability to perform the task or skills specified by the objective.

You use the Readiness Review electronic assessment and the book together to determine how well-prepared you are and to identify your needed areas of study. Use the electronic assessment to determine the exam objectives that you need to study, and then use the Readiness Review book to learn more about those particular objectives and discover additional study materials to supplement your knowledge. You can also use the Readiness Review book to research the answers to specific sample test questions. Keep in mind that to pass the exam, you should understand not only the answer to the question, but the concepts on which the correct answer is based.

MCP Exam Prerequisites

No exams or classes are required before you take the Implementing and Supporting Microsoft Windows NT Workstation 4.0 exam. However, in addition to the administration, installation, configuration, and troubleshooting skills tested by the exam, you should have a working knowledge of the administration, operation, and support of hardware and software in stand-alone computers. This knowledge should include:

- Using an operating system with a graphical user interface, such as Microsoft Windows 95, Microsoft Windows 98, or Microsoft Windows NT 4.0.

- Recognizing networking components, including clients, servers, local area networks (LANs), network adapter cards, drivers, protocols, services, and network operating systems.

- Recognizing basic computer hardware components, including memory, hard disks, CPUs, communication and printer ports, display adapters, and pointing devices.

- Installing application software.

- Installing hardware, such as memory, communication peripherals, and disk drives.

- Recognizing common Windows NT administrative tasks, including creating user and group accounts, assigning permissions, sharing folders, and auditing.

- Identifying network and end-user support issues.

Note After you have used the Readiness Review and determined that you are ready for the exam, see the "Test Registration and Fees" section in the Appendix for information on scheduling for the exam. You can schedule exams up to six weeks in advance, or as late as one working day before the exam date.

Know the Products

Microsoft's certification program relies on exams that measure your ability to perform a specific job function or set of tasks. Microsoft develops the exams by analyzing the tasks performed by people who are currently performing the job function. Therefore, the specific knowledge, skills, and abilities relating to the job are reflected in the certification exam.

Because the certification exams are based on real-world tasks, you need to gain hands-on experience with the applicable technology in order to master the exam. In a sense, you might consider hands-on experience in an organizational environment to be a prerequisite for passing an MCP exam. Many of the questions relate directly to Microsoft products or technology, so use opportunities at your organization or home to practice using the relevant tools.

Using the MCSE Readiness Review

Although you can use the Readiness Review in a number of ways, you might start your studies by taking the electronic assessment as a pretest. After completing the exam, review your results for each Objective Domain and focus your studies first on the Objective Domains where you received the lowest scores. The electronic assessment allows you to print your results, and a printed report of how you fared can be useful when reviewing the exam material in this book.

After you have taken the Readiness Review electronic assessment, use the Readiness Review book to learn more about the Objective Domains that you find difficult and to find listings of appropriate study materials that may supplement your knowledge. By reviewing why the answers are correct or incorrect, you can determine if you made a simple comprehension answer or if you need to study the objective topics more.

Alternatively, you can use the Learn Now feature of the electronic assessment to re- view your answer to each question. This feature provides you with the correct answer and a reference to the *Microsoft Windows NT Network Administration Training* and *Microsoft Windows NT Technical Support Training* kits (purchased separately) or other resources. If you use this method, and you need additional information to under- stand an answer, you can also reference the question in the Readiness Review book.

You can also use the Readiness Review book to focus on the exact objectives that you need to master. Each objective in the book contains several questions that help you determine if you understand the information related to that particular skill. The book is designed so that you can answer each question before turning the page to review the correct answer.

The best method to prepare for the MCP exam is to use the Readiness Review book in conjunction with the electronic assessment and other study material. Thoroughly studying and practicing the material combined with substantial real-world experi- ence can help you fully prepare for the MCP exam.

Understanding the Readiness Review Conventions

Before you start using the Readiness Review, it is important that you understand the terms and conventions used in the electronic assessment and book.

Question Numbering System

The Readiness Review electronic assessment and book contain reference numbers for each question. Understanding the numbering format will help you use the Readi- ness Review more effectively. When Microsoft creates the exams, the questions are grouped by job skills called Objectives. These Objectives are then organized by sec- tions known as Objective Domains. Each question can be identified by the Objective Domain and Objective it covers. The question numbers follow this format:

Test Number.Objective Domain.Objective.Question Number

For example, question number 70-073.02.01.003 means this is question three (3) for Objective one (1) in Objective Domain two (2) of the *Implementing and Supporting Microsoft Windows NT Workstation 4.0* exam (70-073). Refer to the "Exam Objectives

Summary" section later in this introduction to locate the numbers associated with particular objectives. Each question is numbered based on its presentation in the printed book. You can use this numbering system to reference questions on the electronic assessment or in the Readiness Review book. Even though the questions in the book are organized by objective, you will see questions in random order during the electronic assessment and actual certification exam.

Notational Conventions

- Characters or commands that you type appear in MONOSPACE.

- Variable information is *italicized*. *Italic* is also used to identify new terms and book titles.

- Acronyms, utilities, and file names appear in FULL CAPITALS.

Icons

The following table describes the icons that are used throughout this book.

Icon	Description
	References a book resource that contains more information pertinent to the discussed subject.
	References a compact disc resource that contains more information pertinent to the discussed subject.
	References a Microsoft Press training kit or Resource Kit that contains more information pertinent to the discussed subject.
	References a Web site that contains more information pertinent to the discussed subject.

Using the Readiness Review Electronic Assessment

The Readiness Review electronic assessment is designed to provide you with an experience that simulates that of the actual MCP exam. The electronic assessment material mirrors the type and nature of the questions you will see on the certification exam. Furthermore, the electronic assessment format approximates the certification exam format and includes additional features to help you prepare for the real examination.

Each iteration of the electronic assessment consists of 60 question covering all the objectives for the *Implementing and Supporting Microsoft Windows NT Workstation 4.0* exam. (The actual certification exams generally consist of 50 to 70 questions.) Just like a real certification exam, you see questions from the objectives in random order during the practice test. Similar to the certification exam, the electronic assessment allows you to mark questions and review them after you finish the test.

To increase its value as a study aid, you can take the electronic assessment multiple times. Each time you are presented with a different set of questions in a revised order; however, some questions may be repeated from exams you may have taken earlier.

If you have used one of the certification exam preparation tests available from Microsoft, then the Readiness Review electronic assessment should look familiar. The difference is that the electronic assessment covers more questions, and it provides you with the ability to learn as you take the exam.

Installing and Running the Electronic Assessment Software

Before you begin using the electronic assessment, you need to install the software. You need a computer with the following minimum configuration:

- 486 or higher Intel-based processor.

- Microsoft Windows 95 or later (including Windows NT).

- 4 MB of RAM.

- 15 MB of available disk space.

- CD-ROM drive.

- Mouse or other pointing device (recommended).

▶   **To install the electronic assessment**

1. Insert the Readiness Review compact disc into your CD-ROM drive.

2. From the root directory of the compact disc, open the Assess folder and double-click the Setup.exe file.

   A dialog box appears indicating you will install the MCSE Readiness Review test.

3. Click Next.

   The Select Destination Directory dialog box appears showing a default installation directory (named C:\MP073, where C: is the name assigned to your hard disk).

4. Either accept the default or change the installation directory if needed, and then click Next.

   The electronic assessment software installs.

Note These procedures describe using the electronic assessment on a computer running Windows 95, Windows 98, or Windows NT 4.0.

▶ **To start the electronic assessment**

1. From the Start menu, point to Programs, point to MCSE Readiness Review, and then click (70-073) Windows NT Workstation 4.0.

   The electronic assessment program starts.

2. Click Start Test, or from the main menu, double-click the test name.

   Information about the MCSE Readiness Review series appears.

3. Click Start Test.

Taking the Electronic Assessment

The Readiness Review electronic assessment consists of 60 multiple-choice questions, and as in the certification exam, you can skip, or mark, questions for later review. Each exam question contains a reference number that you can use to refer back to the Readiness Review book, and, if you want, you can pause and continue taking the exam at a later time. Before you end the electronic assessment, you should make sure to answer all the questions. When the exam is graded, unanswered questions are counted as incorrect and will lower your score. Similarly, on the actual certification exam you should complete all questions or they will be counted as incorrect.

No trick questions appear on the exam. The correct answer will always be among the list of choices. Some questions may require more than one response, and this will be indicated in the question. A good strategy is to eliminate the most obvious incorrect answers first to make it easier for you to select the correct answer.

You have 75 minutes to complete the electronic assessment. During the exam you will see a timer indicating the amount of time you have remaining. This will help you to gauge the amount of time you should use to answer each question and to complete the exam. The amount of time you are given on the actual certification exam varies with each exam. Generally, certification exams take approximately 90 minutes to complete.

During the electronic assessment, you can find the answer to each question by clicking the Learn Now button as you review the question. You see the correct answer and a reference to the applicable section of the Microsoft Press *Microsoft Windows NT Network Administration Training* and *Microsoft Windows NT Technical Support Training* kits and other resources, which can be purchased separately.

Ending and Grading the Electronic Assessment

By clicking the Grade Now button, you have the opportunity to review the questions you marked or left incomplete. This format is similar to the actual certification exam. When you are satisfied with your answers, click the Grade Test button. The electronic assessment is graded, and the software presents your section and total score.

Note You can always end a test without grading your electronic assessment by clicking the Quit Test button.

After your electronic assessment is graded, you can view a list of Microsoft Press references by clicking the Replay button. You can then click Review Incorrect Answers to view the questions you have missed.

Interpreting the Electronic Assessment Results

The Section Scoring screen shows you the number of questions in each Objective Domain section, the number of questions you answered correctly, and a percentage grade for each section. You can use the Section Scoring screen to determine where to spend additional time studying. On the actual certification exam, the number of questions and passing score will depend on the exam you are taking. The electronic assessment records your score each time you grade an exam so you can track your progress over time.

▶ **To view your progress and exam records**

1. From the electronic assessment main menu, select File, then select History, and then choose View.

2. Click View History.

   Each attempt score and your total score appears.

3. Select an attempt, and then click View Details.

   The section score for each attempt appears. You can review the section score information to determine which Objective Domains you should study further. You can also use the scores to determine your progress as you continue to study and prepare for the real exam.

Ordering More Questions

Self Test Software offers practice tests to help you prepare for a variety of MCP certification exams. These practice tests contain hundreds of additional questions and are similar to the Readiness Review electronic assessment. For a fee, you can order exam practice tests for this exam and other Microsoft certification exams. Click on the To Order More Questions button on the electronic assessment main menu for more information.

Using the Readiness Review Book

You can use the Readiness Review book as a supplement to the Readiness Review electronic assessment, or as a stand-alone study aid. If you decide to use the book as a stand-alone study aid, review the Table of Contents or the list of objectives to find topics of interest or an appropriate starting point for you. To get the greatest benefit from the book, use the electronic assessment as a pretest to determine the Objective Domains where you should spend the most study time. Or, if you would like to re-search specific questions while taking the electronic assessment, you can use the question number located on the question screen to reference the question number in the Readiness Review book.

One way to determine areas where additional study may be helpful is to carefully review your individual section scores from the electronic assessment and note objec-tive areas where your score could be improved. The section scores correlate to the Objective Domains listed in the Readiness Review book.

Reviewing the Objectives

Each Objective Domain in the book contains an introduction and a list of practice skills. Each list of practice skills describes suggested tasks you can perform to help you understand the objectives. Some of the tasks suggest reading additional material, while others are hands-on practices with software or hardware. You should pay par-ticular attention to the hands-on suggestions, as the certification exam reflects real-world knowledge you can gain only by working with the software or technology. Increasing your real-world experience with the relevant products and technologies will greatly enhance your performance on the exam.

Once you have determined the objectives you would like to study, you can use the Table of Contents to locate the objectives in the Readiness Review book. When re-viewing a specific objective, you should make sure you understand the purpose of the objective and the skill or knowledge it is measuring on the certification exam. You can study each objective separately, but you may need to understand the concepts explained in other objectives.

Make sure you understand the key terms for each objective. You will need a thorough understanding of these terms to answer the objective's questions correctly. Key term definitions are located in the Glossary of this book.

Reviewing the Questions

Each odd-numbered page contains one or two questions followed by the possible answers. After you review the question and select a probable answer, you can turn to the following page to determine if you answered the question correctly. (For information about the question numbering format, see "Question Numbering System," earlier in this introduction.)

The Readiness Review briefly discusses each possible answer and provides a specific reason why each answer is correct or incorrect. You should review the discussion of each possible answer to help you understand why the correct answer is the best answer among the choices given. You should understand not only the answer to the question, but the concepts on which the correct answer is based. If you feel you need more information about a topic or you do not understand the answer, use the Further Reading section in each objective to learn where you can find more information.

The answers to the questions in the Readiness Review are based on current industry specifications and standards. However, the information provided by the answers is subject to change as technology improves and changes.

Exam Objectives Summary

The *Implementing and Supporting Microsoft Windows NT Workstation 4.0* (70-073) exam measures your ability to administer, implement, support, and troubleshoot Windows NT Workstation 4.0. Before taking the exam, you should be proficient with the job skills presented in the following sections. The sections provide the exam objectives and the corresponding objective numbers (which you can use to reference the questions in the Readiness Review electronic assessment and book) grouped by Objective Domains.

Objective Domain 1: Planning

The objectives in Objective Domain 1 are as follows:

- Objective 1.1 (70-073.01.01)—Create unattended installation files.

- Objective 1.2 (70-073.01.02)—Plan strategies for sharing and securing resources.

- Objective 1.3 (70-073.01.03)—Choose the appropriate file system to use in a given situation. File systems and situations include: NTFS, FAT, HPFS, security, and dual-boot systems.

Objective Domain 2: Installation and Configuration

The objectives in Objective Domain 2 are as follows:

- Objective 2.1 (70-073.02.01)—Install Windows NT Workstation on an Intel platform in a given situation.

- Objective 2.2 (70-073.02.02)—Set up a dual-boot system in a given situation.

- Objective 2.3 (70-073.02.03)—Remove Windows NT Workstation in a given situation.

- Objective 2.4 (70-073.02.04)—Install, configure, and remove hardware components for a given situation. Hardware components include: network adapter drivers, SCSI device drivers, tape device drivers, UPS, multimedia devices, display drivers, keyboard drivers, and mouse drivers.

- Objective 2.5 (70-073.02.05)—Use Control Panel applications to configure a Windows NT Workstation computer in a given situation.

- Objective 2.6 (70-073.02.06)—Upgrade to Windows NT Workstation 4.0 in a given situation.

- Objective 2.7 (70-073.02.07)—Configure server-based installation for wide-scale deployment in a given situation.

Objective Domain 3: Managing Resources

The objectives in Objective Domain 3 are as follows:

- Objective 3.1 (70-073.03.01)—Create and manage local user accounts and local group accounts to meet given requirements.

- Objective 3.2 (70-073.03.02)—Set up and modify user profiles.

- Objective 3.3 (70-073.03.03)—Set up shared folders and permissions.

- Objective 3.4 (70-073.03.04)—Set permissions on NTFS partitions, folders, and files.

- Objective 3.5 (70-073.03.05)—Install and configure printers in a given environment.

Objective Domain 4: Connectivity

The objectives in Objective Domain 4 are as follows:

- Objective 4.1 (70-073.04.01)—Add and configure the network components of Windows NT Workstation.

- Objective 4.2 (70-073.04.02)—Use various methods to access network resources.

- Objective 4.3 (70-073.04.03)—Implement Windows NT Workstation as a client in a NetWare environment.

- Objective 4.4 (70-073.04.04)—Use various configurations to install Windows NT Workstation as a TCP/IP client.

- Objective 4.5 (70-073.04.05)—Configure and install Dial-Up Networking in a given situation.

- Objective 4.6 (70-073.04.06)—Configure Microsoft Peer Web Services in a given situation.

Objective Domain 5: Running Applications

The objectives in Objective Domain 5 are as follows:

- Objective 5.1 (70-073.05.01)—Start applications on Intel and RISC platforms in various operating system environments.

- Objective 5.2 (70-073.05.02)—Start applications at various priorities.

Objective Domain 6: Monitoring and Optimization

The objectives in Objective Domain 6 are as follows:

- Objective 6.1 (70-073.06.01)—Monitor system performance by using various tools.

- Objective 6.2 (70-073.06.02)—Identify and resolve a given performance problem.

- Objective 6.3 (70-073.06.03)—Optimize system performance in various areas.

Objective Domain 7: Troubleshooting

The objectives in Objective Domain 7 are as follows:

- Objective 7.1 (70-073.07.01) — Choose the appropriate course of action to take when the boot process fails.

- Objective 7.2 (70-073.07.02) — Choose the appropriate course of action to take when a print job fails.

- Objective 7.3 (70-073.07.03) — Choose the appropriate course of action to take when the installation process fails.

- Objective 7.4 (70-073.07.04) — Choose the appropriate course of action to take when an application fails.

- Objective 7.5 (70-073.07.05) — Choose the appropriate course of action to take when a user cannot access a resource.

- Objective 7.6 (70-073.07.06) — Modify the registry using the appropriate tool in a given situation.

- Objective 7.7 (70-073.07.07) — Implement advanced techniques to resolve various problems.

Getting More Help

A variety of resources are available to help you study for the exam. Your options include instructor-led classes, seminars, self-paced kits, or other learning materials. The materials described here are created to prepare you for MCP exams. Each training resource fits a different type of learning style and budget.

Microsoft Official Curriculum (MOC)

Microsoft Official Curriculum (MOC) courses are technical training courses developed by Microsoft product groups to educate computer professionals who use Microsoft technology. The courses are developed with the same objectives used for Microsoft certification, and MOC courses are available to support most exams for the MCSE certification. The courses are available in instructor-led, online, or self-paced formats to fit your preferred learning style.

Self-Paced Training

Microsoft Press self-paced training kits cover a variety of Microsoft technical products. The self-paced kits, which are based on MOC courses, feature self-paced lessons, hands-on practices, multimedia presentations, practice files, and demonstration software. They can help you understand the concepts and get the experience you need to prepare for the corresponding MCP exam.

To help you prepare for the *Implementing and Supporting Microsoft Windows NT Workstation 4.0* 70-073 MCP exam, Microsoft has written the *Microsoft Windows NT Network Administration Training* and *Microsoft Windows NT Technical Support Training* kits. With these official self-paced training kits, you can learn how to implement and support Microsoft Windows NT Workstation 4.0. These kits give you training for the real world by offering hands-on training through CD-ROM-based network simulation exercises.

MCP Approved Study Guides

MCP Approved Study Guides, available through several organizations, are learning tools that help you prepare for MCP exams. The study guides are available in a variety of formats to match your learning style, including books, compact discs, online content, and videos. These guides come in a wide range of prices to fit your budget.

Microsoft Seminar Series

Microsoft Solution Providers and other organizations are often a source of information to help you prepare for an MCP exam. For example, many solution providers will present seminars to help industry professionals understand a particular product technology such as networking. For information on all Microsoft-sponsored events, visit http://www.microsoft.com/events.

Planning

The Planning Domain examines the basic steps necessary for implementing Windows NT Workstation in an organization. These steps include:

- Creating unattended installation files.

- Planning strategies for sharing and securing resources.

- Choosing the appropriate file system to use in a given situation.

Unattended Windows NT Workstation installation can reduce the cost of migration by allowing you to predefine responses to prompts that appear during setup. If you need to conduct a similar installation more than five times, you should consider planning for an unattended installation.

Sharing resources, such as printers and folders, can reduce network traffic and save hard-disk space on the server. If the security needs at your site allow resource sharing, you should consider planning which resources may be shared.

When implementing Windows NT Workstation, you must choose one of two supported file systems, either the *Windows NT File System* (NTFS) or *file allocation table* (FAT) file system, for each partition you create. The system you choose depends entirely on the system configuration and the needs of your organization. For example, situations requiring the highest security levels must use NTFS, while situations requiring dual-boot capability between Windows NT and other operating systems must use the FAT file system.

Before implementing Windows NT Workstation in your organization, you must gather the information and resources you need to make the necessary decisions regarding these steps.

Tested Skills and Suggested Practices

- Creating unattended installation files. You should be able to create unattended installation files used to automate a Windows NT Workstation installation.

  - Practice 1: Using the Windows NT Setup Manager, create an unattended answer file that predefines responses to prompts that appear during Windows NT Workstation setup.

  - Practice 2: Learn the purpose and structure of uniqueness data files (UDFs) and how they work with unattended answer files during a Windows NT Workstation installation. Read about how these files are indexed using uniqueness IDs.

  - Practice 3: Learn the purpose and structure of device information files and how they may be required to work with unattended answer files during a Windows NT Workstation installation. Read about how these files allow remote installation of software for hardware devices or applications.

- Planning strategies for sharing and securing resources. Be able to determine the folders and resources, such as printers, that may be shared for a given configuration, depending on user and security needs.

  - Practice 1: Determine how to configure computers using various operating systems and Windows NT Workstation computers to share folders. Learn the folder share permissions and how they work when assigned to users, groups, or both.

  - Practice 2: Determine how to set printer user permissions and printer priority levels based on user and security needs. Learn the printer user permissions and how they work when assigned to users, groups, or both.

- Choosing the appropriate file system to use in a given situation. You must be able to determine the appropriate file system (either NTFS or FAT) for a situation.

  - Practice 1: Learn the requirements, advantages, and disadvantages of the NTFS and FAT file systems. Read why NTFS is the preferred Windows NT file system.

  - Practice 2: Contrast the effects of copying and moving a folder between or within NTFS and FAT file systems on the folder's disk compression attribute. Read how to manage NTFS file compression.

OBJECTIVE   1.1

Create unattended installation files.

Running an unattended installation of Windows NT Workstation can help reduce the cost of migration by providing for a fast remote installation. Begin planning for unattended installations when you are specifying the preferred client configuration. Make sure that you document each feature needed, so that you can automate the selection of those features.

There are three types of unattended installation files: answer files, uniqueness database files, and device information files. Unattended answer files let you predefine responses to prompts that appear during Windows NT Workstation Setup. UDFs work along with unattended answer files and let users provide information specific to their computers or groups of computers during setup. Device information files provide the Windows NT Setup program with information needed to install software that supports a specific hardware device or to install software applications that must be installed interactively.

Questions related to this objective are designed to determine if you have an awareness of these issues. To successfully answer the questions for this objective, you need a firm understanding of several key terms. For definitions of these terms, refer to the Glossary in this book.

Key Terms

- Answer file

- Difference file

- GUI-mode setup

- Text-mode setup

- Unattended installation

- Uniqueness database file

- Uniqueness IDs

70-073.01.01.001

Which two methods can you use to create answer files for unattended installation of Windows NT Workstation on Pentium-based computers?

A. Modifying the sample SETUP.TXT file located on the Windows NT Server compact disc

B. Modifying the sample UNATTEND.TXT file located on the Windows NT Server compact disc

C. Using the Setup Manager utility located in the LANGPACK folder on the Windows NT Workstation compact disc

D. Using the Setup Manager utility located in the SUPPORT\DEPTOOLS\I386 folder on the Windows NT Server compact disc

70-073.01.01.001

Which two methods can you use to create answer files for unattended installation of Windows NT Workstation on Pentium-based computers?

▶ **Correct Answers: B and D**

A. **Incorrect:** SETUP.TXT cannot be used to create an answer file. This file contains important material pertaining to the Windows NT Setup program that is not available in documentation or in Help, as well as information on changes that occurred after publicationYou may modify the UNATTEND.TXT file to create answer files for an unattended installation.

B. **Correct:** Modifying the sample UNATTEND.TXT file (located on the Windows NT Server compact disc) for your platform is one method of creating an answer file for unattended installation. The unattended answer file consists of several sections that contain information used during the installation.

C. **Incorrect:** The Setup Manager utility is not located in the LANGPACK folder and cannot be used to create an answer file from this folder. The LANGPACK folder allows you to add additional language support. You may use the Setup Manager utility located in the SUPPORT\DEPTOOLS\I386 folder to create answer files for an unattended installation.

D. **Correct:** Using the Setup Manager utility located in the SUPPORT\DEPTOOLS\I386 folder is one method of creating an answer file for unattended installation. The unattended answer file consists of several sections that contain information used during the installation.

70-073.01.01.002

You want to perform an unattended installation of Windows NT Workstation on 20 Pentium-based computers. Which installation file should you create to specify data, such as network settings, used during text-mode setup?

A. An answer file

B. A difference file

C. A setup table file

D. A uniqueness database file

70-073.01.01.002

You want to perform an unattended installation of Windows NT Workstation on 20 Pentium-based computers. Which installation file should you create to specify data, such as network settings, used during text-mode setup?

▶ **Correct Answer: A**

A. **Correct:** The answer file is a script you create to run an unattended installation. The file can provide answers during text-mode setup that a user would otherwise be prompted for during the GUI-mode setup. You can make unattended answer files for the various setup configurations used in your organization, such as network settings, and then customize them with UDFs as needed.

B. **Incorrect:** The difference file is used along with the SYSDIFF utility in the OEM directory to allow you to preinstall applications that do not support a scripted installation.

C. **Incorrect:** The setup table file contains setup parameters for Internet Explorer 4.0 and Microsoft Office 97 Professional and is not used in an unattended installation to specify data, such as network settings, used during text-mode setup.

D. **Incorrect:** In an unattended installation, uniqueness database files work along with the answer file to provide replacements for sections of the answer file or to supply additional sections. These replacements or additional sections would be necessary when the information (such as the computer name) must be unique to each computer. You can use an answer file for information that applies to all users (such as network settings) and one or more uniqueness database files to supply information that is specific to a single computer or a small group of computers.

70-073.01.01.003

You are planning an unattended installation of Windows NT Workstation on Alpha-based computers connected to a local area network (LAN). How should the answer file be configured if you want to include additional files and applications in the installation process?

A. The line `OEMBootFiles=Yes` should be added to the [Network] section.

B. The line `OEMPreinstall=Yes` should be added to the [Unattended] section.

C. A section for each computer that contains the username and computer name should be created.

D. A section for each computer that contains the media access control (MAC) address of the network adapter should be created.

70-073.01.01.003

You are planning an unattended installation of Windows NT Workstation on Alpha-based computers connected to a local area network (LAN). How should the answer file be configured if you want to include additional files and applications in the installation process?

▶ **Correct Answer: B**

A. **Incorrect:** Adding the line OEMBootFiles=Yes to the [Network] section allows you to install onto *x*86 computers. This action would not allow you to include additional files and applications.

B. **Correct:** To include additional files and applications in the installation process, the line OEMPreinstall=Yes must be present in the [Unattended] section. A Yes value indicates that the Windows NT Setup program might need to install some original equipment manufacturer-(OEM-) supplied files located in subdirectories of OEM. A No value implies that the Windows NT Setup program will perform a regular unattended installation. The [Unattended] section can be specified only in the answer file, not in the UDF.

C. **Incorrect:** Creating a section for each computer that contains the username and computer name results in customizing individual user and computer names for the installation and is more effective when configured in the UDF file rather than the answer file. This action would not allow you to include additional files and applications.

D. **Incorrect:** Creating a section for each computer that contains the MAC address of the network adapter results in customizing the MAC address for the installation and is more effective when configured in the UDF file rather than the answer file. This action would not allow you to include additional files and applications.

70-073.01.01.004

You are planning an unattended installation of Windows NT Workstation on Intel-based computers connected to a LAN. How should the uniqueness database file be configured if you want to customize individual user and computer names?

A. The line `OEMBootFiles=Yes` should be added to the [Network] section.

B. The line `OEMPreinstall=Yes` should be added to the [Unattended] section.

C. A section that contains the username and computer name should be created for each computer.

D. A section that contains the MAC address of the network adapter should be created for each computer.

70-073.01.01.004

You are planning an unattended installation of Windows NT Workstation on Intel-based computers connected to a LAN. How should the uniqueness database file be configured if you want to customize individual user and computer names?

▶ **Correct Answer: C**

A. **Incorrect:** Adding the line OEMBootFiles=Yes to the [Network] section allows you to install onto *x*86 computers and must be configured in the UDF file, not the answer file. This action would not allow you to customize individual usernames and computer names.

B. **Incorrect:** Adding the line OEMPreinstall=Yes to the [Unattended] section allows you to include additional files and applications in the installation process and must be configured in the UDF file, not the answer file. This action would not allow you to customize individual usernames and computer names.

C. **Correct:** To customize individual usernames and computer names for the installation you must create a UDF for each computer with a section that contains the username and computer name. The user can then run a customized installation by specifying the appropriate answer and UDF file when running WINNT.EXE or WINNT32.EXE.

D. **Incorrect:** Creating a section for each computer that contains the MAC address of the network adapter results in customizing the MAC address for the installation. This action would not allow you to customize individual usernames and computer names.

70-073.01.01.005

Which unattended installation file is used by the Windows NT Workstation Setup program to install software to support a hardware device?

A. The *device information file* (INF)

B. The *text* (TXT) file

C. The *uniqueness database file* (UDF)

D. The *setup table file* (STF)

70-073.01.01.005

Which unattended installation file is used by the Windows NT Workstation Setup program to install software to support a hardware device?

▶ **Correct Answer: A**

A. **Correct:** Device information files (INF files) provide information used by the Windows NT Workstation Setup program to install software that supports a given hardware device. You create the INF and place it in the OEM directory.

B. **Incorrect:** The TXT file is the answer file that automates the installation. You cannot install software to support a hardware device using the TXT file; the INF file is used. However, for the INF file to be invoked, you must edit the answer (TXT) file, adding the line `OEMPreinstall=Yes` to the Unattended section.

C. **Incorrect:** The UDF file works with the answer file to provide customized sections of the unattended installation. You cannot install software to support a hardware device using the UDF file.

D. **Incorrect:** You cannot install software to support a hardware device using the STF file.

Further Reading

 The *Microsoft Windows NT Technical Support* volume of the *Microsoft Windows NT Technical Support Training* kit Chapter 2, Lesson 5 contains basic information on performing an unattended installation, including creating answer files and creating uniqueness database files. Practice in creating an unattended TXT file and performing an unattended setup is included on the CD provided in this training kit.

 The *Microsoft Windows NT Workstation Resource Kit* Chapter 2 contains detailed information on customizing the installation of Windows NT Workstation, including information on answer files, uniqueness database files, the OEM directory, the OEM\$$ directory, and the SYSDIFF utility. Appendix A contains in-depth information on the structure of answer files and UDFs.

Use Microsoft Technical Support Online (http://support.microsoft.com) to search for "Windows NT Workstation" and for the question "unattended installation." Then when the results list is displayed, click "Windows NT Server and Workstation Deployment and Unattended Setup Questions."

OBJECTIVE 1.2

Plan strategies for sharing and securing resources.

Sharing lets you share folders and resources, such as printers, with other computers. Begin planning for sharing needs when you are specifying the preferred client configuration.

Shared folders save disk space by providing authorized users with centralized access to network programs, data, and user home programs. Centralized network programs allow you to configure and upgrade software in one location and avoid maintenance in multiple client locations. Centralized data allows users to access and store common files. Centralized user home programs provide a secure backup area for users' data. You can assign folder share permissions—Full Control, Change, Read, and No Access—to specific users, groups, or both.

Shared printers allow greater flexibility in the print process by allowing you to set printer permissions and printer priority depending on user needs. Printer permissions—Full Control, Manage Documents, Print, and No Access—control who can print and which tasks they can perform. However, most users require only the print permission.

Printer priority determines which documents are printed first. You can assign various printer priorities from 1 (low) to 99 (high) to two or more printers (software interfaces) for the same print device (printer hardware). Users can be set up to print automatically to the appropriate priority-based printer, depending on their needs, or they can manually select the printer with the appropriate priority.

Questions related to this objective are designed to determine if you have an awareness of these issues. To successfully answer the questions for this objective, you need a firm understanding of several key terms. For definitions of these terms, refer to the Glossary in this book.

Key Terms

- Group

- Print device

- Printer

- Printer permissions

- Printer priority

- Shared resource

- Workgroup

70-073.01.02.001

You have a Windows NT Workstation–based computer that participates in a workgroup. The only operating systems in use on the workgroup are Windows 95 and Windows NT Workstation. If you want to access a shared folder on a computer running Windows 95, what should you do? (Choose all that apply.)

A. Install File and Printer Sharing for Microsoft Networks.

B. Ensure that both computers are running a common protocol.

C. Configure the computer running Windows 95 for share-level security.

D. Edit the access control list on the computer running Windows 95 to include your username and password.

70-073.01.02.002

You want to share the printer connected to a Windows NT Workstation computer with ten other users. How should you configure the user permissions if you want to allow users to send print jobs to the printer and to pause, resume, or delete only their own jobs?

A. Assign Print permission to the individual users.

B. Assign Manage Documents permission to the individual users.

C. Assign Print permission to a user group, and add the users to the group.

D. Assign Manage Documents permission to a user group, and add the users to the group.

70-073.01.02.001

You have a Windows NT Workstation–based computer that participates in a workgroup. The only operating systems in use on the workgroup are Windows 95 and Windows NT Workstation. If you want to access a shared folder on a computer running Windows 95, what should you do? (Choose all that apply.)

▶ **Correct Answers: A, B, and C**

    A. **Correct:** Before a Windows NT Workstation user can share a folder or other resource on a computer running Windows 95, the computer must have File and Printer Sharing services installed, using the Network option in the Control Panel.

    B. **Correct:** Before a Windows NT Workstation user can share a folder or other resource on a computer running Windows 95, all the computers must be running a common protocol.

    C. **Correct:** Before a Windows NT Workstation user can share a folder or other resource on a computer running Windows 95, the computer must be configured for share-level or user-level security.

    D. **Incorrect:** The access control list for the computer running Windows 95 is actually stored on a server in a centralized database. Therefore, you must have a Windows NT Server or NetWare domain controller running to use an access control list to access a shared folder on the Windows 95 computer. This scenario uses a workgroup and does not use a domain controller.

70-073.01.02.002

You want to share the printer connected to a Windows NT Workstation computer with ten other users. How should you configure the user permissions if you want to allow users to send print jobs to the printer and to pause, resume, or delete only their own jobs?

▶ **Correct Answer: C**

    A. **Incorrect:** The Print permission does allow users to send print jobs to the printer and to pause, resume, or delete their own jobs. However, assigning this permission to individuals is less efficient than assigning the permission to a user group and then assigning individuals to that user group.

    B. **Incorrect:** The Manage Documents permission allows users to change the status of any print job submitted by any user, which is not what this scenario requires. In addition, assigning this permission to individuals is less efficient than assigning the permission to a user group and then assigning individuals to that user group.

    C. **Correct:** The Print permission allows users to send print jobs to the printer and to pause, resume, or delete their own jobs. Selecting the Print permission, assigning this permission to a user group, and then adding the users to the group is the most efficient way to establish printer security.

    D. **Incorrect:** The Manage Documents permission allows users to change the status of any print job submitted by any user, which is not what this scenario requires.

70-073.01.02.003

The printer connected to your Windows NT Workstation computer is shared with ten other users. There are often many large print jobs in the queue when you need to print a report. While still sharing the printer, how can you ensure that your print jobs are printed before those of other users?

A. Create your own printer. Set the printer priority to 1.

B. Create your own printer. Set the printer priority to 99.

C. Grant Change permission to the Everyone group for the default spool directory.

D. Change the spool directory location to a folder on an NTFS partition to which only you have Change permission.

70-073.01.02.004

Your Windows NT Workstation computer participates in a workgroup and has a connected print device. The workgroup consists of Windows NT Workstation 4.0 and Windows 95 computers, and your network uses TCP/IP as its only protocol.

The required result is to share your printer with other members of the workgroup. The first optional result is to allow user RandyA to take ownership of the printer. The second optional result is to allow user RonS to add additional printers.

The proposed solution is to use the SHARE share_name command from the command prompt, make RandyA a member of the Administrators group, and make RonS a member of the Power Users group. What does the proposed solution provide?

A. The required result and all the optional results.

B. The required result and the first optional result.

C. The required result and the second optional result.

D. The proposed solution does not provide the required result.

70-073.01.02.003

The printer connected to your Windows NT Workstation computer is shared with ten other users. There are often many large print jobs in the queue when you need to print a report. While still sharing the printer, how can you ensure that your print jobs are printed before those of other users?

▶ **Correct Answer: B**

A. **Incorrect:** While it is correct to create your own printer, setting the printer priority to 1 prints your document after printers set from priorities 2–99. One is the lowest printer priority.

B. **Correct:** Creating your own printer and setting the printer priority to 99 prints your document before printers set from priorities 1–98. Ninety-nine is the highest printer priority.

C. **Incorrect:** By default, the Everyone group has Change permission in the default spool directory. This allows all user print jobs write access to the default spooler directory. This does not ensure that your print jobs will be printed before those of others.

D. **Incorrect:** A print job that cannot be spooled to disk during processing does not print. If the spool directory location is changed, all users who need to print must have Change permission for the new spool directory. Your print jobs will be printed before those of others, but you will no longer be sharing the printer.

70-073.01.02.004

Your Windows NT Workstation computer participates in a workgroup and has a connected print device. The workgroup consists of Windows NT Workstation 4.0 and Windows 95 computers, and your network uses TCP/IP as its only protocol.

The required result is to share your printer with other members of the workgroup. The first optional result is to allow user RandyA to take ownership of the printer. The second optional result is to allow user RonS to add additional printers.

The proposed solution is to use the SHARE share_name command from the command prompt, make RandyA a member of the Administrators group, and make RonS a member of the Power Users group. What does the proposed solution provide?

▶ **Correct Answer: D**

A. **Incorrect:** See the explanation for answer D.

B. **Incorrect:** See the explanation for answer D.

C. **Incorrect:** See the explanation for answer D.

D. **Correct:** The SHARE share_name command is an MS-DOS subsystem command and no longer has any effect because share functionality is automatic in Windows NT. The SHARE share_name command will not allow you to share your printer with other members of the workgroup or RandyA to take ownership of the printer, nor will this command allow RonS to add printers.

70-073.01.02.005

Your Windows NT Workstation client computer participates in a workgroup and has a connected print device.

The required result is to share your printer with other members of the workgroup. The first optional result is to allow user RandyA to take ownership of the printer. The second optional result is to allow user RonS to add additional printers.

The proposed solution is to log on as Administrator and use the printer sharing properties sheet to share the printer. Add user RandyA and RonS to the Power Users group.

What does the proposed solution provide?

A. The required result and all the optional results.

B. The required result and the first optional result.

C. The required result and the second optional result.

D. The proposed solution does not provide the required result.

70-073.01.02.005

Your Windows NT Workstation client computer participates in a workgroup and has a connected print device.

The required result is to share your printer with other members of the workgroup. The first optional result is to allow user RandyA to take ownership of the printer. The second optional result is to allow user RonS to add additional printers.

The proposed solution is to log on as Administrator and use the printer sharing properties sheet to share the printer. Add user RandyA and RonS to the Power Users group.

What does the proposed solution provide?

▶ **Correct Answer: A**

A. **Correct:** By logging on as an Administrator and using the Printer Sharing tab on the Printer properties sheet, you can share your printer with other members of the workgroup. And by adding the users RandyA and RonS to the Power Users group you can allow RandyA to take ownership of the printer and RonS to add printers.

B. **Incorrect:** See the explanation for answer A.

C. **Incorrect:** See the explanation for answer A.

D. **Incorrect:** See the explanation for answer A.

Further Reading

 Microsoft Windows NT Workstation Resource Kit Chapter 7 provides detailed procedures on print security. Chapter 4 provides basic information on sharing resources when you're using both Windows NT Workstation and Windows 95 in the same environment.

 The *Microsoft Windows NT Network Administration* volume of the *Microsoft Windows NT Network Administration Training* kit Chapter 7, Lesson 2 contains detailed information and procedures on sharing new and existing printers. Chapter 7, Lesson 3 contains detailed information and procedures for setting printer priority. Practice in adding and sharing a printer and setting printer priority is included on the CD provided in this kit. Chapter 8, Lesson 1 contains a table showing the levels of administration required to perform specific printer administration tasks.

OBJECTIVE 1.3

Choose the appropriate file system to use in a given situation.

This objective focuses on file systems and situations that include NTFS, FAT, HPFS, security, and dual-boot systems. Before installing Windows NT Workstation, you must plan whether to use the Windows NT File System (NTFS) or the file allocation table file (FAT) system. Only computers running Windows NT can use NTFS. FAT is required for computers running Windows 95 and MS-DOS. The High-Performance File System (HPFS) is designed for the OS/2 version 1.2 operating system and partitions cannot be accessed by Windows NT 4.0.

NTFS is the preferred Windows NT file system mainly because it provides a higher level of security than FAT does. While Windows NT provides for permissions on shared folders, using NTFS provides permissions on files as well, whether or not they are shared. In addition, NTFS provides file and folder compression, which can reduce file sizes by 40 to 50 percent. Because NTFS has a higher file-system overhead, it is most efficient for partitions greater than 400 MB in size. The maximum file size is between 4 and 64 GB, while the maximum partition size is 2 TB.

FAT is required for dual-boot computers running Windows NT and Windows 95 or MS-DOS. FAT is also required for running Windows NT on RISC-based computers. Because the FAT file system has less file-system overhead, it is most efficient, and preferred, when partitions are less than 400 MB in size. The maximum file and partition size is 4 GB. The FAT32 file system provides support for logical drives larger than 2 GB; however, FAT32 is not supported by MS-DOS, older versions of Windows 95, or Windows NT.

Questions related to this objective are designed to determine if you have an awareness of these issues. To successfully answer the questions for this objective, you need a firm understanding of several key terms. For definitions of these terms, refer to the Glossary in this book.

Key Terms

- Dual-boot computer

- File system

- NTFS compression

- System partition

70-073.01.03.001

You want to configure a Pentium-based computer to dual-boot Windows NT Workstation with Windows 95. Which file system should you use for the system partition on the hard disk?

A. FAT

B. NTFS

C. HPFS

D. FAT32

70-073.01.03.002

You are planning to deploy Windows NT on a new network. The company wants computers on the network to have the highest security possible. Which file system should be used?

A. FAT

B. HPFS

C. NTFS

D. FAT32

70-073.01.03.001

You want to configure a Pentium-based computer to dual-boot Windows NT Workstation with Windows 95. Which file system should you use for the system partition on the hard disk?

▶ **Correct Answer: A**

    A. **Correct:** The FAT file system is required for computers running Windows 95. So if you want to dual-boot Windows NT Workstation and Windows 95 on a Pentium-based computer, you should use the FAT file system.

    B. **Incorrect:** NTFS can be used only on computers running Windows NT. You cannot boot Windows 95 with NTFS.

    C. **Incorrect:** HPFS is designed for the OS/2 version 1.2 operating system and cannot be used to dual-boot Windows NT Workstation and Windows 95 on a Pentium-based computer.

    D. **Incorrect:** The FAT32 file system can only be used on computers running some older versions of Windows 95. You cannot boot Windows NT with the FAT32 file system.

70-073.01.03.002

You are planning to deploy Windows NT on a new network. The company wants computers on the network to have the highest security possible. Which file system should be used?

▶ **Correct Answer: C**

    A. **Incorrect:** A FAT file system partition is protected only through Windows NT directory-level sharing mechanisms. The local file or folder security features of Windows NT do not protect a FAT partition.

    B. **Incorrect:** HPFS is designed for the OS/2 version 1.2 operating system and cannot be used for Windows NT.

    C. **Correct:** NTFS provides the highest level of network security. In addition to providing directory-level security, NTFS allows permissions to be assigned to individual files and folders, whether or not they are shared.

    D. **Incorrect:** The FAT32 file system can be used only on computers running some OEM versions of Windows 95 and cannot be used for Windows NT.

70-073.01.03.003

Some of the folders on an NTFS volume are compressed and others are not compressed. What happens if an uncompressed file is moved to a compressed folder on the same volume?

A. The move fails.

B. The file is compressed.

C. The file remains uncompressed.

D. The user is prompted to specify the compression attribute.

70-073.01.03.004

You have acquired a used Pentium-based computer, and you want to install Windows NT Workstation on it. The existing hard disk has a small capacity, so you will replace it with a 4.3-GB Integrated Device Electronics (IDE) hard disk. You want the file system on the computer to have the highest reliability, and you want to assign permissions to individual files. Which file system should be used?

A. FAT

B. HPFS

C. NTFS

D. FAT32

70-073.01.03.003

Some of the folders on an NTFS volume are compressed and others are not compressed. What happens if an uncompressed file is moved to a compressed folder on the same volume?

▶ **Correct Answer: C**

    A. **Incorrect:** The move succeeds. On an NTFS volume, the file retains its compression attribute, meaning it remains uncompressed regardless of the compression of the target folder.

    B. **Incorrect:** The file is not compressed. On an NTFS volume, the file retains its compression attribute, meaning it remains uncompressed regardless of the compression of the target folder.

    C. **Correct:** On an NTFS volume, the file retains its compression attribute, meaning it remains uncompressed regardless of the compression of the target folder. However, when you move a file from one NTFS volume to another, it inherits the compression attributes of the target folder.

    D. **Incorrect:** The user is not prompted to specify the compression attribute. On an NTFS volume, the move succeeds and the file retains its compression attribute, meaning it remains uncompressed regardless of the compression of the target folder.

70-073.01.03.004

You have acquired a used Pentium-based computer, and you want to install Windows NT Workstation on it. The existing hard disk has a small capacity, so you will replace it with a 4.3-GB Integrated Device Electronics (IDE) hard disk. You want the file system on the computer to have the highest reliability, and you want to assign permissions to individual files. Which file system should be used?

▶ **Correct Answer: C**

    A. **Incorrect:** The FAT file system partition is protected only through Windows NT directory-level sharing mechanisms. The local file or folder security features of Windows NT do not protect a FAT partition.

    B. **Incorrect:** HPFS is designed for the OS/2 version 1.2 operating system and partitions cannot be accessed in Windows NT 4.0.

    C. **Correct:** Windows NTFS provides the highest level of network security. In addition to providing directory-level security, NTFS allows permissions to be assigned to individual files and folders, whether or not they are shared.

    D. **Incorrect:** The FAT32 file system can be used only on computers running some OEM versions of Windows 95 and cannot be used for Windows NT.

70-073.01.03.005

You have acquired a used Pentium-based computer, and you want to install Windows NT Workstation on it. The existing hard disk has failed, so you have replaced it with a single 4.3-GB IDE hard disk.

The required result is to create and format a single 4.3-GB partition on the hard disk. The first optional result is to allow the disk to support dual booting between Windows NT Workstation and Windows 95. The second optional result is to allow the use of Services for Macintosh for file sharing.

The proposed solution is to boot the computer from an MS-DOS 6.22 boot disk, use FDISK to set a single primary FAT partition, and format the hard disk.

What does the proposed solution provide?

A. The required result and all optional results.

B. The required result and one optional result.

C. The required result but none of the optional results.

D. The proposed solution does not provide the required result.

70-073.01.03.005

You have acquired a used Pentium-based computer, and you want to install Windows NT Workstation on it. The existing hard disk has failed, so you have replaced it with a single 4.3-GB IDE hard disk.

The required result is to create and format a single 4.3-GB partition on the hard disk. The first optional result is to allow the disk to support dual booting between Windows NT Workstation and Windows 95. The second optional result is to allow the use of Services for Macintosh for file sharing.

The proposed solution is to boot the computer from an MS-DOS 6.22 boot disk, use FDISK to set a single primary FAT partition, and format the hard disk.

What does the proposed solution provide?

▶ **Correct Answer: D**

A. **Incorrect:** See the explanation for answer D.

B. **Incorrect:** See the explanation for answer D.

C. **Incorrect:** See the explanation for answer D.

D. **Correct:** The maximum FAT partition that DOS 6.22 FDISK can create is 2 GB, so this solution does not provide the required result of formatting a single 4.3-GB partition on the hard disk. Although setting a FAT partition would allow you to support dual booting between Windows NT Workstation and Windows 95, it would not allow you use of Services for Macintosh for file sharing, so at most only one of the optional results would be provided for this problem.

Further Reading

 The *Microsoft Windows NT Technical Support* volume of the *Microsoft Windows NT Technical Support Training* kit Chapter 2, Lesson 1 contains basic information on selecting FAT or NTFS during setup. Chapter 5, Lesson 1 contains more detailed information on selecting a file system and information on converting or changing file systems. Chapter 5, Lesson 3 contains detailed information on file compression on NTFS partitions. Practice in compressing files and folders on an NTFS partition is included on the CD provided in this kit.

 Microsoft Windows NT Workstation Resource Kit Chapter 18 contains further information on the capabilities and limitations of FAT and NTFS.

 Custer, Helen: *Inside the Windows NT File System.* Microsoft Press, 1994. ISBN 1-55615-660-X. Provides more information about the NTFS design.

 Use Microsoft Technical Support Online (http://support.microsoft.com) by clicking "Frequently Asked Questions," choosing the Windows NT Workstation product, and clicking "Setup and Upgrading Questions."

Installation and Configuration

The Installation and Configuration domain examines the issues involved in the installation and configuration of Windows NT Workstation. These issues include:

- Installation requirements and options.

- Dual-boot procedures.

- Procedures for removing Windows NT Workstation and partitions.

- Installing, configuring, and removing hardware components.

- Configuring Windows NT Workstation using the Control Panel.

- Procedures for upgrading to Windows NT Workstation.

- Procedures for configuring a server-based installation.

Tested Skills and Suggested Practices

- Installing Windows NT Workstation on an Intel platform. Given a situation, you must be able to determine installation strategies.

  - Practice 1: Learn the minimum hardware requirements for installing Windows NT Workstation on an Intel platform. Use the *Hardware Compatibility List* (HCL) to determine if your hardware configuration is supported by Microsoft.

  - Practice 2: Distinguish between the WINNT.EXE and WINNT32.EXE Setup program commands. Learn which command to use for a given situation.

  - Practice 3: Select the appropriate WINNT.EXE and WINNT32.EXE switches for a given situation. Learn how each switch is used in a given situation.

- Setting up a dual-boot system. Given a situation, you must be able to determine dual-boot strategies.

  - Practice 1: Determine the operating systems for dual booting and their configuration requirements. Read about how dual booting affects domains, computer names, and applications.

  - Practice 2: Set up operating system selection capability using the BOOT.INI file. Learn how the [Operating Systems] section of this command supports dual booting and the [Boot Loader] section sets a time limit for operating system selection.

- Removing Windows NT Workstation. Given a situation, you must be able to determine the method for removing Windows NT Workstation.

  - Practice 1: Learn how to use the SYS C command to remove Windows NT Workstation from a *file allocation table* (FAT) partition. Read about how to delete the remaining unused Windows NT files to free hard-disk space.

  - Practice 2: Learn how the setup boot disk is used to remove the partition on which Windows NT is installed. Note that this method also removes any other information on the partition.

- Installing, configuring, and removing hardware components. Given a situation, you must be able to install, configure, and remove network adapter drivers, *Small Computer System Interface* (SCSI) device drivers, tape device drivers, *uninterruptible power supplies* (UPSs), multimedia devices, display drivers, keyboard drivers, and mouse drivers.

  - Practice 1: Using the appropriate programs in the Control Panel, learn how to install, configure, and remove network adapter drivers, SCSI device drivers, tape device drivers, UPSs, multimedia devices, display drivers, keyboard drivers, and mouse drivers. Learn which tabs in the Control Panel programs are used for installation, configuration, and removal.

  - Practice 2: Recognize the scsi() syntax that must be added to the *Advanced RISC Computing Specification* (ARC) pathname when setting up a SCSI drive. Read about the meaning of each of the four scsi() syntax parameters.

- Using Control Panel applications to configure a Windows NT Workstation computer. Given a situation, you must be able to use the Control Panel to configure user settings (which affect only a specific Windows NT Workstation user) and computer settings (which affect all Windows NT Workstation users).

  - Practice 1: Using the appropriate programs in the Control Panel, learn how to configure system policy, domains, modems, application performance, and virtual memory. Learn which tabs in the Control Panel programs are used for each configuration.

- Upgrading to Windows NT Workstation 4.0. Given a situation, you must be able to determine upgrade strategies.

    - Practice 1: Learn how to use WINNT32.EXE to upgrade Windows 3.*x*, Windows for Workgroups, or an earlier version of Windows NT Workstation to Windows NT Workstation 4.0. Determine whether to create boot floppies, where to install version 4.0, and whether to use the CONVERT utility for a given situation.

    - Practice 2: Learn why you cannot upgrade to Windows NT Workstation 4.0 from Windows 95. Read about ways to convert a Windows 95 machine to Windows NT Workstation 4.0.

- Configuring server-based installation for wide-scale deployment. Given a situation, you must be able to determine server-based installation strategies for wide-scale systems.

    - Practice 1: Develop an answer file for an unattended installation. Determine the computers for the installation, the desired configuration, and the applications to be installed to determine the answer file.

    - Practice 2: Develop a uniqueness data file (UDF) and possibly use the SYSDIFF utility (if the application requires an interactive installation). Determine the computers for the installation, the desired configuration, and the applications to be installed to determine the uniqueness data file and components of the SYSDIFF utility.

Install Windows NT Workstation on an Intel platform in a given situation.

Before installing Windows NT Workstation, you must determine if your computer meets the minimum hardware requirements. Once it meets the requirements, you can install Windows NT Workstation directly from the boot floppies and Windows NT Workstation CD-ROM or run a server-based installation.

Hardware Requirements

The minimum hardware requirements for installing Windows NT Workstation on an Intel platform are displayed in this table.

Hardware component	Minimum hardware requirement
CPU	One of the following microprocessors:
	■ 32-bit Intel *x*86-based (80486/33 or higher) processor or compatible
	■ Intel Pentium- or Pentium Pro–based processor
Memory	12 MB RAM
Free hard-disk space	110 MB
Display	VGA resolution or better
Mouse	Microsoft mouse or other pointing device
Other drives	High-density 3.5-inch floppy disk drive and a CD-ROM drive (unless you have access to a network CD-ROM drive)

In addition, you can use the Hardware Compatibility List to determine if your hardware configuration is supported by Microsoft. The list is provided on your Windows NT Workstation compact disc and is located on the Internet at the following Web site: http://www.microsoft.com/ntserver under Solutions & Demos, Hardware Compatibility.

Direct and Server-based Installation

If you need to install Windows NT Workstation on only a few computers, you may use the boot floppies and the Windows NT CD-ROM. For computers with an existing operating system, you can skip the boot floppies and run the Setup program from the CD-ROM.

To install Windows NT Workstation to multiple computers, simplify the installation process by copying the installation files to a network server. Then you can log on to each of the computers and run the setup program from the server. This process is known as a *server-based installation*.

The two setup programs used for server-based installations are as follows:

- WINNT.EXE, used to install Windows NT Workstation on a computer running Windows 95 or MS-DOS.

- WINNT32.EXE, used to install or upgrade Windows NT Workstation on a computer already running Windows NT Workstation.

Various switches can be used with the setup programs to determine how they run:

- **/S** specifies the location of the Windows NT files. Using this switch bypasses the source file location prompt that occurs during Setup.

- **/I:INF_FILE** specifies the filename (no path) of the setup information file. The default is DOSNET.INF.

- **/T:DRIVE_LETTER** forces Setup to place temporary files on the specified drive.

- **/X** prevents Setup from creating Setup boot floppies. Use this when you already have Setup boot floppies (from your administrator, for example).

- **/B** causes the boot files to be loaded on the system's hard drive rather than on floppy disks, so that floppy disks do not need to be loaded or removed by the user.

- **/O** specifies that Setup only create boot floppies, allowing you to create floppy disks without installing Windows NT.

- **/OX** specifies that Setup create boot floppies for CD-ROM or floppy-based installation.

- **/U:ANSWER_FILE** specifies the location of a file that provides answers the user would otherwise be prompted for during Setup.

- **/UDF:ID [,UDF_FILE]** specifies the identifier used by the Setup program to apply sections of the uniqueness database file (UDF) in place of the same section in the answer file. If no UDF is specified, the Setup program prompts the user to insert a disk that contains a file called $UNIQUE$.UDF. If a UDF is specified, Setup looks for the identifier in that file.

Questions related to this objective are designed to determine if you have an awareness of these issues. To successfully answer the questions for this objective, you need a firm understanding of several key terms. For definitions of these terms, refer to the Glossary in this book.

Key Terms

- Setup boot disks

- WINNT command

- WINNT32 command

70-073.02.01.001

Your network has the following workstations:

Ten Windows NT Workstation 3.51 computers, each with a 233-MHz Pentium processor, 4-GB hard drive, 24 MB of RAM, one 3.5-inch floppy drive, and a CD-ROM drive

Ten Windows 95 computers, each with a 66-MHz 486 processor, 2-GB hard drive, 8 MB of RAM, one 3.5-inch floppy drive, and a CD-ROM drive

Five Windows 95 computers, each with a 33-MHz 486 processor, 1-GB hard drive, 16 MB of RAM, one 3.5-inch floppy drive, and a CD-ROM drive

Five MS-DOS workstations, each with a 33-MHz 486 processor, 1-GB hard drive, 12 MB of RAM, but no floppy or CD-ROM drive

On how many computers may Windows NT Workstation 4.0 be installed without purchasing new hardware?

A. 10

B. 15

C. 20

D. 25

E. 30

70-073.02.01.001

Your network has the following workstations:

Ten Windows NT Workstation 3.51 computers, each with a 233-MHz Pentium processor, 4-GB hard drive, 24 MB of RAM, one 3.5-inch floppy drive, and a CD-ROM drive

Ten Windows 95 computers, each with a 66-MHz 486 processor, 2-GB hard drive, 8 MB of RAM, one 3.5-inch floppy drive, and a CD-ROM drive

Five Windows 95 computers, each with a 33-MHz 486 processor, 1-GB hard drive, 16 MB of RAM, one 3.5-inch floppy drive, and a CD-ROM drive

Five MS-DOS workstations, each with a 33-MHz 486 processor, 1-GB hard drive, 12 MB of RAM, but no floppy or CD-ROM drive

On how many computers may Windows NT Workstation 4.0 be installed without purchasing new hardware?

▶ **Correct Answer: C**

    A. **Incorrect:** More than ten computers meet the minimum hardware requirements for a Windows NT Workstation installation.

    B. **Incorrect:** More than fifteen computers meet the minimum hardware requirements for a Windows NT Workstation installation.

    C. **Correct:** Twenty computers meet the minimum hardware requirements. The first group of ten Windows NT Workstation 3.51 computers meets hardware requirements, the second group of ten Windows 95 computers does not have sufficient memory, the third group of five Windows 95 computers meets hardware requirements, and the fourth group of five MS-DOS workstations meets hardware requirements since the computers are all on a network and a network installation can be performed.

    D. **Incorrect:** Less than twenty-five computers meet the minimum hardware requirements for a Windows NT Workstation installation. Ten computers do not have sufficient memory.

    E. **Incorrect:** All thirty computers do not meet the minimum hardware requirements for a Windows NT Workstation installation. Ten computers do not have sufficient memory.

70-073.02.01.002

The following machines have been removed from your company's network and your supervisor asks that you install Windows NT Workstation 4.0 on as many of these machines as possible:

Ten Windows NT Workstation 3.51 computers, each with a 233-MHz Pentium processor, 4-GB hard drive, 24 MB of RAM, one 3.5-inch floppy drive, and a CD-ROM drive

Ten Windows 95 computers, each with a 66-MHz 486 processor, 2-GB hard drive, 8 MB of RAM, one 3.5-inch floppy drive, and a CD-ROM drive

Five Windows 95 computers, each with a 33-MHz 486 processor, 1-GB hard drive, 16 MB of RAM, one 3.5-inch floppy drive, and a CD-ROM drive

Five MS-DOS workstations, each with a 33-MHz 486 processor, 1-GB hard drive, 12 MB of RAM, but no floppy or CD-ROM drive

On how many computers may Windows NT Workstation 4.0 be installed without purchasing any new hardware except additional memory?

A. 10

B. 15

C. 20

D. 25

E. 30

70-073.02.01.002

The following machines have been removed from your company's network and your supervisor asks that you install Windows NT Workstation 4.0 on as many of these machines as possible:

Ten Windows NT Workstation 3.51 computers, each with a 233-MHz Pentium processor, 4-GB hard drive, 24 MB of RAM, one 3.5-inch floppy drive, and a CD-ROM drive

Ten Windows 95 computers, each with a 66-MHz 486 processor, 2-GB hard drive, 8 MB of RAM, one 3.5-inch floppy drive, and a CD-ROM drive

Five Windows 95 computers, each with a 33-MHz 486 processor, 1-GB hard drive, 16 MB of RAM, one 3.5-inch floppy drive, and a CD-ROM drive

Five MS-DOS workstations, each with a 33-MHz 486 processor, 1-GB hard drive, 12 MB of RAM, but no floppy or CD-ROM drive

On how many computers may Windows NT Workstation 4.0 be installed without purchasing any new hardware except additional memory?

▶ **Correct Answer: B**

A. **Incorrect:** More than ten computers meet the minimum hardware requirements for a Windows NT Workstation installation without purchasing any new hardware.

B. **Correct:** Fifteen computers meet the minimum hardware requirements. The first group of ten Windows NT Workstation 3.51 computers meets hardware requirements, the second group of ten Windows 95 computers does not have sufficient memory, the third group of five Windows 95 computers meets hardware requirements, and the fourth group of five MS-DOS workstations does not have a CD-ROM drive. Since the computers are not on a network, a network installation cannot be performed for the computers without a CD-ROM drive.

C. **Incorrect:** Less than twenty computers meet the minimum hardware requirements for a Windows NT Workstation installation. Ten computers do not have sufficient memory and five computers do not have a CD-ROM drive.

D. **Incorrect:** Less than twenty-five computers meet the minimum hardware requirements for a Windows NT Workstation installation. Ten computers do not have sufficient memory and five computers do not have a CD-ROM drive.

E. **Incorrect:** Less than thirty computers meet the minimum hardware requirements for a Windows NT Workstation installation. Ten computers do not have sufficient memory and five computers do not have a CD-ROM drive.

70-073.02.01.003

You need to install Windows NT Workstation 4.0 on a Windows NT Workstation 3.51 computer. Your network administrator has given you the Setup boot floppies, so you do not want to create another set. Which switch should you use when you run WINNT32.EXE?

A. /X

B. /B

C. /O

D. /OX

70-073.02.01.003

You need to install Windows NT Workstation 4.0 on a Windows NT Workstation 3.51 computer. Your network administrator has given you the Setup boot floppies, so you do not want to create another set. Which switch should you use when you run WINNT32.EXE?

▶ **Correct Answer: A**

A. **Correct:** The /X switch prevents the Setup program from creating Setup boot floppies. This is the switch to use when you already have Setup boot floppies and do not want to create another set.

B. **Incorrect:** While the /B switch prevents Setup boot floppies from being created, it causes boot files to be loaded on the hard drive of the computer where Windows NT Workstation is being installed. This action requires 4 to 5 MB of space, and is not required since boot files already exist on boot floppies.

C. **Incorrect:** The /O switch causes the Setup program to only create boot floppies, allowing you to create floppy disks without installing Windows NT. This is not the switch to use when you already have Setup boot floppies and do not want to create another set.

D. **Incorrect:** The /OX switch causes the Setup program to create boot disks for installing from compact disc. This switch is used to replace Windows NT Workstation disks if they have been lost or damaged. This is not the switch to use when you already have Setup boot floppies and do not want to create another set.

70-073.02.01.004

You need to install Windows NT Workstation 4.0 on three Windows NT Workstation 3.51 machines. Rather than create the Setup boot disks during each installation, you would like to create a set in advance so you can be sure no time is wasted when you perform the actual installation.

Which switch can you use with WINNT32.EXE to specify that Setup only creates the boot floppies, allowing you to create floppy disks without installing Windows NT?

A. /X

B. /B

C. /U

D. /O

70-073.02.01.004

You need to install Windows NT Workstation 4.0 on three Windows NT Workstation 3.51 machines. Rather than create the Setup boot disks during each installation, you would like to create a set in advance so you can be sure no time is wasted when you perform the actual installation.

Which switch can you use with WINNT32.EXE to specify that Setup only creates the boot floppies, allowing you to create floppy disks without installing Windows NT?

▶ **Correct Answer: D**

    A. **Incorrect:** The /X switch prevents the Setup program from creating Setup boot floppies. This is not the switch to use to specify that Setup only creates the boot floppies, allowing you to create floppy disks without installing Windows NT.

    B. **Incorrect:** The /B switch causes boot files to be loaded on the hard drive of the computer where Windows NT Workstation is being installed, and requires 4 to 5 MB of space. This is not the switch to use to specify that Setup only creates the boot floppies, allowing you to create floppy disks without installing Windows NT.

    C. **Incorrect:** The /U switch is used to specify the location of the answer file used in an unattended installation. The /U switch does not create boot floppies.

    D. **Correct:** The /O switch causes the Setup program to only create boot floppies, allowing you to create floppy disks without installing Windows NT.

70-073.02.01.005

You want to install Windows NT Workstation on a stand-alone Pentium-based computer running MS-DOS. However, the CD-ROM drive is not supported by Windows NT.

The required result is to install Windows NT Workstation on the computer.

The first optional result is to install Windows NT Workstation 4.0 without creating Setup floppy disks. The second optional result is to enable the CD-ROM drive to work with Windows NT Workstation 4.0.

The proposed solution is to boot the computer in MS-DOS, copy the \I386 directory from the CD-ROM drive to the hard disk, and run WINNT.EXE with the /B switch from the hard disk.

What does the proposed solution provide?

A. The required result and both optional results.

B. The required result and one optional result.

C. The required result but none of the optional results.

D. The proposed solution does not provide the required result.

70-073.02.01.005

You want to install Windows NT Workstation on a stand-alone Pentium-based computer running MS-DOS. However, the CD-ROM drive is not supported by Windows NT.

The required result is to install Windows NT Workstation on the computer.

The first optional result is to install Windows NT Workstation 4.0 without creating Setup floppy disks. The second optional result is to enable the CD-ROM drive to work with Windows NT Workstation 4.0.

The proposed solution is to boot the computer in MS-DOS, copy the \I386 directory from the CD-ROM drive to the hard disk, and run WINNT.EXE with the /B switch from the hard disk.

What does the proposed solution provide?

▶ **Correct Answer: B**

A. **Incorrect:** See the explanation for answer B.

B. **Correct:** The Setup program installs Windows NT Workstation and the /B switch prevents Setup floppy disks from being created. The /B switch causes the boot files to be written to a temporary directory on the hard drive. Since the Windows NT Workstation cannot use the unsupported CD-ROM drive, the drive cannot be enabled to work with Windows NT.

C. **Incorrect:** See the explanation for answer B.

D. **Incorrect:** See the explanation for answer B.

70-073.02.01.006

You want to install Windows NT Workstation on a stand-alone Pentium-based computer running MS-DOS. However, the CD-ROM drive is not supported by Windows NT.

The required result is to install Windows NT Workstation on the computer.

The first optional result is to install Windows NT Workstation 4.0 without creating Setup floppy disks. The second optional result is to enable the CD-ROM drive to work with Windows NT Workstation 4.0.

The proposed solution is to boot the computer in MS-DOS, copy the \I386 directory from the CD-ROM drive to the hard disk, and run WINNT32.EXE from the hard disk.

What does the proposed solution provide?

A. The required result and both optional results.

B. The required result and one optional result.

C. The required result but none of the optional results.

D. The proposed solution does not provide the required result.

70-073.02.01.006

You want to install Windows NT Workstation on a stand-alone Pentium-based computer running MS-DOS. However, the CD-ROM drive is not supported by Windows NT.

The required result is to install Windows NT Workstation on the computer.

The first optional result is to install Windows NT Workstation 4.0 without creating Setup floppy disks. The second optional result is to enable the CD-ROM drive to work with Windows NT Workstation 4.0.

The proposed solution is to boot the computer in MS-DOS, copy the \I386 directory from the CD-ROM drive to the hard disk, and run WINNT32.EXE from the hard disk.

What does the proposed solution provide?

▶ **Correct Answer: D**

A. **Incorrect:** See the explanation for answer D.

B. **Incorrect:** See the explanation for answer D.

C. **Incorrect:** See the explanation for answer D.

D. **Correct:** The WIN32.EXE command is the 32-bit version of the Setup program and is used to upgrade from an earlier version of Windows NT Workstation. Since the WIN32.EXE command does not run under MS-DOS, Windows NT Workstation cannot be installed on the computer, and the CD-ROM drive cannot be enabled to work with Windows NT using this command.

70-073.02.01.007

You want to install Windows NT Workstation on a stand-alone Pentium-based computer running MS-DOS. However, the CD-ROM drive is not supported by Windows NT.

The required result is to install Windows NT Workstation on the computer.

The first optional result is to install Windows NT Workstation 4.0 without creating Setup floppy disks. The second optional result is to enable the CD-ROM drive to work with Windows NT Workstation 4.0.

The proposed solution is to boot the computer in MS-DOS and run WINNT.EXE with the /B switch from the CD-ROM.

What does the proposed solution provide?

A. The required result and both optional results.

B. The required result and one optional result.

C. The required result but none of the optional results.

D. The proposed solution does not provide the required result.

70-073.02.01.007

You want to install Windows NT Workstation on a stand-alone Pentium-based computer running MS-DOS. However, the CD-ROM drive is not supported by Windows NT.

The required result is to install Windows NT Workstation on the computer.

The first optional result is to install Windows NT Workstation 4.0 without creating Setup floppy disks. The second optional result is to enable the CD-ROM drive to work with Windows NT Workstation 4.0.

The proposed solution is to boot the computer in MS-DOS and run WINNT.EXE with the /B switch from the CD-ROM.

What does the proposed solution provide?

▶ **Correct Answer: B**

A. **Incorrect:** See the explanation for answer B.

B. **Correct:** The Setup program installs Windows NT Workstation, and the /B switch prevents Setup floppy disks from being created. The /B switch causes the boot files to be written to a temporary directory on the hard drive. Since the Windows NT Workstation cannot use the unsupported CD-ROM drive, the drive cannot be enabled to work with Windows NT.

C. **Incorrect:** See the explanation for answer B.

D. **Incorrect:** See the explanation for answer B.

70-073.02.01.008

You want to install Windows NT Workstation on a stand-alone Pentium-based computer running MS-DOS. However, the CD-ROM drive is not supported by Windows NT.

The required result is to install Windows NT Workstation on the computer.

The first optional result is to install Windows NT Workstation 4.0 without creating Setup floppy disks. The second optional result is to enable the CD-ROM drive to work with Windows NT Workstation 4.0.

The proposed solution is to boot the computer in MS-DOS, copy the \I386 directory from the CD-ROM drive to the hard disk, and run WINNT.EXE from the hard disk.

What does the proposed solution provide?

A. The required result and both optional results.

B. The required result and one optional result.

C. The required result but none of the optional results.

D. The proposed solution does not provide the required result.

70-073.02.01.008

You want to install Windows NT Workstation on a stand-alone Pentium-based computer running MS-DOS. However, the CD-ROM drive is not supported by Windows NT.

The required result is to install Windows NT Workstation on the computer.

The first optional result is to install Windows NT Workstation 4.0 without creating Setup floppy disks. The second optional result is to enable the CD-ROM drive to work with Windows NT Workstation 4.0.

The proposed solution is to boot the computer in MS-DOS, copy the \I386 directory from the CD-ROM drive to the hard disk, and run WINNT.EXE from the hard disk.

What does the proposed solution provide?

▶ **Correct Answer: C**

A. **Incorrect:** See the explanation for answer C.

B. **Incorrect:** See the explanation for answer C.

C. **Correct:** The Setup program installs Windows NT Workstation. Because the /B switch was not specified, Setup floppy disks are created. In addition, the Windows NT Workstation cannot use the unsupported CD-ROM drive, so the drive cannot be enabled to work with Windows NT.

D. **Incorrect:** See the explanation for answer C.

Further Reading

The *Microsoft Windows NT Technical Support* volume of the *Microsoft Windows NT Technical Support Training* kit Chapter 2, Lesson 2 contains procedures for creating Windows NT Server Setup disks. Lesson 3 contains procedures for creating Windows NT Workstation Setup disks. Practice for creating Setup disks is included using the CD provided in this kit. Lesson 5 describes the switches that can be used with WINNT.EXE and WINNT32.EXE to control how the Setup program runs.

The *Microsoft Windows NT Workstation 4.0 Resource Kit* Chapter 2 contains detailed information on the switches that can be used with WINNT.EXE and WINNT32.EXE to control how the Setup program runs.

Use Microsoft Technical Support Online (http://support.microsoft.com) by searching for "Windows NT Workstation" and for the "WINNT command." Then click "View Windows NT 4.0 Setup Troubleshooting Guide."

Use Microsoft Technical Support Online (http://support.microsoft.com) by searching for "Windows NT Workstation" and for "WINNT.EXE." Then click "How to Create Windows NT Boot Floppy Disks."

OBJECTIVE   2.2

Set up a dual-boot system in a given situation.

Dual booting allows you the flexibility to choose an operating system from which various applications are run. A user might want to retain the previous operating system in order to run a legacy program. You can dual-boot Windows NT Workstation 4.0 with Windows NT Workstation 3.51, Windows 95, Windows 3.1, Windows 3.11, and MS-DOS.

To set up a dual-boot system, you must determine:

- The operating systems you want to run.

- The file systems required by the operating systems (NT File System [NTFS], FAT).

- How the operating systems will start as determined by the BOOT.INI file.

- How applications should be configured on each operating system.

The following rules apply when setting up dual booting:

- If the two versions of Windows NT coexist in the same domain, you must assign each version a unique computer name.

- You must install Windows NT Workstation 4.0 interactively using the WINNT command (not /U).

- You must install Windows-based application programs to each operating system.

- Windows NT must be installed in folders different from the ones containing Windows 95 and other versions of Windows NT.

- Windows NT can be installed in the same folders as Windows 3.1 or Windows 3.11 or in different folders.

- When dual booting with MS-DOS or Windows 95, install MS-DOS or Windows 95 first for best results.

Questions related to this objective are designed to determine if you have an awareness of these issues. To successfully answer the questions for this objective, you need a firm understanding of several key terms. For definitions of these terms, refer to the Glossary in this book.

Key Terms

- Computer name

- Dual-boot computer

- Registry

- Registry Editor

- Triple-boot computer

70-073.02.02.001

You are responsible for testing software applications using Windows NT Workstation, and you need to set up a system to dual-boot Windows NT Workstation 3.51 and Windows NT Workstation 4.0. Both installations will be members of the same domain, and Windows NT Workstation 3.51 has been installed with the computer name MYWORK.

How should Windows NT Workstation 4.0 be installed?

A. You should install Windows NT Workstation 4.0 using WINNT and assign the computer name MYWORK.

B. You should install Windows NT Workstation 4.0 using WINNT32 /U and assign the computer name MYWORK.

C. You should install Windows NT Workstation 4.0 using WINNT and assign a unique computer name to the 4.0 installation.

D. You should install Windows NT Workstation 4.0 using WINNT32 /U and assign a unique computer name to the 4.0 installation.

70-073.02.02.001

You are responsible for testing software applications using Windows NT Workstation, and you need to set up a system to dual-boot Windows NT Workstation 3.51 and Windows NT Workstation 4.0. Both installations will be members of the same domain, and Windows NT Workstation 3.51 has been installed with the computer name MYWORK.

How should Windows NT Workstation 4.0 be installed?

▶ **Correct Answer: C**

    A. **Incorrect:** While you should install Windows NT Workstation 4.0 interactively using the WINNT command, you should not assign the computer name MYWORK. Since both the Windows NT Workstation 3.51 installation and the Windows NT Workstation 4.0 installation are members of the same domain, they must have different computer names.

    B. **Incorrect:** You must install Windows NT Workstation 4.0 interactively using the WINNT command, not the WINNT32 /U (unattended setup) command. In addition, you should not assign the computer name MYWORK. Since both the Windows NT Workstation 3.51 installation and the Windows NT Workstation 4.0 installation are members of the same domain, they must have different computer names.

    C. **Correct:** You must install Windows NT Workstation 4.0 interactively using the WINNT command, and you must assign a unique computer name when both the Windows NT Workstation 3.51 installation and the Windows NT Workstation 4.0 installation are members of the same domain.

    D. **Incorrect:** You must install Windows NT Workstation 4.0 interactively using the WINNT command, not the WINNT32 /U (unattended setup) command. However, assigning a unique computer name when both the Windows NT Workstation 3.51 installation and the Windows NT Workstation 4.0 installation are members of the same domain is correct.

70-073.02.02.002

Your computer running Windows NT Workstation 3.51 is a member of the TECHPUB domain. You need to set up the system to dual-boot Windows NT Workstation 3.51 and Windows NT Workstation 4.0 so your word processing and publishing applications are available under both versions.

How can this be accomplished?

A. Install Windows NT Workstation 4.0 and add the line WINVER=4.0 to the BOOT.INI file.

B. Install Windows NT Workstation 4.0 to the same directory where version 3.51 is installed.

C. Install Windows NT Workstation 4.0 to a separate directory and reinstall all application programs under version 4.0.

D. Install Windows NT Workstation 4.0 to a separate directory and use REGEDT32 to migrate application Registry entries for use with version 4.0.

70-073.02.02.003

You have acquired a new Pentium-based computer and are considering the use of multiple operating systems. In which order should you proceed if you want to triple-boot MS-DOS, Windows 95, and Windows NT?

A. Install MS-DOS first, then Windows 95, and then Windows NT Workstation.

B. Install Windows 95 first, then Windows NT Workstation, and then MS-DOS.

C. Install Windows NT Workstation first, then MS-DOS, and then Windows 95.

D. Install MS-DOS first, then Windows NT Workstation, and then Windows 95.

70-073.02.02.002

Your computer running Windows NT Workstation 3.51 is a member of the TECHPUB domain. You need to set up the system to dual-boot Windows NT Workstation 3.51 and Windows NT Workstation 4.0 so your word processing and publishing applications are available under both versions.

How can this be accomplished?

▶ **Correct Answer: C**

A. **Incorrect:** The BOOT.INI file is used to determine the operating system options to display during the boot process. This file cannot provide word processing and publishing applications in Windows NT Workstation versions 3.51 and 4.0. In addition, the line WINVER=4.0 is an MS-DOS command and cannot be added to the BOOT.INI file.

B. **Incorrect:** To set up dual booting, you must install different versions of Windows NT Workstation in different directories.

C. **Correct:** To set up dual booting of Windows NT Workstation 3.51 and 4.0 and have word processing and publishing applications available under both versions, you must install Windows NT Workstation 4.0 in a separate directory and reinstall the applications under version 4.0.

D. **Incorrect:** Wherever possible, you should use the administrative tools, in this case those that install the application software, rather than REGEDT32 (the Registry Editor). Using the Registry Editor incorrectly can cause serious problems that may require reinstallation of Windows NT.

70-073.02.02.003

You have acquired a new Pentium-based computer and are considering the use of multiple operating systems. In which order should you proceed if you want to triple-boot MS-DOS, Windows 95, and Windows NT?

▶ **Correct Answer: A**

A. **Correct:** You should Install MS-DOS first, then Windows 95, and then Windows NT Workstation.

B. **Incorrect:** Install MS-DOS first, then Windows 95, and then Windows NT Workstation.

C. **Incorrect:** Install MS-DOS first, then Windows 95, and then Windows NT Workstation.

D. **Incorrect:** Install MS-DOS first, then Windows 95, and then Windows NT Workstation.

70-073.02.02.004

Your computer dual-boots MS-DOS and Windows NT Workstation. If you do not choose an operating system when starting the computer, it waits 30 seconds and then loads Windows NT Workstation automatically. You want the computer to wait indefinitely for your selection. Which file can you modify to force the computer to wait for an operating system selection?

A. SYS.INI

B. HAL.DLL

C. BOOT.INI

D. NTDETECT.COM

70-073.02.02.004

Your computer dual-boots MS-DOS and Windows NT Workstation. If you do not choose an operating system when starting the computer, it waits 30 seconds and then loads Windows NT Workstation automatically. You want the computer to wait indefinitely for your selection. Which file can you modify to force the computer to wait for an operating system selection?

▶ **Correct Answer: C**

   A. **Incorrect:** The SYS.INI file does not exist in Windows NT and cannot force the computer to wait for an operating system selection.

   B. **Incorrect:** The HAL.DLL file hides the characteristics of the platform from Windows NT Workstation, allowing the operating system to run on different platforms with different processors. You cannot modify the HAL.DLL file to force the computer to wait for an operating system selection.

   C. **Correct:** The BOOT.INI file is used to determine the operating system options to display during the boot process. To force the computer to wait indefinitely for an operating system selection, set the timeout parameter in the Boot Loader section to –1.

   D. **Incorrect:** NTDETECT.COM is the hardware detector for $x86$-based computers. It collects a list of currently installed components and returns this information to NTLDR. You cannot modify the NDETECT.COM file to force the computer to wait for an operating system selection.

Further Reading

 The *Microsoft Windows NT Workstation 4.0 Resource Kit* Chapter 2 contains basic information on setting up a computer to dual boot Windows NT Workstation 3.51 and Windows NT Workstation 4.0. Chapter 19 contains details on configuring the computer for various dual- and triple-booting scenarios.

 Use Microsoft Technical Support Online (http://support.microsoft.com) by searching for "Windows NT Workstation" and for "BOOT.INI." Then click "Purpose of the BOOT.INI File."

 Use Microsoft Technical Support Online (http://support.microsoft.com) by searching for "Windows NT Workstation" and for "dual boot." Then click various entries.

O B J E C T I V E   2 . 3

Remove Windows NT Workstation in a given situation.

There are two methods for removing Windows NT:

- Remove the partition on which Windows NT is installed (NTFS and FAT partitions).

- Remove only Windows NT (FAT partitions only).

Removing a Partition

If you are using the NTFS file system for the Windows NT partition, the *only* way you can remove Windows NT from the computer is to remove the partition. As well, if you are using the FAT file system for the Windows NT partition, you can remove Windows NT from the computer by removing the partition. This method also *removes all information* from the partition.

▶ **To remove a partition:**

1. Start the computer from the Setup boot disk.

2. Click the partition where the Windows NT Workstation files are located and press D to delete the partition.

3. Exit Setup.

Removing Windows NT Workstation from a FAT Partition

If you are using a FAT file system for the Windows NT partition, you can remove Windows NT from the computer without removing the entire partition.

▶ **To remove Windows NT Workstation from a FAT partition:**

1. Start the computer from a Windows 95 or MS-DOS system disk containing the SYS.COM file.

2. From drive A, type **SYS C:**

   This command replaces the Windows NT boot files with the MS-DOS or Windows 95 boot files, allowing you to boot MS-DOS or Windows 95.

3. After the system files are transferred, restart the computer.

4. To free space on the hard disk, delete the following:

   - C:\PAGEFILE.SYS

   - C:\BOOT.INI

   - C:\NT*.*

   - C:\BOOTSECT.DOS

   - The SYSTEMROOT folder

   - Windows NT program files

Questions related to this objective are designed to determine if you have an awareness of these issues. To successfully answer the questions for this objective, you need a firm understanding of several key terms. For definitions of these terms, refer to the Glossary in this book.

Key Terms

- FDISK utility

- System partition

70-073.02.03.001

Your computer has one FAT partition and is set up to dual-boot MS-DOS and Windows NT Workstation. What is the easiest way to change the system configuration to boot MS-DOS only?

A. Edit BOOT.INI to place a semicolon before the Windows NT line.

B. Click the Add/Remove Programs icon in Control Panel and uninstall Windows NT.

C. Boot the computer from an MS-DOS boot floppy, run FDISK, run FORMAT, and reinstall MS-DOS.

D. Boot the computer from an MS-DOS boot floppy and run SYS C:. Restart from the hard disk and delete the Windows NT files.

70-073.02.03.002

Your Windows NT Workstation-based computer has one hard disk with a single partition formatted as NTFS. You want to configure the system to run only MS-DOS 6.22. How should you proceed?

A. Edit BOOT.INI to replace all references to Windows NT with references to MS-DOS.

B. Use FDISK to change the partition to FAT32, format the hard disk, and install MS-DOS from the setup disks.

C. Use the CONVERT utility to convert the partition to FAT, boot from an MS-DOS boot disk, run SYS C:, restart, and remove the Windows NT files.

D. Boot from an MS-DOS boot disk, use FDISK to delete the non-DOS partition and create a FAT partition, format the hard disk, and install MS-DOS from the setup disks.

70-073.02.03.001

Your computer has one FAT partition and is set up to dual-boot MS-DOS and Windows NT Workstation. What is the easiest way to change the system configuration to boot MS-DOS only?

▶ **Correct Answer: D**

  A. **Incorrect:** Placing a semicolon before the Windows NT line does not change the system configuration to MS-DOS only. BOOT.INI determines the system options to display during the startup process.

  B. **Incorrect:** You cannot install or uninstall Windows NT from the Add/Remove Programs icon in the Control Panel.

  C. **Incorrect:** Running FDISK removes the entire FAT partition and all of the information on the partition. You want to run MS-DOS on the FAT partition.

  D. **Correct:** To remove Windows NT from a FAT partition and boot MS-DOS only, you must boot the computer from the MS-DOS boot floppy and run SYS C: to transfer the MS-DOS system files to the boot track on drive C. You must then restart the system and delete the Windows NT files.

70-073.02.03.002

Your Windows NT Workstation-based computer has one hard disk with a single partition formatted as NTFS. You want to configure the system to run only MS-DOS 6.22. How should you proceed?

▶ **Correct Answer: D**

  A. **Incorrect:** BOOT. INI is used to determine the operating system options to display during Windows NT startup. Replacing all references to Windows NT with references to MS-DOS in BOOT.INI does not change that the computer is running Windows NT on an NTFS partition.

  B. **Incorrect:** MS-DOS does not recognize FAT32 partitions, and is unable to boot from a FAT32 volume.

  C. **Incorrect:** There is no way to convert an NTFS partition to FAT; the CONVERT utility only converts an existing FAT (or *High Performance File System* [HPFS]) hard-disk partition to NTFS.

  D. **Correct:** To configure the system to run only MS-DOS 6.22, first boot MS-DOS 6.22 from the boot disk, and use the FDISK utility to delete the NTFS partition, create a FAT partition, and format the hard disk. Then install MS-DOS 6.22 from the setup disks.

70-073.02.03.003

Your computer has an NTFS partition and a FAT partition set up to dual-boot MS-DOS and Windows NT Workstation. How can you remove Windows NT from the NTFS partition?

A. Edit BOOT.INI, and replace references to Windows NT with references to MS-DOS.

B. Edit MSDOS.SYS, and replace references to Windows NT with references to MS-DOS.

C. Start the computer from the Setup boot disk. Select the NTFS partition, and press D to delete it. Exit Setup.

D. Start the computer from the Setup boot disk. Select the FAT partition, and press D to delete it. Exit Setup.

70-073.02.03.003

Your computer has an NTFS partition and a FAT partition set up to dual-boot MS-DOS and Windows NT Workstation. How can you remove Windows NT from the NTFS partition?

▶ **Correct Answer: C**

A. **Incorrect:** BOOT. INI is used to determine the operating system options to display during Windows NT startup. Replacing all references to Windows NT with references to MS-DOS in BOOT.INI does not remove Windows NT from an NTFS partition.

B. **Incorrect:** MSDOS.SYS provides the operating system software for MS-DOS and does not contain references to Windows NT. Changing MSDOS.SYS will not remove Windows NT from the NTFS partition.

C. **Correct:** To delete Windows NT and the NTFS partition, start the computer with the Setup boot disk, select the NTFS partition, and press D. Exit Setup and the partition and its contents are removed from the system.

D. **Incorrect:** You do not want to delete the FAT partition; you want to remove Windows NT from the NTFS partition.

70-073.02.03.004

A company executive's laptop computer has been recently upgraded from Windows 95 to Windows NT Workstation. During the upgrade process, the Windows 95 files were not removed or overwritten.

The executive wants to change back to Windows 95 so he can use a scheduling program that will not run well under Windows NT Workstation. He also wants to free hard-disk space by removing Windows NT from the hard drive once Windows 95 is restored.

Which steps should you complete to revert to Windows 95? (Choose three.)

A. Reinstall Windows 95 on the hard drive.

B. Delete the BOOT.SYS file from the hard drive.

C. Delete the root directory for Windows NT from the hard drive.

D. Delete the PAGEFILE.SYS, BOOTSECT.DOS, and BOOT.INI files from the hard drive.

E. Transfer the system files from the Windows 95 system disk to the hard drive.

F. Use the Windows NT emergency disk's option to remove Windows NT Workstation.

70-073.02.03.004

A company executive's laptop computer has been recently upgraded from Windows 95 to Windows NT Workstation. During the upgrade process, the Windows 95 files were not removed or overwritten.

The executive wants to change back to Windows 95 so he can use a scheduling program that will not run well under Windows NT Workstation. He also wants to free hard-disk space by removing Windows NT from the hard drive once Windows 95 is restored.

Which steps should you complete to revert to Windows 95? (Choose three.)

▶ **Correct Answers: C, D, E**

   A. **Incorrect:** It is not necessary to reinstall Windows 95; the scenario states that Windows 95 files were not removed or overwritten.

   B. **Incorrect:** BOOT.SYS allows you to maintain and select system configurations in Windows 3.1. This file does not exist in Windows 95 or Windows NT and will not allow you to revert to Windows 95.

   C. **Correct:** Deleting the root directory for Windows NT (C:\NT*.*) from the hard drive is one step to free space on the hard disk.

   D. **Correct:** Deleting PAGEFILE.SYS, BOOTSECT.DOS, and BOOT.INI is one step to free space on the hard disk.

   E. **Correct:** Transferring the Windows 95 system files from the system disk to the hard drive using the SYS.COM file (SYS C:) is one step in reverting back to Windows 95.

   F. **Incorrect:** The Windows NT emergency disk is used to recover a bootable system in case of failure, not to remove Windows NT Workstation.

Further Reading

 The *Microsoft Windows NT Technical Support* volume of the *Microsoft Technical Support Training* kit Chapter 2, Lesson 5 describes how to remove Windows NT from a computer, including removing the partition on which Windows NT is installed and removing only Windows NT (from FAT systems only).

 Use Microsoft Technical Support Online (http://support.microsoft.com) by searching for "Windows NT Workstation" and for "uninstall." Then click "How to Uninstall Windows NT 4.0 Workstation from NTFS."

 Use Microsoft Technical Support Online (http:/support.microsoft.com) by clicking "Frequently Asked Questions," choosing the Windows NT Workstation product, and clicking "Windows NT 4.0 Setup and Upgrading Questions" and "How do I remove Windows NT from my computer?"

O B J E C T I V E   2 . 4

Install, configure, and remove hardware components for a given situation.

The Control Panel allows you to install, configure, and remove hardware components without using the Registry. While some Control Panel programs allow users to configure their own settings on their Windows NT Workstation, only an administrator can perform the installation, configuration, and removal of hardware components.

Network Adapter Drivers

Network adapter card drivers are typically included with Windows NT and installed during Setup. Using the Adapters tab in the Network program in the Control Panel, an administrator can add, remove, view, and change properties for a network adapter card or update a card.

SCSI Device Drivers

Small Computer System Interface (SCSI) device drivers are used to install and start the drivers for the SCSI devices connected to Windows NT Workstation. SCSI devices may include peripheral devices such as hard disks, scanners, printers, CD-ROM, and optical drives, and are configurable only by an administrator. Before you install a SCSI device, make sure it is compatible with Windows NT Workstation. Check the latest Hardware Compatibility List, located at http://www.microsoft.com/ntserver under Solutions & Demos, Hardware Compatibility.

After you have physically installed the SCSI device driver, you must install it on the Drivers tab in the SCSI Adapters program in the Control Panel. You must restart the computer for the changes to take effect. You can then see the SCSI adapters and their associated devices on the Device tab in the SCSI Adapters program in the Control Panel.

When Windows NT Workstation needs to load a SCSI device driver and use that driver to access the boot partition, the scsi()syntax is required in the BOOT.INI file. The scsi() syntax indicates the location of the SCSI disk.

Tape Device Drivers

Windows NT automatically detects tape devices when you click the Detect button on the Devices tab in the Tape Devices program in the Control Panel. Click on the Properties button to specify further information on the tape device. Windows NT need not be restarted when a tape device is added or deleted.

UPS

An uninterruptible power supply provides power to your Windows NT Workstation in the event of a main power outage. During a power outage, a UPS pauses the Server, warns users of a shutdown, and then performs the shutdown. A command file can be executed before the shutdown. Using the UPS program in the Control Panel, an administrator can specify UPS settings, including Configuration, Command File to Execute, Characteristics, and Service.

Multimedia Devices

Multimedia devices, such as *Musical Instrument Digital Interface* (MIDI) instruments and sound cards, are added and configured by an administrator from the Multimedia program in the Control Panel. The Devices tab allows a user to view all of the multimedia devices installed on the system.

Display Drivers

The Display program in the Control Panel allows you to configure the appearance of the Windows NT Workstation desktop, screen saver, dialog boxes, and icons. The Settings tab allows you to add and remove display adapters. Only system administrators can change the display adapters, which are display settings configured for all users of the system.

Keyboard Drivers

The Keyboard program in the Control Panel allows you to configure three keyboard settings:

- Speed determines the character repeat and cursor blink rates.

- Input Locales determines keyboard layout for languages.

- General determines the keyboard driver and can be set by a system administrator only.

Mouse Drivers

The Mouse program in the Control Panel allows you to configure three mouse settings:

- Buttons determines the primary button location (right or left) and the double-click speed.

- Pointers determines the pointer appearance.

- Motion controls pointer speed.

- General determines mouse driver and can be set by a system administrator only.

Questions related to this objective are designed to determine if you have an awareness of these issues. To successfully answer the questions for this objective, you need a firm understanding of several key terms. For definitions of these terms, refer to the Glossary in this book.

Key Terms

- *Advanced RISC Computing Specification* (ARC) pathname

- Control Panel

- Control Panel applications

- Device driver

- Network adapter card

- Registry

- Small Computer System Interface (SCSI)

- scsi() syntax

- Uninterruptible Power Supply (UPS)

70-073.02.04.001

You have purchased an EIDE backup tape drive for your Windows NT Workstation computer. Which Control Panel application should you use to install this device?

A. System

B. Devices

C. Tape Devices

D. SCSI Adapters

70-073.02.04.002

You have installed a new network adapter card for use with your computer running Windows NT Workstation. Which Control Panel application should you use to install and configure drivers for this device?

A. System

B. Devices

C. Network

D. Add/Remove Programs

70-073.02.04.001

You have purchased an EIDE backup tape drive for your Windows NT Workstation computer. Which Control Panel application should you use to install this device?

▶ **Correct Answer: C**

   A. **Incorrect:** The System application controls the computer's startup settings, shows the operating systems installed on a computer, and lets you choose which operating system to load for a session. You cannot install a tape backup device from this application.

   B. **Incorrect:** The Devices application starts and stops device drivers and configures the startup type for each driver. You cannot install a tape backup device from this application.

   C. **Correct:** The Tape Devices application lists the installed tape backup devices and drivers.

   D. **Incorrect:** The SCSI Adapters application lists the SCSI adapters, drivers, and connected devices. You cannot install a tape backup device from this application.

70-073.02.04.002

You have installed a new network adapter card for use with your computer running Windows NT Workstation. Which Control Panel application should you use to install and configure drivers for this device?

▶ **Correct Answer: C**

   A. **Incorrect:** The System application controls the computer's startup settings, shows the operating systems installed on a computer, and lets you choose which operating system to load for a session. You cannot install a network adapter card from this application.

   B. **Incorrect:** The Devices application starts and stops device drivers and configures the startup type for each driver. You cannot install a network adapter card from this application.

   C. **Correct:** The Network application allows you to install and remove network adapter cards. Use the Adapters tab to configure network adapter card drivers.

   D. **Incorrect:** The Add/Remove Programs function allows you to add or remove Windows NT components (accessibility options, accessories, communications programs, games, multimedia, and Windows messaging) and install or uninstall applications. You cannot install a network adapter card from this function.

70-073.02.04.003

Your location has many power outages, usually lasting from a few seconds to a minute. If the outages last longer, you need to shut down your applications. You have purchased a UPS with an expected battery life of 10 minutes for your system.

The required result is to install the UPS on your Windows NT Workstation based computer.

The first optional result is to run a command file just before the UPS shuts down your system. The second optional result is to configure the UPS service to wait 2 minutes after a power failure before sending an alert.

The proposed solution is to connect the UPS and specify the port to which the UPS is connected in the Control Panel UPS application. Then specify the name of the command file in the Execute Command File field and a value of 120 in The Time Between Power Failure and Initial Warning Message box.

What does the proposed solution provide?

A. The required result and both optional results.

B. The required result and one optional result.

C. The required result but none of the optional results.

D. The proposed solution does not provide the required result.

70-073.02.04.003

Your location has many power outages, usually lasting from a few seconds to a minute. If the outages last longer, you need to shut down your applications. You have purchased a UPS with an expected battery life of 10 minutes for your system.

The required result is to install the UPS on your Windows NT Workstation based computer.

The first optional result is to run a command file just before the UPS shuts down your system. The second optional result is to configure the UPS service to wait 2 minutes after a power failure before sending an alert.

The proposed solution is to connect the UPS and specify the port to which the UPS is connected in the Control Panel UPS application. Then, specify the name of the command file in the Execute Command File field and a value of 120 in The Time Between Power Failure and Initial Warning Message box.

What does the proposed solution provide?

▶ **Correct Answer: A**

A. **Correct:** Connecting the UPS and specifying the port to which it is connected installs the UPS on a Windows NT Workstation–based computer. Specifying the name of the command file (extension .BAT, .CMD, .EXE, or .COM) in the Execute Command File field runs the command file just before system shutdown. Such a file might run a command to close remote connections. Specifying 120 in the Time Between Power Failure and Initial Warning Message box makes the UPS wait 2 minutes before sending an alert to users.

B. **Incorrect:** See the explanation for answer A.

C. **Incorrect:** See the explanation for answer A.

D. **Incorrect:** See the explanation for answer A.

70-073.02.04.004

When setting up a SCSI drive on either a RISC-based or Intel-based computer, what is the correct scsi() syntax for the ARC pathname?

A. scsi(W)rdisk(X)disk(Y)partition(Z)

B. scsi(W)partition(X)disk(Y)rdisk(Z)

C. scsi(W)disk(X)rdisk(Y)partition(Z)

D. multi(W)partition(X)disk(Y)rdisk(Z)

70-073.02.04.004

When setting up a SCSI drive on either a RISC-based or Intel-based computer, what is the correct scsi() syntax for the ARC pathname?

▶ **Correct Answer: C**

A. **Incorrect:** The physical disk (disk) is stated first in the scsi() syntax for the ARC pathname.

B. **Incorrect:** The partition is stated last in the scsi() syntax for the ARC pathname.

C. **Correct:** This scsi() syntax for the ARC pathname is scsi(W)disk(X)rdisk(Y)partition(Z), where W indicates the primary controller number as identified by the NTBOOTDD.SYS driver, X is the SCSI ID of the target disk, Y is the SCSI logical unit number, and Z is the partition number.

D. **Incorrect:** We want to know the correct scsi() syntax for the ARC pathname on either a RISC-based or Intel-based computer. This answer shows an incorrect multi() syntax. Multi() syntax is valid for setting up SCSI disks in Windows NT versions 3.5 and higher, but is only used on *x*86-based computers.

Further Reading

The *Microsoft Windows NT Technical Support* volume of the *Microsoft Windows NT Technical Support Training* kit Chapter 3, Lesson 2 contains detailed information on the Control Panel applications, including tape device drivers, UPSs, multimedia devices, display drivers, keyboard drivers, and mouse drivers. Chapter 10, Lesson 1 contains detailed information on installing and configuring network adapter card drivers.

The *Microsoft Windows NT Workstation 4.0 Resource Kit* Chapter 20 contains detailed information on understanding scsi() syntax used in the ARC path for loading a SCSI device driver.

Use Microsoft Technical Support Online (http:/support.microsoft.com) by clicking "Frequently Asked Questions," choosing the Windows NT Workstation product, and clicking "Windows NT 4.0 Hardware and Multimedia Questions" and "How do I install and configure a third party network adapter driver in Windows NT?."

Windows NT Workstation 4.0 Study Guide. Osborne McGraw-Hill, Berkeley, CA, 1998. ISBN 0-07-882492-3. Chapter 3 contains detailed information on installing SCSI adapters and the SCSI Adapters program in the Control Panel.

Use Control Panel applications to configure a Windows NT Workstation computer in a given situation.

In addition to providing a means for installing hardware components for Windows NT Workstation, the Control Panel allows you to configure Windows NT Workstation settings without using the Registry. Some Control Panel programs allow users to personalize settings based on their unique logon name. Other Control Panel programs are set by an administrator to control configurations for the computer. These settings are used for any user logged on to the computer running Windows NT.

Some examples of using the Control Panel to configure a Windows NT Workstation are:

- Adding a path to a user environment.

- Configuring domains.

- Configuring modems.

- Configuring application performance.

- Configuring virtual memory.

Questions related to this objective are designed to determine if you have an awareness of these issues. To successfully answer the questions for this objective, you need a firm understanding of several key terms. For definitions of these terms, refer to the Glossary in this book.

Key Terms

- Control Panel

- Domain

- Environment variables

- Paging file

- Path

- Process

- Registry

- Registry Editor

- Thread

70-073.02.05.001

How can you add a path to a user environment?

A. Use User Manager.

B. Use System Policy Editor.

C. From the System icon in Control Panel, select the Environment tab.

D. From the System icon in Control Panel, select the User Profiles tab.

70-073.02.05.001

How can you add a path to a user environment?

▶ **Correct Answer: C**

A. **Incorrect:** User Manager allows you to manage security (create and maintain user accounts and groups) for a computer running Windows NT Workstation. You cannot add a path to a user environment with User Manager.

B. **Incorrect:** Use the System Policy Editor to create the system policy, a set of rules that controls what a user sees on their desktop and what they can do with their computer. The system policy allows you to restrict options in the Control Panel, customize parts of the desktop, and control network logon and access. You cannot add a path to a user environment with the System Policy Editor.

C. **Correct:** The Environment tab in the System Properties dialog box displays all of the system and user environment variables in effect. Environment variables contain information such as a drive, path, or filename. System environment variables remain the same no matter who logs on to the computer and can only be changed by an administrator. User environment variables are set by the user (such as the path for the TEMP directory) or by programs (such as the path where application files are located).

D. **Incorrect:** The User Profiles tab in the System Properties dialog box is used to copy, delete, or modify user profiles. The user profile contains user-definable settings for Windows NT Explorer, including settings for the Taskbar, printers, Control Panel, accessories, online help bookmarks, and more. You cannot add a path to a user environment on the User Profiles tab.

70-073.02.05.002

Your computer running Windows NT Workstation is a member of a domain. What is the simplest way to configure the computer to participate in a different domain?

A. Reinstall Windows NT Workstation.

B. Log off and select a different domain from the drop-down list in the Logon dialog box.

C. Use Registry Editor to overwrite the existing domain name with the desired domain name.

D. From the Network properties box in Control Panel, click the Identification tab and the Change button.

70-073.02.05.003

You need to configure a modem for use with a computer running Windows NT Workstation. Which Control Panel application should you use?

A. Ports

B. Modems

C. Telephony

D. SCSI Adapters

70-073.02.05.002

Your computer running Windows NT Workstation is a member of a domain. What is the simplest way to configure the computer to participate in a different domain?

▶ **Correct Answer: D**

    A. **Incorrect:** Although you can select another domain during setup, reinstalling Windows NT Workstation is not the simplest way to configure the computer to participate in a different domain.

    B. **Incorrect:** Selecting a domain from the drop-down list box is valid only when you want to log on to a domain from a computer that is a domain member. The scenario asks you the simplest way to configure the computer to participate (join, be a member) in a new domain.

    C. **Incorrect:** Although you can use the Registry Editor to overwrite the existing domain name with the desired domain name, this practice is extremely dangerous, and should be avoided.

    D. **Correct:** Clicking the Change button on the Identification tab in Network dialog box is the simplest way to configure the computer to join a different domain.

70-073.02.05.003

You need to configure a modem for use with a computer running Windows NT Workstation. Which Control Panel application should you use?

▶ **Correct Answer: B**

    A. **Incorrect:** The Ports application allows you to specify communications settings such as baud rate, data bits, parity, and stop bits for a selected serial port. This application does not contain modem information.

    B. **Correct:** The Modems application allows you to install and configure a new modem. In addition, this application can detect modem hardware and will prompt you for Windows NT to try to detect the modem each time you attempt to add a modem.

    C. **Incorrect:** The Telephony application provides information about your current location so that calls can be dialed properly and does not include modem information.

    D. **Incorrect:** The SCSI Adapters application lists the SCSI adapters, drivers, and connected devices and does not include modem information.

70-073.02.05.004

In Windows NT Workstation's Control Panel, which icon is used to change a paging file from 22 MB to 30 MB?

A. Server

B. System

C. Devices

D. Network

E. Services

70-073.02.05.004

In Windows NT Workstation's Control Panel, which icon is used to change a paging file from 22 MB to 30 MB?

▶ **Correct Answer: B**

A. **Incorrect:** The Server application allows you to view and manage the server properties of the computer. You can display the available shared resources, determine which of these resources are in use, and determine who is using them. A paging file is not a shared resource.

B. **Correct:** The Performance tab on the System Properties dialog box is used to change the paging file size. The paging file is used to hold information temporarily swapped into virtual memory. The default paging file size is equal to the total amount of RAM plus 12 MB. A typical paging file is around 24 MB.

C. **Incorrect:** The Devices application starts and stops device drivers and configures the startup type for each driver. A paging file is not a device.

D. **Incorrect:** The Network application allows you to configure network hardware and software for Windows NT Workstation. Specifically, you can specify a workgroup or domain, establish a domain account, configure protocols, install and configure a network adapter, and configure bindings from the Network application. A paging file is not network software.

E. **Incorrect:** The Services application displays the services running on the system and allows you to configure, start, pause, and stop services. A service is a process that performs a specific system function and often provides an application programming interface for other processes to call. A paging file is not a service.

70-073.02.05.005

In Windows NT Workstation's Control Panel, which icon is used to decrease the priority of a thread?

A. Server

B. System

C. Devices

D. Network

E. Services

70-073.02.05.005

In Windows NT Workstation's Control Panel, which icon is used to decrease the priority of a thread?

▶ **Correct Answer: B**

A. **Incorrect:** The Server application allows you to view and manage the server properties of the computer. You can display the available shared resources, determine which resources are in use, and determine who is using them. Thread priority is not a shared resource.

B. **Correct:** The Boost selection on the Performance tab in the System Properties dialog box is used to change the priority of a foreground process (active window) relative to the background programs. Since a thread inherits its priority from the process in which it runs, you can decrease the Boost, which will in turn decrease the priority of a thread when the process is active. There are three Boost settings: Maximum increases the foreground process by two priorities; Middle increases the foreground process by one priority; and None gives foreground and background processes the same priority.

C. **Incorrect:** The Devices application starts and stops device drivers and configures the startup type for each driver. Thread priority is not a device.

D. **Incorrect:** The Network application allows you to configure network hardware and software for Windows NT Workstation. Specifically, you can specify a workgroup or domain, establish a domain account, configure protocols, install and configure a network adapter, and configure bindings from the Network application. A thread priority is not network software.

E. **Incorrect:** The Services application displays the services running on the system and allows you to configure, start, pause, and stop services. A service is a process that performs a specific system function and often provides an application programming interface for other processes to call. A thread priority is not a service.

Further Reading

 The *Microsoft Windows NT Technical Support* volume of the *Microsoft Windows NT Technical Support Training* kit Chapter 2, Lesson 3 contains information on joining a computer to a domain. Chapter 3, Lesson 3 explains how to configure virtual memory and environment variables. Chapter 12, Lesson 1 explains how to implement remote access service and modems.

 Chapters 5 and 13 of the *Microsoft Windows NT Workstation 4.0 Resource Kit* explain application and thread priority.

 Use Microsoft Technical Support Online (http://support.microsoft.com) by searching for "Windows NT Workstation" and for "thread priority." Then click "SQL Server and Windows NT Thread Scheduling" and "Program Priority and Multithreaded Applications."

OBJECTIVE 2.6

Upgrade to Windows NT Workstation 4.0 in a given situation.

When you upgrade to Windows NT Workstation, many existing Windows settings are simply copied to the new configuration. You can upgrade from Windows 3.*x*, Windows for Workgroups, or an earlier version of Windows NT Workstation. Because Windows NT and Windows 95 do not use the same Registry settings, you cannot upgrade a Windows 95 installation. Instead, you must install Windows NT to a separate folder, reinstall all applications (which updates the Windows NT Registry), and then delete the Windows 95 folder.

Recall that the WINNT32.EXE setup program is used to upgrade to Windows NT Workstation 4.0 on a computer already running Windows NT Workstation. Various switches can be used with the setup program to determine how they run; these switches are discussed in Objective 2.1.

To upgrade to Windows NT Workstation 4.0 on a computer running Windows 3.*x*, click Yes in response to the upgrade question during the Windows NT Workstation 4.0 setup process and follow the upgrade instructions.

Depending on the situation, to perform an upgrade you may have to determine:

- The folder in which to install Windows NT Workstation.

- Whether to convert an existing partition.

- Whether to create boot floppies.

- Whether to install from boot floppies, the installation CD-ROM, or both.

- Whether to upgrade from the server.

Questions related to this objective are designed to determine if you have an awareness of these issues. To successfully answer the questions for this objective, you need a firm understanding of several key terms. For definitions of these terms, refer to the Glossary in this book.

Key Terms

- CONVERT utility

- Registry

70-073.02.06.001

Your Pentium-based computer runs only Windows 95. The computer is equipped with 32 MB of RAM, a 5-GB hard drive, and a 24-speed CD-ROM drive.

The required result is to upgrade the computer to Windows NT Workstation.

The first optional result is to retain Registry settings for software applications so they do not have to be reinstalled. The second optional result is to migrate user profiles to operate with Windows NT.

The proposed solution is to install Windows NT Workstation to the folder where Windows 95 is installed using WINNT32.

What does the proposed solution provide?

A. The required result and both optional results.

B. The required result and one optional result.

C. The required result but none of the optional results.

D. The proposed solution does not provide the required result.

70-073.02.06.001

Your Pentium-based computer runs only Windows 95. The computer is equipped with 32 MB of RAM, a 5-GB hard drive, and a 24-speed CD-ROM drive.

The required result is to upgrade the computer to Windows NT Workstation.

The first optional result is to retain Registry settings for software applications so they do not have to be reinstalled. The second optional result is to migrate user profiles to operate with Windows NT.

The proposed solution is to install Windows NT Workstation to the folder where Windows 95 is installed using WINNT32.

What does the proposed solution provide?

▶ **Correct Answer: D**

A. **Incorrect:** See the explanation for answer D.

B. **Incorrect:** See the explanation for answer D.

C. **Incorrect:** See the explanation for answer D.

D. **Correct:** Installing Windows NT Workstation in the Windows 95 folder using WINNT32 will not accomplish the required result or any of the optional results. You cannot upgrade from Windows 95 to Windows NT Workstation 4.0 because the two operating systems do not use the same Registry settings or hardware device support. You must install Windows NT to a separate folder, restart the computer in Windows NT, and reinstall all applications.

70-073.02.06.002

Your computer running Windows NT Workstation 3.51 has one partition formatted as HPFS. How can you upgrade the installation to version 4.0 while retaining desktop settings, configuration settings, and file system security attributes?

A. Use the CONVERT utility to convert the partition to FAT, and use WINNT to install Windows NT Workstation 4.0 in the same directory as Windows NT Workstation 3.51.

B. Use the CONVERT utility to convert the partition to FAT, and use WINNT32 to install Windows NT Workstation 4.0 in a directory different from that used by Windows NT Workstation 3.51.

C. Use the CONVERT utility to convert the partition to NTFS, and use WINNT to install Windows NT Workstation 4.0 in a directory different from that used by Windows NT Workstation 3.51.

D. Use the CONVERT utility to convert the partition to NTFS, and use WINNT32 to install Windows NT Workstation 4.0 in the same directory as Windows NT Workstation 3.51.

70-073.02.06.002

Your computer running Windows NT Workstation 3.51 has one partition formatted as HPFS. How can you upgrade the installation to version 4.0 while retaining desktop settings, configuration settings, and file system security attributes?

▶ **Correct Answer: D**

A. **Incorrect:** There is no way to convert an HPFS partition to FAT; the CONVERT utility only converts an HPFS (or FAT) partition to NTFS. In addition, the WINNT setup program is used to install Windows NT on a computer running Windows 95 or MS-DOS. Since your computer is running Windows NT Workstation 3.51, you should use the WINNT32 setup program.

B. **Incorrect:** There is no way to convert an HPFS partition to FAT; the CONVERT utility only converts an HPFS (or FAT) partition to NTFS. However, since your computer is running Windows NT Workstation 3.51, you should use the WINNT32 setup program.

C. **Incorrect:** Using the CONVERT utility to convert the partition to NTFS is the correct way to convert the HPFS partition. However, the WINNT setup program is used to install Windows NT on a computer running Windows 95 or MS-DOS. Since your computer is running Windows NT Workstation 3.51, you should use the WINNT32 setup program.

D. **Correct:** Using the CONVERT utility to convert the partition to NTFS is the correct way to convert the HPFS partition. Since your computer is running Windows NT Workstation 3.51, you should use the WINNT32 setup program. To retain desktop settings, configuration settings, and file system security attributes, you must install Windows NT Workstation 4.0 in the same folder where Windows 3.51 was installed.

70-073.02.06.003

You are running Windows NT Workstation 3.51, and you want to upgrade to version 4.0. How should you install version 4.0 from a Windows NT Server computer to preserve your desktop and configuration settings?

A. Use WINNT.EXE and install version 4.0 in a new folder.

B. Use WINNT32.EXE and install version 4.0 in a new folder.

C. Use WINNT.EXE and install version 4.0 in the same folder where version 3.51 is installed.

D. Use WINNT32.EXE and install version 4.0 in the same folder where version 3.51 is installed.

70-073.02.06.003

You are running Windows NT Workstation 3.51, and you want to upgrade to version 4.0. How should you install version 4.0 from a Windows NT Server computer to preserve your desktop and configuration settings?

▶ **Correct Answer: D**

A. **Incorrect:** The WINNT setup program is used to install Windows NT on a computer running Windows 95 or MS-DOS. Since your computer is running Windows NT Workstation 3.51, you should use the WINNT32 setup program. In addition, to preserve your desktop and configuration settings, you must install Windows NT Workstation 4.0 in the same folder where Windows NT Workstation 3.51 was installed, not in a new folder.

B. **Incorrect:** Since your computer is running Windows NT Workstation 3.51, you should use the WINNT32 setup program. However, to preserve your desktop and configuration settings, you must install Windows NT Workstation 4.0 in the same folder where Windows NT Workstation 3.51 was installed, not in a new folder.

C. **Incorrect:** The WINNT setup program is used to install Windows NT on a computer running Windows 95 or MS-DOS. Since your computer is running Windows NT Workstation 3.51, you should use the WINNT32 setup program. By installing Windows NT Workstation 4.0 in the same folder where Windows NT Workstation 3.51 was installed, you can preserve your desktop and configuration settings.

D. **Correct:** Since your computer is running Windows NT Workstation 3.51, you should use the WINNT32 setup program. And, by installing Windows NT Workstation 4.0 in the same folder where Windows NT Workstation 3.51 was installed, you can preserve your desktop and configuration settings.

70-073.02.06.004

You are upgrading a client from Windows NT Workstation 3.51 to Windows NT Workstation 4.0 and want to preserve your desktop and configuration settings. The \I386 directory has been copied to a network server, and you want to run the installation yourself from the workstation. You do not, however, want to create Setup boot disks for this computer.

The required result is to install Windows NT Workstation 4.0 on the computer.

The first optional result is to avoid creating Setup boot disks during installation. The second optional result is to preserve desktop and configuration settings.

You propose to run WINNT32 on the network share from the workstation and install Windows NT Workstation 4.0 in a different directory than the Windows NT Workstation 3.51 installation.

What does this solution provide?

A. The required result and both optional results.

B. The required result and one optional result.

C. The required result but none of the optional results.

D. The proposed solution does not provide the required result.

70-073.02.06.004

You are upgrading a client from Windows NT Workstation 3.51 to Windows NT Workstation 4.0 and want to preserve your desktop and configuration settings. The \I386 directory has been copied to a network server, and you want to run the installation yourself from the workstation. You do not, however, want to create Setup boot disks for this computer.

The required result is to install Windows NT Workstation 4.0 on the computer.

The first optional result is to avoid creating Setup boot disks during installation. The second optional result is to preserve desktop and configuration settings.

You propose to run WINNT32 on the network share from the workstation and install Windows NT Workstation 4.0 in a different directory than the Windows NT Workstation 3.51 installation.

What does this solution provide?

▶ **Correct Answer: C**

A. **Incorrect:** See the explanation for answer C.

B. **Incorrect:** See the explanation for answer C.

C. **Correct:** Running a network share from the workstation and installing Windows NT Workstation 4.0 in a directory different from the one containing Windows NT Workstation 3.51 installs Windows NT Workstation 4.0 on the computer. However, Setup boot disks are created and desktop and configurations settings are not preserved.

D. **Incorrect:** See the explanation for answer C.

70-073.02.06.005

You are upgrading a client from Windows NT Workstation 3.51 to Windows NT Workstation 4.0 and you do not want to create or use the three floppy boot disks. Which command should you use to perform the upgrade?

A. WINNT

B. WINNT /B

C. WINNT /OX

D. WINNT32 /X

E. WINNT32 /B

70-073.02.06.005

You are upgrading a client from Windows NT Workstation 3.51 to Windows NT Workstation 4.0 and you do not want to create or use the three floppy boot disks. Which command should you use to perform the upgrade?

▶ **Correct Answer: E**

A. **Incorrect:** The WINNT setup program is used to install Windows NT Workstation on a computer running Windows 95 or MS-DOS. Since your computer is running Windows NT Workstation 3.51, you should use the WINNT32 setup program.

B. **Incorrect:** The WINNT setup program is used to install Windows NT Workstation on a computer running Windows 95 or MS-DOS, although the /B switch causes the boot files to be loaded onto the computer's hard disk rather than creating floppies. Since your computer is running Windows NT Workstation 3.51, you should use the WINNT32 setup program.

C. **Incorrect:** The WINNT setup program is used to install Windows NT Workstation on a computer running Windows 95 or MS-DOS. In addition, the /OX switch creates boot floppies. Since your computer is running Windows NT Workstation 3.51, you should use the WINNT32 setup program.

D. **Incorrect:** While you should use the WINNT32 setup program to upgrade from Windows NT Workstation 3.51 to Windows NT Workstation 4.0, the /X switch should be used to prevent creation of boot floppies only when they already exist. The boot floppies should exist either as disks or be loaded on the computer's hard disk.

E. **Correct:** You should use the WINNT32 setup program to upgrade from Windows NT Workstation 3.51 to Windows NT Workstation 4.0. The /B switch causes the boot files to be loaded onto the computer's hard disk rather than creating floppies. The boot floppies should exist either as disks or be loaded on the computer's hard disk.

70-073.02.06.006

You are upgrading a client from Windows NT Workstation 3.51 to Windows NT Workstation 4.0 and want to preserve your desktop and configuration settings. The \I386 directory has been copied to a network server, and you want to run the installation yourself from the workstation. You do not, however, want to create Setup boot disks for this computer.

The required result is to install Windows NT Workstation 4.0 on the computer.

The first optional result is to avoid creating Setup boot disks during installation. The second optional result is to preserve desktop and configuration settings.

You propose to run WINNT32 on the network share from the workstation and install Windows NT Workstation 4.0 in the same directory as the Windows NT Workstation 3.51 installation.

What does this solution provide?

A. The required result and both optional results.

B. The required result and one optional result.

C. The required result but none of the optional results.

D. The proposed solution does not provide the required result.

70-073.02.06.006

You are upgrading a client from Windows NT Workstation 3.51 to Windows NT Workstation 4.0 and want to preserve your desktop and configuration settings. The \I386 directory has been copied to a network server, and you want to run the installation yourself from the workstation. You do not, however, want to create Setup boot disks for this computer.

The required result is to install Windows NT Workstation 4.0 on the computer.

The first optional result is to avoid creating Setup boot disks during installation. The second optional result is to preserve desktop and configuration settings.

You propose to run WINNT32 on the network share from the workstation and install Windows NT Workstation 4.0 in the same directory as the Windows NT Workstation 3.51 installation.

What does this solution provide?

▶ **Correct Answer: B**

A. **Incorrect:** See the explanation for answer B.

B. **Correct:** Running WINNT32 on a network share from the workstation and installing Windows NT Workstation 4.0 in the same directory as Windows NT Workstation 3.51 results in the installation of Windows NT Workstation 4.0 on the computer and the preservation of desktop and configuration settings. Because no switch was specified for the WINNT32 setup program, Setup boot disks are created.

C. **Incorrect:** See the explanation for answer B.

D. **Incorrect:** See the explanation for answer B.

70-073.02.06.007

You are upgrading a client from Windows NT Workstation 3.51 to Windows NT Workstation 4.0 and want to preserve your desktop and configuration settings. The \I386 directory has been copied to a network server, and you want to run the installation yourself from the workstation. You do not, however, want to create Setup boot disks for this computer.

The required result is to install Windows NT Workstation 4.0 on the computer.

The first optional result is to avoid creating Setup boot disks during installation. The second optional result is to preserve desktop and configuration settings.

You propose to run Winnt32 /B on the network share from the workstation and install Windows NT Workstation 4.0 in a different directory than the Windows NT Workstation 3.51 installation.

What does this solution provide?

A. The required result and both optional results.

B. The required result and one optional result.

C. The required result but none of the optional results.

D. The proposed solution does not provide the required result.

70-073.02.06.007

You are upgrading a client from Windows NT Workstation 3.51 to Windows NT Workstation 4.0 and want to preserve your desktop and configuration settings. The \I386 directory has been copied to a network server, and you want to run the installation yourself from the workstation. You do not, however, want to create Setup boot disks for this computer.

The required result is to install Windows NT Workstation 4.0 on the computer.

The first optional result is to avoid creating Setup boot disks during installation. The second optional result is to preserve desktop and configuration settings.

You propose to run Winnt32 /B on the network share from the workstation and install Windows NT Workstation 4.0 in a different directory than the Windows NT Workstation 3.51 installation.

What does this solution provide?

▶ **Correct Answer: B**

A. **Incorrect:** See the explanation for answer B.

B. **Correct:** Running WINNT32 /B on a network share from the workstation and installing Windows NT Workstation 4.0 in a directory different from the one containing Windows NT Workstation 3.51 results in the installation of Windows NT Workstation 4.0 on the computer. Because the /B switch was specified for the WINNT32 setup program, the program loads boot files on the system's hard disk rather than creating Setup boot disks. However, because Windows NT Workstation 4.0 was installed on a directory different from the one containing Windows NT Workstation 3.51, desktop and configuration settings are not preserved.

C. **Incorrect:** See the explanation for answer B.

D. **Incorrect:** See the explanation for answer B.

70-073.02.06.008

You are upgrading a client from Windows NT Workstation 3.51 to Windows NT Workstation 4.0 and want to preserve your desktop and configuration settings. The \I386 directory has been copied to a network server, and you want to run the installation yourself from the workstation. You do not, however, want to create Setup boot disks for this computer.

The required result is to install Windows NT Workstation 4.0 on the computer.

The first optional result is to avoid creating Setup boot disks during installation. The second optional result is to preserve desktop and configuration settings.

You propose to run WINNT32 /B on the network share from the workstation and install Windows NT Workstation 4.0 in the same directory as the Windows NT Workstation 3.51 installation.

What does this solution provide?

A. The required result and both optional results.

B. The required result and one optional result.

C. The required result but none of the optional results.

D. The proposed solution does not provide the required result.

70-073.02.06.008

You are upgrading a client from Windows NT Workstation 3.51 to Windows NT Workstation 4.0 and want to preserve your desktop and configuration settings. The \I386 directory has been copied to a network server, and you want to run the installation yourself from the workstation. You do not, however, want to create Setup boot disks for this computer.

The required result is to install Windows NT Workstation 4.0 on the computer.

The first optional result is to avoid creating Setup boot disks during installation. The second optional result is to preserve desktop and configuration settings.

You propose to run WINNT32 /B on the network share from the workstation and install Windows NT Workstation 4.0 in the same directory as the Windows NT Workstation 3.51 installation.

What does this solution provide?

▶ **Correct Answer: A**

A. **Correct:** Running WINNT32 /B on a network share from the workstation and installing Windows NT Workstation 4.0 in the same directory as Windows NT Workstation 3.51 results in the installation of Windows NT Workstation 4.0 on the computer. Because the /B switch was specified for the WINNT32 setup program, the program loads boot files on the system's hard disk rather than creating Setup boot disks. And, since Windows NT Workstation 4.0 was installed in the same directory as Windows NT Workstation 3.51, desktop and configuration settings are preserved.

B. **Incorrect:** See the explanation for answer A.

C. **Incorrect:** See the explanation for answer A.

D. **Incorrect:** See the explanation for answer A.

Further Reading

 The *Microsoft Windows NT Technical Support* volume of the *Microsoft Windows NT Technical Support Training* kit Chapter 2, Lesson 1 provides information on file system selection. Lesson 5 provides information on using the WINNT and WINNT32 setup programs and upgrading to Windows 4.0 from Windows 95 and Windows NT 3.*x*. Chapter 5, Lesson 1 provides details on converting to NTFS from FAT.

 Use Microsoft Technical Support Online (http:/support.microsoft.com) by clicking "Frequently Asked Questions," choosing the Windows NT Workstation product and clicking "Setup and Upgrading Questions" and "What are the differences between the FAT, NTFS, and HPFS file systems?"

OBJECTIVE 2.7

Configure a server-based installation for wide-scale deployment in a given situation.

A server-based installation is the most efficient way to deploy Windows NT Workstation in wide-scale situations. By customizing the server-based installation you can further streamline the setup process. To customize an installation you need to determine:

- The computers for the installation.

- How the operating system should be configured.

- What other applications should also be installed.

- The contents of the answer file for an unattended installation.

- The contents of a uniqueness database file.

- Whether applications to be installed will require use of the SYSDIFF utility.

- The contents of the SYSDIFF utility (if required).

Questions related to this objective are designed to determine if you have an awareness of these issues. To successfully answer the questions for this objective, you need a firm understanding of several key terms. For definitions of these terms, refer to the Glossary in this book.

Key Terms

- Automated installation

- Domain

- Server-based installation

- Uniqueness database file

70-073.02.07.001

You need to install Windows NT Workstation on 40 desktop computers and 20 laptops on your network. You also need to install a group of applications for all users.

The required result is to automate the installation of Windows NT Workstation on these computers.

The first optional result is to join the SOUTHEAST domain. The second optional result is to automate the installation of a group of 32-bit applications.

The proposed solution is to install Windows NT Workstation on one of the desktop computers. Install all needed applications and join the SOUTHEAST domain. Copy the contents of the primary boot partition of this computer to a shared folder on a server, including hidden and system files. Boot the other computers from DOS, connect to the server, and copy the shared folder to the other client computers.

What does the proposed solution provide?

A. The required result and both optional results.

B. The required result and one optional result.

C. The required result but none of the optional results.

D. The proposed solution does not provide the required result.

70-073.02.07.001

You need to install Windows NT Workstation on 40 desktop computers and 20 laptops on your network. You also need to install a group of applications for all users.

The required result is to automate the installation of Windows NT Workstation on these computers.

The first optional result is to join the SOUTHEAST domain. The second optional result is to automate the installation of a group of 32-bit applications.

The proposed solution is to install Windows NT Workstation on one of the desktop computers. Install all needed applications and join the SOUTHEAST domain. Copy the contents of the primary boot partition of this computer to a shared folder on a server, including hidden and system files. Boot the other computers from DOS, connect to the server, and copy the shared folder to the other client computers.

What does the proposed solution provide?

▶ **Correct Answer: D**

A. **Incorrect:** See the explanation for answer D.

B. **Incorrect:** See the explanation for answer D.

C. **Incorrect:** See the explanation for answer D.

D. **Correct:** An automated installation requires creation of an answer file. Joining the SOUTHEAST domain requires the domain to be specified in the answer file. Automating the installation of a group of 32-bit applications requires the applications to be set up in the OEM directory on the distribution sharepoint. Since the proposed solution does not involve the creation of an answer file, neither the required result nor any of the optional results has been provided.

70-073.02.07.002

You need to install Windows NT Workstation on 40 desktop computers and 20 laptops on your network. You also need to install a group of applications for all users.

The required result is to automate the installation of Windows NT Workstation on these computers.

The first optional result is to join the SOUTHEAST domain. The second optional result is to automate installation of 32-bit applications.

The proposed solution is to create one answer file for the desktop computers and another answer file for the laptop computers. In the [Unattended] section, add the entry OEMPREINSTALL=YES. In the [Network] section, add the entry JOINDOMAIN=SOUTHEAST. Create a UDF that specifies the setup path for the applications as well as user and computer names for each computer. Start the installation by running the WINNT.EXE command and specifying the applicable answer file and UDF.

What does the proposed solution provide?

A. The required result and both optional results.

B. The required result and one optional result.

C. The required result but none of the optional results.

D. The proposed solution does not provide the required result.

70-073.02.07.002

You need to install Windows NT Workstation on 40 desktop computers and 20 laptops on your network. You also need to install a group of applications for all users.

The required result is to automate the installation of Windows NT Workstation on these computers.

The first optional result is to join the SOUTHEAST domain. The second optional result is to automate installation of 32-bit applications.

The proposed solution is to create one answer file for the desktop computers and another answer file for the laptop computers. In the [Unattended] section, add the entry OEMPREINSTALL=YES. In the [Network] section, add the entry JOINDOMAIN=SOUTHEAST. Create a UDF that specifies the setup path for the applications as well as user and computer names for each computer. Start the installation by running the WINNT.EXE command and specifying the applicable answer file and UDF.

What does the proposed solution provide?

▶ **Correct Answer: B**

A. **Incorrect:** See the explanation for answer B.

B. **Correct:** An automated installation requires creation of an answer file, and the solution provides one answer file for the desktop computers and another for the laptop computers. Joining the SOUTHEAST domain requires the domain to be specified in the answer file, and the solution provides the entry JOINDOMAIN=SOUTHEAST in the [Network] section of the answer file. Automating the installation of a group of 32-bit applications requires the applications to be set up in the OEM directory on the distribution sharepoint. Since the solution does not provide this requirement, only one optional result is provided.

C. **Incorrect:** See the explanation for answer B.

D. **Incorrect:** See the explanation for answer B.

70-073.02.07.003

You want to install Windows NT Workstation on 75 Pentium-based computers connected to a LAN. The computers are grouped into four departments, and each department has configured their computers differently.

Which files are required? (Choose all that apply.)

A. SYSDIFF.INF

B. SYSDIFF.EXE

C. UNATTEND.TXT

D. Uniqueness database file

70-073.02.07.003

You want to install Windows NT Workstation on 75 Pentium-based computers connected to a LAN. The computers are grouped into four departments, and each department has configured their computers differently.

Which files are required? (Choose all that apply.)

▶ **Correct Answers: C and D**

    A. **Incorrect:** You only need to use SYSDIFF.INF if you want to preinstall applications that do not support a scripted installation (those that must be installed interactively). Specifically, the SYSDIFF.INF file provides information used by the Windows NT Workstation Setup program to install software that supports a given hardware device. Since the scenario does not mention the need to install such applications, the SYSDIFF.INF file is not required.

    B. **Incorrect:** You only need to use SYSDIFF.EXE if you want to preinstall applications that do not support a scripted installation (those that must be installed interactively. Since the scenario does not mention the need to install such applications, the SYSDIFF.EXE file is not required.

    C. **Correct:** The most efficient way to install Windows NT Workstation on the 75 computers in the scenario is to employ an automated installation, which requires an UNATTEND.TXT (answer) file.

    D. **Correct:** Because the scenario requires not only an automated installation but also four different configurations for the four departments, a uniqueness database file is required to work with the UNATTEND.TXT (answer) file to customize the installation.

70-073.02.07.004

A company is planning to create a new domain for their marketing department. When planning the installation, you decide that an unattended server-based installation from the Network Distribution Server is the most effective method of installation. You create an answer file, but you also need to customize user information for each machine. Which file can you use to customize user information?

A. User data file

B. Unique data file

C. User database file

D. Uniqueness database file

70-073.02.07.004

A company is planning to create a new domain for their marketing department. When planning the installation, you decide that an unattended server-based installation from the Network Distribution Server is the most effective method of installation. You create an answer file, but you also need to customize user information for each machine. Which file can you use to customize user information?

▶ **Correct Answer: D**

   A. **Incorrect:** The user data file does not exist in Windows NT Workstation and cannot be used to customize user information in an unattended server-based installation.

   B. **Incorrect:** The unique data file does not exist in Windows NT Workstation and cannot be used to customize user information in an unattended server-based installation.

   C. **Incorrect:** The user database file does not exist in Windows NT Workstation and cannot be used to customize user information in an unattended server-based installation.

   D. **Correct:** Because the scenario requires an unattended installation and customized user information for each machine, a uniqueness database file is required to work with the UNATTEND.TXT (answer) file to customize each installation.

Further Reading

 The *Microsoft Windows NT Technical Support* volume of the *Microsoft Windows NT Technical Support Training* kit Chapter 2, Lesson 5 provides information on performing an unattended installation. Practice for creating an unattended installation is included on the CD provided in this kit.

 The *Microsoft Windows NT Workstation 4.0 Resource Kit* Chapter 2 contains detailed information on performing an unattended installation, including answer files, uniqueness database files, and the SYSDIFF utility. Appendix A contains details on each section in the answer file and UDF.

 Use Microsoft Technical Support Online (http://support.microsoft.com) by searching for "Windows NT Workstation" and for "unattended installation." Then click "Unattended Installation of Microsoft Windows NT 4.0."

Managing Resources

The Managing Resources domain examines how resources are set up and managed in the Windows NT Workstation environment. Resources include:

- Local user accounts.

- Local group accounts.

- NT file system (NTFS) permissions.

- Printers.

- Shared folders.

- Share permissions.

- User profiles.

Tested Skills and Suggested Practices

- Creating and managing local user accounts and local group accounts to meet given requirements. You must be able to determine the best strategy for setting up local user and group accounts that give users access to resources while considering security needs.

  - Practice 1: Create a local user account that limits hours and dates of account access and provides for a daily backup location. Learn where to specify logon hours and an expiration date. Create a home folder for the user.

  - Practice 2: Create local and global group accounts. Create three local group accounts for three applications. Assign each group access to the application. Create a global group, and add all users to the global group. Then add the global group to each of the three local groups.

  - Practice 3: Rename existing user accounts. Use an existing user account to reflect a new user's name, and change the password.

- Setting up and modifying user profiles. You must be able to configure a local user profile and a roaming user profile.

    - Practice 1: Using a template user profile, set up local user profiles for a group. Copy the template user profile to a network server, and specify the users permitted to use the profile.

    - Practice 2: Distinguish between default, roaming personal, and roaming mandatory user profiles. Learn which profiles can be changed by users.

    - Practice 3: Using a template user profile, set up roaming user profiles for a group. Copy the template user profile to a network server, and specify the path to the roaming user profile.

- Setting up shared folders and permissions. You should be able to set up shared folders and assign share permissions to users and groups.

    - Practice 1: Learn the four share permissions and the rules for applying share permissions. Read how user and group share permissions work together. Read how the No Access permission overrides all other permissions assigned to users and groups.

    - Practice 2: Using the Sharing tab, set up a shared folder. Assign a share permission of Change to a group.

- Setting permissions on NTFS partitions, folders, and files. Learn how permissions for partitions, files, and folders are affected by moving and copying.

    - Practice 1: Learn the individual, folder, and file NTFS permissions. Read the rules for moving and copying files with NTFS permissions.

    - Practice 2: Move folders and files between partitions. Observe how permissions are affected.

- Installing and configuring printers in a given environment. Be able to configure printing to a local computer or to printers on the network. Use configuration settings to customize printing setups.

    - Practice 1: Install a network print server. Confirm your print device compatibility, and use the Add Printer Wizard to install a printer driver for the print device on the print server. Use the Sharing tab to provide network printing for clients.

    - Practice 2: Using the tabs on the Printer Properties window, configure a printing pool. Learn the configuration information contained in the Printer Properties tabs.

O B J E C T I V E   3 . 1

Create and manage local user accounts and local group accounts to meet given requirements.

Local user accounts and local group accounts work together to provide Windows NT security and simplify administration tasks.

User Accounts

User accounts are the basis for Windows NT security. Persons who access the system must have a user account containing their unique information; this account controls their level of access to various system resources. Each account is assigned a unique *security identifier* (SID) number that is used to identify the account to Windows NT. For its internal processes, Windows NT uses the SID rather than the user's name or other personal information. There are three types of user accounts:

Account type	Description	How created
Default User	Allows user to log on to a local computer, domain, or network resource, depending on permissions.	Must be created
Guest	Allows occasional users to log on to a local computer. This account is disabled by default; it can be renamed but not deleted.	Automatically upon installation
Administrator	Allows user to perform administrative tasks and manage the computer, domain configuration, and resources. This account can be renamed but not deleted.	Automatically upon installation

The two types of default user accounts are as follows:

- Domain user account

- Local user account

The domain user account contains information that allows a user to log on to a domain from any computer on the network. You should create domain user accounts for all users. The User Manager for Domains account management tool in Windows NT Server is used to set up domain user accounts. Windows NT Workstation does not include the User Manager for Domains tool. However, you can install User Manager for Domains by installing the Windows NT Server client-based administration tools on the Windows NT Workstation.

The local user account contains information that allows a user to log on to the local computer only. To log on to another computer, a user must have a separate user account. Local user accounts should be created only for users in a workgroup environment (rather than a domain environment). The User Manager account management tool in Windows NT Workstation or the User Manager for Domains account management tool (discussed earlier) is used to set up local user accounts.

You can rename existing user accounts simply by changing the username and password information. Windows NT retains the permissions and rights settings from the original account because the SID is not deleted.

Group Accounts

Group accounts allow you to organize user accounts by need, simplifying administrative tasks. Instead of assigning user rights or permissions to each user account, you can place users with similar needs in a group and assign rights or permissions only once. The two kinds of groups are as follows:

- Local groups

- Global groups

Local Groups

Local groups allow users to access a network resource on the local computer. The rules for local groups are:

- They can contain user accounts and global groups from any domain.

- They cannot contain other local groups.

Local groups must be created where the needed resource resides. For example, if the local group needs access to a common printer that resides on the *primary domain controller* (PDC), the local group must be created on the PDC. User Manager or User Manager for Domains is used to create local groups on member servers or Windows NT Workstation. User Manager for Domains is used to create local groups on the PDC. Recall that Windows NT Workstation does not include User Manager for Domains. However, you can install User Manager for Domains by installing the Windows NT Server client-based administration tools on the Windows NT Workstation.

Global Groups

Global groups are used only for grouping domain user accounts, often by function or location. The rules for global groups are:

- They can contain only user accounts from the domain where the global group is created.

- They cannot contain local groups.

- They cannot contain other global groups.

Global groups are always created on the PDC in the domain where the user accounts reside. User Manager for Domains is used to create global groups.

Questions related to this objective are designed to determine if you have an awareness of these issues. To successfully answer the questions for this objective, you need a firm understanding of several key terms. For definitions of these terms, refer to the Glossary in this book.

Key Terms

- Backup domain controller (BDC)

- Domain

- Domain user account

- Global groups

- Local group account

- Local user account

- Permissions

- Primary domain controller (PDC)

- Security identifier (SID)

- Trust relationship

- User rights

- Workgroup

70-073.03.01.001

You are planning to hire three new employees who will use the same Windows NT Workstation–based computer connected to your Windows NT domain in a 24-hour, three-shift environment.

The required result is to provide security for each user's data.

The first optional result is to restrict users from logging on to the network during non-working hours. The second optional result is to ensure that all user files are backed up on a daily basis.

The proposed solution is to create a password-protected domain user account for each of the three users, configure the applicable logon hours for each account, and create a home folder for each user on a server with a tape device and backup software installed. You will also schedule a daily backup routine.

What does the proposed solution provide?

A. The required result and all optional results.

B. The required result and one optional result.

C. The required result but none of the optional results.

D. The proposed solution does not provide the required result.

70-073.03.01.001

You are planning to hire three new employees who will use the same Windows NT Workstation–based computer connected to your Windows NT domain in a 24-hour, three-shift environment.

The required result is to provide security for each user's data.

The first optional result is to restrict users from logging on to the network during non-working hours. The second optional result is to ensure that all user files are backed up on a daily basis.

The proposed solution is to create a password-protected domain user account for each of the three users, configure the applicable logon hours for each account, and create a home folder for each user on a server with a tape device and backup software installed. You will also schedule a daily backup routine.

What does the proposed solution provide?

▶ **Correct Answer: A**

A. **Correct:** Because the employees must be connected to your Windows NT domain, you must set up domain user accounts, which require User Manager for Domains. User Manager for Domains is the account management tool on computers running Windows NT Server; you can install User Manager for Domains on a computer running Windows NT Workstation or Windows 95 by installing the Windows NT Server client-based administration tools. By creating a password-protected domain user account, you provide security for each user's data. Configuring appropriate logon hours restricts users from logging on during non-working hours. And by creating a home folder and scheduling a daily backup routine, you ensure that all user files are backed up on a daily basis.

B. **Incorrect:** See the explanation for answer A.

C. **Incorrect:** See the explanation for answer A.

D. **Incorrect:** See the explanation for answer A.

70-073.003.01.002

A user is leaving your company, and you must ensure that she can no longer access any computer resources. Her Windows NT Workstation–based computer has permissions set at the file level for sensitive company data. A new user is being hired to fill the position and will need the same access to these files.

How should you proceed?

A. Delete the user account and create a new account with a different name and password.

B. Rename the existing user account to reflect the new user's name and change the password.

C. Rename the existing user account to reflect the new user's name and leave the password unchanged.

D. Delete the old user account, create a new account for the new hire, and transfer ownership of all sensitive files to the new user account.

70-073.003.01.002

A user is leaving your company, and you must ensure that she can no longer access any computer resources. Her Windows NT Workstation–based computer has permissions set at the file level for sensitive company data. A new user is being hired to fill the position and will need the same access to these files.

How should you proceed?

▶ **Correct Answer: B**

A. **Incorrect:** Deleting the user account removes the security identifier that Windows NT uses to refer to the user's account, along with the permissions and rights associated with the account. By creating a new account with a different name and password, you have not provided the permissions for access to the sensitive company data files for the new user.

B. **Correct:** If you change the user's name and password for the existing account, permissions associated with the account remain unchanged for the new user because the SID was not deleted. Windows NT uses the SID to refer to an account rather than the account's user or group name.

C. **Incorrect:** Changing the user account name but leaving the password for the existing user's account unchanged does not prevent the old user from accessing computer resources.

D. **Incorrect:** Deleting the user account removes the SID that Windows NT uses to refer to the user's account, along with the permissions and rights associated with the account. Transferring ownership of sensitive files to the new user account is not acceptable, since it may prevent other authorized users from accessing the files.

70-073.03.01.03

A number of clerical users in the Windows NT domain you administer need to access a word process-ing application on a member server, the REPORTS folder on the PDC, and the DOCUMENTS folder on a BDC. What is the best way to grant access to the resources these users need?

A. Create three local groups on the PDC named WORDP, RPTS, and DOCS. Assign the appropriate access to each group, and add all clerical users to each group.

B. Create a global group on the PDC named CLERKS, and assign the appropriate access to the direc-tories on all three servers. Add all clerical users in the domain to the CLERKS group.

C. Create three local groups, one on the PDC named RPTS, one on the BDC named DOCS, and one on the member server named WORDP. Assign the appropriate access to each group, and add all clerical users to each group.

D. Create three local groups on the PDC named WORDP, RPTS, and DOCS. Assign the appropriate access to each group. Create a global group named CLERKS, and add the clerical users in the do-main to the CLERKS group. Add the CLERKS group to each of the local groups.

E. Create three local groups, two on the PDC named RPTS and DOCS, and one on the member server named WORDP. Assign the appropriate access to each group. Create a global group named CLERKS and add all clerical users in the domain to the CLERKS group. Add the CLERKS group to the three local groups.

70-073.03.01.03

A number of clerical users in the Windows NT domain you administer need to access a word processing application on a member server, the REPORTS folder on the PDC, and the DOCUMENTS folder on a BDC. What is the best way to grant access to the resources these users need?

▶ **Correct Answer: E**

A. **Incorrect:** Creating three local groups on the PDC does not give users access to the word processing application on the member server. Also, adding the same clerical users to three local groups is inefficient.

B. **Incorrect:** Creating a global group on the PDC does not give users access to the word processing application on the member server. Global groups should be used only for grouping domain user accounts, not for assigning access to directories. Members of global groups are assigned resource permissions when the global group is added to a local group.

C. **Incorrect:** It is not necessary to create a local group on the BDC. The PDC provides account and security information to all other domain controllers in the domain, including the backup domain. Also, adding the same clerical users to three local groups is inefficient.

D. **Incorrect:** Creating three local groups on the PDC will not give users access to the word processing application on the member server.

E. **Correct:** Creating three local groups, two on the PDC and one on the member server, gives local groups access to all necessary applications and folders. By setting up a global group, assigning all users to the global group, and then assigning the global group to the local groups, you only have to assign users to a group once, which is the most efficient way to grant access to resources.

70-073.03.01.004

A consultant is going to visit your office next week, and she will require access to your Windows NT Workstation computer for one week during normal business hours. You have administrative permissions on your department's Windows NT domain, but there are no servers located in your area.

The required result is to create a user account for the consultant on your Windows NT Workstation.

The first optional result is to allow the consultant to log on only during working hours (8 A.M. to 5 P.M.). The second optional result is to limit the account access to one week.

The proposed solution is to install Windows NT Server client-based administrative tools on the computer, start User Manager for Domains, and create a user account with a unique user name. Use the Logon Hours dialog box to only allow logons from 8 A.M. to 5 P.M. Use the Account Information dialog box to set an expiration date for the account.

What does the proposed solution provide?

A. The required result and all optional results.

B. The required result and one optional result.

C. The required result but none of the optional results.

D. The proposed solution does not provide the required result.

70-073.03.01.004

A consultant is going to visit your office next week, and she will require access to your Windows NT Workstation computer for one week during normal business hours. You have administrative permissions on your department's Windows NT domain, but there are no servers located in your area.

The required result is to create a user account for the consultant on your Windows NT Workstation.

The first optional result is to allow the consultant to log on only during working hours (8 A.M. to 5 P.M.). The second optional result is to limit the account access to one week.

The proposed solution is to install Windows NT Server client-based administrative tools on the computer, start User Manager for Domains, and create a user account with a unique user name. Use the Logon Hours dialog box to only allow logons from 8 A.M. to 5 P.M. Use the Account Information dialog box to set an expiration date for the account.

What does the proposed solution provide?

▶ **Correct Answer: A**

A. **Correct:** Because you need to set logon hours and an account expiration date, you will require User Manager for Domains on your Windows NT Workstation. You can install User Manager for Domains by installing the Windows NT Server client-based administration tools. By creating a user account with a unique user name, you create the account on the Windows NT Workstation. Setting the Logon Hours dialog box to only allow logons from 8 A.M. to 5 P.M. ensures access only during working hours. And setting an expiration date in the Account Information dialog box limits the account access to one week.

B. **Incorrect:** See the explanation for answer A.

C. **Incorrect:** See the explanation for answer A.

D. **Incorrect:** See the explanation for answer A.

70-073.03.01.005

You are the administrator of a Windows NT Workstation–based computer. A consultant is going to visit your office next week, and she will require access to your computer.

The required result is to create a new user account for the consultant.

The first optional result is to allow the consultant to log on only during working hours (8 A.M. to 5 P.M.). The second optional result is to limit the account access to a one-week time period only.

The proposed solution is to start User Manager and create a user account with a unique user name, use the Logon Hours dialog box to only allow logons from 8 A.M. to 5 P.M., and use the Account Information dialog box to set an expiration date for the account.

What does the proposed solution provide?

A. The required result and all optional results.

B. The required result and one optional result.

C. The required result but none of the optional results.

D. The proposed solution does not provide the required result.

70-073.03.01.005

You are the administrator of a Windows NT Workstation–based computer. A consultant is going to visit your office next week, and she will require access to your computer.

The required result is to create a new user account for the consultant.

The first optional result is to allow the consultant to log on only during working hours (8 A.M. to 5 P.M.). The second optional result is to limit the account access to a one-week time period only.

The proposed solution is to start User Manager and create a user account with a unique user name, use the Logon Hours dialog box to only allow logons from 8 A.M. to 5 P.M., and use the Account Information dialog box to set an expiration date for the account.

What does the proposed solution provide?

▶ **Correct Answer: C**

A. **Incorrect:** See the explanation for answer C.

B. **Incorrect:** See the explanation for answer C.

C. **Correct:** User Manager does not allow you to set logon hours or to set an account expiration date. The proposed solution only accomplishes the required result—creating a new user account for the consultant. To set logon hours and an account expiration date, you will require User Manager for Domains on your Windows NT Workstation. You can install User Manager for Domains by installing the Windows NT Server client-based administration tools.

D. **Incorrect:** See the explanation for answer C.

Further Reading

 The *Microsoft Windows NT Network Administration* volume of the *Microsoft Windows NT Network Administration Training* kit Chapter 2, Lesson 1 discusses the types of user accounts and how they are created. Lesson 2 examines planning of user accounts and provides a user accounts planning worksheet to be completed in a scenario exercise. Lesson 3 provides procedures for setting up user accounts. Chapter 3, Lesson 1 discusses the use of local and global groups and includes a short video and exercises explaining how they are used in single-domain and multiple-domain networks. Lesson 2 examines planning of group accounts and provides a group accounts planning worksheet to be completed in a scenario exercise.

OBJECTIVE 3.2

Set up and modify user profiles.

User profiles allow users to select and store settings for the user environment, including Display settings, Regional settings, Mouse settings, Sounds settings, Network connections, and Printer connections. In addition, the following settings are automatically saved in a user profile:

- Windows NT Explorer
- Taskbar
- Network printer
- Control Panel
- Accessories
- Windows NT–based programs
- Online Help bookmarks

There are two types of user profiles:

- **Local user profile.** The local user profile is created from the default user profile when a user logs on to Windows NT Workstation for the first time. The local user profile stores settings for a user logged on to a specific computer. The stored profile is used the next time the user logs on to the computer.

- **Roaming user profile.** The roaming user profile is used in a domain environment and is stored on a network server rather than locally. This profile allows a user to log on to the same working environment, at any workstation they use, rather than just a local computer. A roaming user profile can be either *personal* or *mandatory*. A roaming personal user profile can be changed by the user; changes are stored when the user logs off. A roaming mandatory user profile is a preconfigured profile that users cannot change. A roaming mandatory user profile is often assigned to many users who require identical desktop configurations.

Questions related to this objective are designed to determine if you have an awareness of these issues. To successfully answer the questions for this objective, you need a firm understanding of several key terms. For definitions of these terms, refer to the Glossary in this book.

Key Terms

- Roaming mandatory user profile

- Roaming personal user profile

- Roaming user profile

- Template user profile

- User profile

70-073.03.02.001

You need to configure the user environment for the clients on your Windows NT Server–based network. Your network has Windows NT Workstation and Windows 3.1 client computers.

The required result is to configure the network environment for Windows NT Workstation and Windows 3.1 clients each time they log on to the network.

The first optional result is to prevent Windows NT Workstation users from changing their configurations. The second optional result is to prevent Windows 3.1 clients from changing their configurations.

The proposed solution is to use the default user profiles created when users log on to the network for the first time.

What does the proposed solution provide?

A. The required result and all optional results.

B. The required result and one optional result.

C. The required result but none of the optional results.

D. The proposed solution does not provide the required result.

70-073.03.02.002

Which type of user profile cannot be changed by users?

A. A default local user profile

B. A roaming personal user profile

C. A roaming mandatory user profile

70-073.03.02.001

You need to configure the user environment for the clients on your Windows NT Server–based network. Your network has Windows NT Workstation and Windows 3.1 client computers.

The required result is to configure the network environment for Windows NT Workstation and Windows 3.1 clients each time they log on to the network.

The first optional result is to prevent Windows NT Workstation users from changing their configurations. The second optional result is to prevent Windows 3.1 clients from changing their configurations.

The proposed solution is to use the default user profiles created when users log on to the network for the first time.

What does the proposed solution provide?

▶ **Correct Answer: D**

A. **Incorrect:** See the explanation for answer D.

B. **Incorrect:** See the explanation for answer D.

C. **Incorrect:** See the explanation for answer D.

D. **Correct:** While default user profiles are created when Windows NT Workstation users log on for the first time, you cannot set user profiles for users who log on from Windows 3.1. For these users, you must write a logon script to configure user network and printer connections.

70-073.03.02.002

Which type of user profile cannot be changed by users?

▶ **Correct Answer: C**

A. **Incorrect:** A default user profile is created automatically when a user logs on for the first time from a Windows NT–based client; however, a user can change the settings.

B. **Incorrect:** A roaming personal user profile can be changed by the user.

C. **Correct:** A roaming mandatory user profile is a preconfigured file that users cannot change. A mandatory user profile can be assigned to many users, so changing one profile affects all users assigned to that profile.

70-073.03.02.003

You need to create roaming user profiles for 25 sales representatives in your division. What is the best way to accomplish this task?

A. No action is required because roaming user profiles are created automatically when a user logs on for the first time.

B. Create a user profile for each sales representative and place the profiles in a shared folder named SALES on a network server.

C. Create a user profile for each sales representative, and place each profile in a shared folder named SALES on the user's workstation.

D. Create a template user profile, copy the template user profile to a shared directory named PROFILES on a network server, specify the users permitted to use the profile, and specify the path to the profile in the User Environment Profile dialog box.

70-073.03.02.004

You need to configure the user environment for the clients on your Windows NT Server–based network. Your network has Windows NT Workstation and Windows 3.11 client computers.

The required result is to configure the network environment for Windows NT Workstation and Windows 3.11 clients each time they log on to the network.

The first optional result is to prevent Windows NT Workstation users from changing their configurations. The second optional result is to prevent Windows 3.11 clients from changing their configurations.

The proposed solution is to create user profiles for each user and remove access to the Administrative Tools folder from all users' configurations.

What does the proposed solution provide?

A. The required result and all optional results.

B. The required result and one optional result.

C. The required result but none of the optional results.

D. The proposed solution does not provide the required result.

70-073.03.02.003

You need to create roaming user profiles for 25 sales representatives in your division. What is the best way to accomplish this task?

▶ **Correct Answer: D**

   A. **Incorrect:** Default user profiles, not roaming user profiles, are created automatically when a user logs on for the first time.

   B. **Incorrect:** It is not necessary, nor is it efficient, to create a user profile for each sales representative. Creating a template user profile allows you to create only one user profile and then select the users permitted to use the profile.

   C. **Incorrect:** It is not necessary, nor is it efficient, to create a user profile for each sales representative. Creating a template user profile allows you to create only one user profile and then select the users permitted to use the profile.

   D. **Correct:** Creating a template user profile, copying it to a shared directory on a network server, selecting the users permitted to use the profile, and specifying a path to the profile is the best way to create roaming profiles for 25 sales representatives. This procedure eliminates creating a user profile for each sales representative.

70-073.03.02.004

You need to configure the user environment for the clients on your Windows NT Server–based network. Your network has Windows NT Workstation and Windows 3.11 client computers.

The required result is to configure the network environment for Windows NT Workstation and Windows 3.11 clients each time they log on to the network.

The first optional result is to prevent Windows NT Workstation users from changing their configurations. The second optional result is to prevent Windows 3.11 clients from changing their configurations.

The proposed solution is to create user profiles for each user and remove access to the Administrative Tools folder from all users' configurations.

What does the proposed solution provide?

▶ **Correct Answer: D**

   A. **Incorrect:** See the explanation for answer D.

   B. **Incorrect:** See the explanation for answer D.

   C. **Incorrect:** See the explanation for answer D.

   D. **Correct:** While default user profiles are created when Windows NT Workstation users log on for the first time, you cannot set user profiles for users who log on from Windows 3.1. For these users, you must write a logon script to configure user network and printer connections.

70-073.03.02.005

You need to configure the user environment for the clients on your Windows NT Server–based network. Your network has Windows NT Workstation and Windows 3.11 client computers.

The required result is to configure the network environment for Windows NT Workstation and Windows 3.11 clients each time they log on to the network.

The first optional result is to prevent Windows NT Workstation users from changing their configurations. The second optional result is to prevent Windows 3.11 clients from changing their configurations.

The proposed solution is to create a user profile for each Windows NT Workstation client and a logon script for each Windows 3.11 client.

What does the proposed solution provide?

A. The required result and all optional results.

B. The required result and one optional result.

C. The required result but none of the optional results.

D. The proposed solution does not provide the required result.

70-073.03.02.005

You need to configure the user environment for the clients on your Windows NT Server–based network. Your network has Windows NT Workstation and Windows 3.11 client computers.

The required result is to configure the network environment for Windows NT Workstation and Windows 3.11 clients each time they log on to the network.

The first optional result is to prevent Windows NT Workstation users from changing their configurations. The second optional result is to prevent Windows 3.11 clients from changing their configurations.

The proposed solution is to create a user profile for each Windows NT Workstation client and a logon script for each Windows 3.11 client.

What does the proposed solution provide?

▶ **Correct Answer: B**

A. **Incorrect:** See the explanation for answer B.

B. **Correct:** While default user profiles are created when Windows NT Workstation users log on for the first time, and you have created a logon script to configure user network and printer connections for Windows 3.11 users, no steps have been taken to prevent Windows NT Workstation users from changing their configurations.

C. **Incorrect:** See the explanation for answer B.

D. **Incorrect:** See the explanation for answer B.

70-073.03.02.006

You need to configure the user environment for the clients on your Windows NT Server–based network. Your network has Windows NT Workstation and Windows 3.11 client computers.

The required result is to configure the network environment for Windows NT Workstation and Windows 3.1 clients each time they log on to the network.

The first optional result is to prevent Windows NT Workstation users from changing their configurations. The second optional result is to prevent Windows 3.11 clients from changing their configurations.

The proposed solution is to create a user profile for each Windows NT Workstation client and a logon script for each Windows 3.11 client. Configure the profiles for Windows NT Workstation users so that they cannot access the Administrative Tools folder.

What does the proposed solution provide?

A. The required result and all optional results.

B. The required result and one optional result.

C. The required result but none of the optional results.

D. The proposed solution does not provide the required result.

70-073.03.02.006

You need to configure the user environment for the clients on your Windows NT Server–based network. Your network has Windows NT Workstation and Windows 3.11 client computers.

The required result is to configure the network environment for Windows NT Workstation and Windows 3.1 clients each time they log on to the network.

The first optional result is to prevent Windows NT Workstation users from changing their configurations. The second optional result is to prevent Windows 3.11 clients from changing their configurations.

The proposed solution is to create a user profile for each Windows NT Workstation client and a logon script for each Windows 3.11 client. Configure the profiles for Windows NT Workstation users so that they cannot access the Administrative Tools folder.

What does the proposed solution provide?

▶ **Correct Answer: A**

A. **Correct:** Default user profiles are created when Windows NT Workstation users log on for the first time, a logon script is created to configure user network and printer connections for Windows 3.11 users, and profiles are configured to prevent Windows NT Workstation users from changing their configurations.

B. **Incorrect:** See the explanation for answer A.

C. **Incorrect:** See the explanation for answer A.

D. **Incorrect:** See the explanation for answer A.

Further Reading

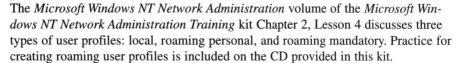

The *Microsoft Windows NT Network Administration* volume of the *Microsoft Windows NT Network Administration Training* kit Chapter 2, Lesson 4 discusses three types of user profiles: local, roaming personal, and roaming mandatory. Practice for creating roaming user profiles is included on the CD provided in this kit.

O B J E C T I V E   3 . 3

Set up shared folders and permissions.

Shared folders allow network users access to files stored in a centralized location. Permissions are assigned to user and group accounts to control access to shared folders.

Shared Folders

Shared folders are set up on the Sharing tab in the Properties dialog box for the folder. Select the button for shared folder, enter a description in the Comment field, specify a user limit, set permissions for the folder, and click OK.

Share Permissions

Share permissions can be assigned to users, groups, or both to control how folders are accessed. These permissions are not the same as NTFS permissions, which will be discussed later in this book. Share permissions are assigned on the Access Through Share Permissions dialog box, which is accessed by clicking the Permissions button in the Properties dialog box for the folder. There are four share permissions, described in the following table.

Permission	Allows users to
Full Control	Modify file permissions
	Take ownership of files on NTFS partitions
	Perform all tasks permitted by the Change and Read permissions
Change	Create and delete folders and add files
	Change data in files
	Change file attributes
	Perform all tasks permitted by the Read permission

(continued)

(continued)

Permission	Allows users to
Read	Display folder names and file names
	Display the data and attributes of files
	Run program files
	Access other folders within that folder
No Access	Establish only a connection to the shared folder. Access is denied and the contents do not appear. The No Access permission overrides other permissions.

There are two rules for applying share permissions:

- If you assign permissions to a user and also to a group of which the user is a member, the user's effective permission is the *least restrictive* of the two permissions. For example, if a user has Read access to a folder and a group the user belongs to has Change permission, the user effectively has the least restrictive permission—Change.

- The No Access permission overrides all other permissions assigned to either the user or a group of which the user is a member.

Questions related to this objective are designed to determine if you have an awareness of these issues. To successfully answer the questions for this objective, you need a firm understanding of several key terms. For definitions of these terms, refer to the Glossary in this book.

Key Terms

- Creator Owner group

- Everyone group

- Permissions

- Share

- Share permissions

70-073.03.03.001

You want to share a folder on the hard disk of your Windows NT Workstation–based computer. What is the recommended procedure?

A. Use User Manager.

B. Use Windows NT Explorer.

C. Use the SHARE command line utility.

D. Use the ATTRIB command line utility.

70-073.03.03.002

What are the rules for applying permissions to a shared directory? (Choose two.)

A. If the No Access permission is assigned to a user, but Full Control is assigned to a group that includes the user as a member, the group permission overrides the No Access permission.

B. If the No Access permission is assigned to a user, but Full Control is assigned to a group that includes the user as a member, the No Access permission overrides all other permissions.

C. If the Full Control permission is assigned to a user, but No Access is assigned to a group that includes the user as a member, the Full Control permission overrides the No Access permission.

D. If permissions are assigned to a user and also to a group that includes the user as a member, the user's effective permissions are the most restrictive permissions resulting from the combination of the user and group permissions.

E. If permissions other than No Access are assigned to a user and also to a group that includes the user as a member, the user's effective permissions are the least restrictive permissions resulting from the combination of the user and group permissions.

70-073.03.03.001

You want to share a folder on the hard disk of your Windows NT Workstation–based computer. What is the recommended procedure?

▶ **Correct Answer: B**

A. **Incorrect:** User Manager is an account management tool used to manage local accounts on the Windows NT Workstation.

B. **Correct:** Use Windows NT Explorer to view the properties for the folder you want to share, click the Sharing tab, and fill in the details for the share.

C. **Incorrect:** The NET SHARE command line utility, not the SHARE command, allows you to share a folder.

D. **Incorrect:** The ATTRIB command is used to display, set, or remove the read-only, archive, system, and hidden attributes assigned to files or directories.

70-073.03.03.002

What are the rules for applying permissions to a shared directory? (Choose two.)

▶ **Correct Answers: B and E**

A. **Incorrect:** The No Access permission overrides all other permissions that are assigned to the user or to the groups of which the user is a member.

B. **Correct:** The No Access permission overrides all other permissions that are assigned to the user or to the groups of which the user is a member.

C. **Incorrect:** The No Access permission overrides all other permissions that are assigned to the user or to the groups of which the user is a member.

D. **Incorrect:** If permissions are assigned to a user and also to a group that includes the user as a member, the user's effective permissions are the least restrictive permissions resulting from the combination of the user and group permissions.

E. **Correct:** If permissions are assigned to a user and also to a group that includes the user as a member, the user's effective permissions are the least restrictive permissions resulting from the combination of the user and group permissions.

70-073.03.03.003

You share your Windows NT Workstation 4.0 computer with another user, JohnP, and you store confidential data in the TECHDATA folder on a FAT partition on this machine.

The required result is to prevent the user JohnP from accessing the TECHDATA folder.

The first optional result is to avoid performance degradation by allowing only five network users to access the share simultaneously. The second optional result is to give the user JohnP the ability to stop sharing this folder when he is logged on to the machine.

The proposed solution is to log on to the computer as Administrator, select the TECHDATA folder properties in Explorer, and share the folder. Then click Permissions, remove the Everyone group, add John P's account name, and specify No Access.

Under the User Limit part of the Sharing properties page, select Allow and enter a value of 5 in the Users box.

What does the proposed solution provide?

A. The required result and all optional results.

B. The required result and one optional result.

C. The required result but none of the optional results.

D. The proposed solution does not provide the required result.

70-073.03.03.003

You share your Windows NT Workstation 4.0 computer with another user, JohnP, and you store confidential data in the TECHDATA folder on a FAT partition on this machine.

The required result is to prevent the user JohnP from accessing the TECHDATA folder.

The first optional result is to avoid performance degradation by allowing only five network users to access the share simultaneously. The second optional result is to give the user JohnP the ability to stop sharing this folder when he is logged on to the machine.

The proposed solution is to log on to the computer as Administrator, select the TECHDATA folder properties in Explorer, and share the folder. Then click Permissions, remove the Everyone group, add John P's account name, and specify No Access.

Under the User Limit part of the Sharing properties page, select Allow and enter a value of 5 in the Users box.

What does the proposed solution provide?

▶ **Correct Answer: D**

A. **Incorrect:** See the explanation for answer D.

B. **Incorrect:** See the explanation for answer D.

C. **Incorrect:** See the explanation for answer D.

D. **Correct:** Share permissions give network users centralized access to network files and do not apply to local files. You cannot use share permissions to prevent users from gaining access to the folders on their local computers.

70-073.03.03.004

You have some proposal documents stored in the \BANK folder on your computer running Windows NT Workstation.

The required result is to copy the \BANK folder to the \WEDGE folder on a server with one NTFS partition, where the Everyone system group has Full Control permission.

The first optional result is to prevent other users from changing the existing files in the \BANK folder after it is copied, but to allow others to read the files. The second optional result is to allow others to create, change, and delete new files in the \BANK folder after it is copied.

The proposed solution is to copy the \BANK folder to the \WEDGE folder on the server. Share the \BANK folder on the server, and set permissions so that the Everyone system group has Read permission, and the Creator Owner system group has Full Control permission. Select the Replace Permissions on Existing Files option.

What does the proposed solution provide?

A. The required result and all optional results.

B. The required result and one optional result.

C. The required result but none of the optional results.

D. The proposed solution does not provide the required result.

70-073.03.03.004

You have some proposal documents stored in the \BANK folder on your computer running Windows NT Workstation.

The required result is to copy the \BANK folder to the \WEDGE folder on a server with one NTFS partition, where the Everyone system group has Full Control permission.

The first optional result is to prevent other users from changing the existing files in the \BANK folder after it is copied, but to allow others to read the files. The second optional result is to allow others to create, change, and delete new files in the \BANK folder after it is copied.

The proposed solution is to copy the \BANK folder to the \WEDGE folder on the server. Share the \BANK folder on the server, and set permissions so that the Everyone system group has Read permission, and the Creator Owner system group has Full Control permission. Select the Replace Permissions on Existing Files option.

What does the proposed solution provide?

▶ **Correct Answer: A**

A. **Correct:** Copying the \BANK folder to the \WEDGE folder on the server automatically provides Full Control permission to the Everyone system group for the \WEDGE folder. Sharing the \BANK folder on the server and setting permissions so the Everyone system group has Read permission prevents other users from changing files in the \BANK folder, but allows them to read the files. Setting the permissions for the Creator Owner system group to Full Control ensures that you will be able to access and change your files. Selecting the Replace Permissions on Existing Files option for the \BANK folder ensures that users can create, change, and delete only new files in the \BANK folder.

B. **Incorrect:** See the explanation for answer A.

C. **Incorrect:** See the explanation for answer A.

D. **Incorrect:** See the explanation for answer A.

Further Reading

The *Microsoft Windows NT Network Administration* volume of the *Microsoft Windows NT Network Administration Training* kit Chapter 5, Lesson 1 discusses the purpose of shared folders, share permissions, limitations of share permissions, and rules for how shared permissions are applied. Lesson 3 contains procedures for sharing

folders and assigning permissions. Practice for sharing folders is included on the CD provided in this kit. Chapter 6, Lesson 4 contains information on setting directory and file permissions.

Windows NT Workstation 4.0 Study Guide. Osborne McGraw-Hill, Berkeley, CA, 1998. ISBN 0-07-882492-3. Chapter 6 contains detailed information on sharing a directory through the command prompt using the NET SHARE command.

O B J E C T I V E   3 . 4

Set up permissions on NTFS partitions, folders, and files.

NTFS permissions allow you to set permissions for both folders and files. This higher level of security is available only on partitions formatted with NTFS. NTFS permissions may apply both to the computer where the file or folder is stored and to shared files or folders accessed through the network.

There are six individual NTFS permissions: Read (R), Write (W), Execute (X), Delete (D), Change Permissions (P), and Take Ownership (O). Descriptions of what these permissions enable a user to do are as follows:

Individual permission	For a folder, a user can	For a file, a user can
Read (R)	Display folder names, attributes, owner, and permissions.	Display file data, attributes, owner, and permissions.
Write (W)	Add files and folders, change a folder's attributes, and display owner and permissions.	Display owner and permissions, change file attributes, create data in and append data to a file.
Execute (X)	Display folder attributes, make changes to folders within a folder, and display owner and permissions.	Display file attributes, owner, and permissions. Run a file if it is an executable.
Delete (D)	Delete a folder.	Delete a file.
Change Permissions (P)	Change a folder's permissions.	Change a file's permissions.
Take Ownership (O)	Take ownership of a folder.	Take ownership of a file.

The NTFS folder-level permissions are:

Permission	Individual folder permission	Individual permission on files in the folder
No Access	None	None
List	RX	N/A
Read	RX	RX
Add	WX	N/A
Add & Read	RWX	RX
Change	RWXD	RWXD
Full Control	RWXDPO	RWXDPO

The NTFS file-level permissions are:

Permission	Individual file permission
No Access	None
Read	RX
Change	RWXD
Full Control	RWXDPO

Moving and Copying Files

There are three rules to remember for moving and copying files:

- If you move a folder or file within an NTFS volume, the folder or file retains its original permissions and owner. However, if you move a folder or file to another NTFS volume, the folder or file inherits the permissions of the destination folder but the owner remains the same.

- If you copy a file from one folder to another, the file inherits the permissions of the destination folder.

- Folders and files copied or moved to FAT partitions lose their permissions, since FAT cannot support NTFS permissions.

Questions related to this objective are designed to determine if you have an awareness of these issues. To successfully answer the questions for this objective, you need a firm understanding of several key terms. For definitions of these terms, refer to the Glossary in this book.

Key Terms

- Individual permissions

- NTFS permissions

- Standard permissions

70-073.03.04.001

Bob has a user account on a Windows NT Workstation–based computer. Bob is a member of the WebUsers and WebDesigners local groups and the Everyone system group. The computer has one hard disk formatted with NTFS. The NTFS permissions for the \DOWNLOAD folder are listed below:

Group name	NTFS permissions	Group type
Everyone	Read	System
WebUsers	Read	Local
WebDesigners	Change	Local

What are Bob's effective permissions for the files in the \DOWNLOAD folder while he is logged onto the computer locally?

A. Read

B. Change

C. No Access

D. Full Control

70-073.03.04.001

Bob has a user account on a Windows NT Workstation–based computer. Bob is a member of the WebUsers and WebDesigners local groups and the Everyone system group. The computer has one hard disk formatted with NTFS. The NTFS permissions for the \DOWNLOAD folder are listed below:

Group name	NTFS permissions	Group type
Everyone	Read	System
WebUsers	Read	Local
WebDesigners	Change	Local

What are Bob's effective permissions for the files in the \DOWNLOAD folder while he is logged onto the computer locally?

▶ **Correct Answer: B**

A. **Incorrect:** While the WebUsers group allows Bob Read permission for the \DOWNLOAD folder, the WebDesigners group allows him Change permission for the \DOWNLOAD folder. NTFS permissions provide effective permissions that are the least restrictive permissions resulting from the combination of the two user groups.

B. **Correct:** While the WebUsers group allows Bob Read permission for the \DOWNLOAD folder, the WebDesigners group allows him Change permission for the \DOWNLOAD folder. Since NTFS permissions provide effective permissions that are the least restrictive permissions resulting from the combination of the two user groups, Bob's permission for the files in the \DOWNLOAD folder is Change.

C. **Incorrect:** For the \DOWNLOAD folder, the WebUsers group allows Bob Read permission, and the WebDesigners group allows him Change permission. Bob is not a member of any local group that provides No Access permission for the \DOWNLOAD folder.

D. **Incorrect:** For the \DOWNLOAD folder, the WebUsers group allows Bob Read permission, and the WebDesigners group allows him Change permission. Bob is not a member of any local group that provides Full Control permission for the \DOWNLOAD folder.

70-073.03.04.002

Bob has a user account on a Windows NT Workstation–based computer. Bob is a member of the WebUsers and WebDesigners local groups and the Everyone system group. He wants to access files in the \DESIGN folder. The NTFS permissions for this folder are listed below:

Group name	NTFS permissions	Group type
Everyone	Read	System
WebUsers	No Access	Local
WebDesigners	Change	Local

The computer has one hard disk formatted as NTFS. What are Bob's effective permissions for the files in the \DESIGN folder while he is logged onto the computer locally?

A. Read

B. Change

C. No Access

D. Full Control

70-073.03.04.002

Bob has a user account on a Windows NT Workstation–based computer. Bob is a member of the WebUsers and WebDesigners local groups and the Everyone system group. He wants to access files in the \DESIGN folder. The NTFS permissions for this folder are listed below:

Group name	NTFS permissions	Group type
Everyone	Read	System
WebUsers	No Access	Local
WebDesigners	Change	Local

The computer has one hard disk formatted as NTFS. What are Bob's effective permissions for the files in the \DESIGN folder while he is logged onto the computer locally?

▶ **Correct Answer: C**

A. **Incorrect:** For the \DESIGN folder, the WebUsers group allows Bob No Access permission, and the WebDesigners group allows him Change permission. Bob is not a member of any local group that provides Read permission for the \DESIGN folder.

B. **Incorrect:** The WebUsers group allows Bob No Access permission for the \DESIGN folder, and the WebDesigners group allows him Change permission for the \DESIGN folder. The No Access permission overrides all other permissions.

C. **Correct:** The WebUsers group allows Bob No Access permission for the \DESIGN folder, and the WebDesigners group allows him Change permission for the \DESIGN folder. Since the No Access permission overrides all other permissions, Bob's permission for the files in the \DESIGN folder is No Access.

D. **Incorrect:** For the \DESIGN folder, the WebUsers group allows Bob No Access permission, and the WebDesigners group allows him Change permission. Bob is not a member of any local group that provides Full Control permission for the \DESIGN folder.

70-073.03.04.003

What will happen to long filenames and file permissions when a folder is moved from an NTFS volume to a FAT volume? (Choose two.)

A. Long filenames will be retained.

B. File permissions will be retained.

C. Long filenames will be discarded.

D. File permissions will be discarded.

70-073.03.04.003

What will happen to long filenames and file permissions when a folder is moved from an NTFS volume to a FAT volume? (Choose two.)

▶ **Correct Answers: A and D**

A. **Correct:** In the Windows NT operating system, the FAT file system is enhanced to support long filenames.

B. **Incorrect:** Files moved from an NTFS volume to a FAT volume lose their permissions because FAT volumes do not support NTFS permissions.

C. **Incorrect:** In the Windows NT operating system, the FAT file system is enhanced to support long filenames.

D. **Correct:** Files moved from an NTFS volume to a FAT volume lose their permissions because FAT volumes do not support NTFS permissions.

Further Reading

 Microsoft Windows NT Network Administration Training kit Chapter 6, Lesson 1 explains the purpose of NTFS permissions and how they are applied. Lesson 2 includes a short video and exercises on combining share permissions and NTFS permissions. Lesson 6 examines what happens when you copy or move a folder or file within an NTFS volume, to another NTFS volume, or to a FAT volume.

 The *Microsoft Windows NT Technical Support* volume of the *Microsoft Windows NT Technical Support Training* kit Chapter 5, Lesson 1 reviews the characteristics of the NTFS and FAT file systems. You can use these features to determine what happens when you copy or move a folder or file within an NTFS volume, to another NTFS volume, or to a FAT volume.

OBJECTIVE 3.5

Install and configure printers in a given environment.

Windows NT allows you to print directly to a local computer or to printers over the network. Configuration settings allow you to customize printer settings.

Installation

To set up a network print server, you must complete the following four tasks:

- **Determine hardware compatibility.** Determine if your print device is included on the Windows NT Hardware Compatibility List (HCL). If your print device is on the list, the required print driver is included in the Windows NT software. If your print device is not on the list, the required print driver is not included with Windows NT software. You must obtain the driver from the manufacturer or use a driver that your device can emulate.

- **Log on with Full Control permission.** You must log on with Full Control print permission to set up a network print server. Logging on as a member of the Administrators, Print Operators, Server Operators, or Power Users built-in groups provides Full Control print permission with varying degrees of ability.

- **Add a printer.** Use the Add Printer Wizard to install a driver for the print device on the print server.

- **Share a printer.** Sharing a printer allows other users to print to a device connected to a local computer. You can share a printer while it is being added or after it has been added.

Configuration

To configure a printer, use the following tabs on the Printer Properties window:

- **General tab**—Allows you to enter a comment about the printer, specify the location of the printer for users, and select the printer driver. You can also choose whether to print a page separating print jobs, change the print processor, or print a test page.

- **Ports tab**—Allows you to choose a printer port and choose whether to add or delete ports from your system. You can also choose whether to create a printing pool, which can automatically distribute print jobs to print devices using the same printer driver.

- **Scheduling tab**—Allows you to specify the times the printer is available and the printer priority.

- **Sharing tab**—Allows you to share the printer on a network.

- **Security tab**—Allows you to set user permissions and manage documents, to track printing activities, and to take ownership of the printer.

- **Device settings tab**—Displays settings specific to the print device.

Questions related to this objective are designed to determine if you have an awareness of these issues. To successfully answer the questions for this objective, you need a firm understanding of several key terms. For definitions of these terms, refer to the Glossary in this book.

Key Terms

- Data link control (DLC)

- NetBIOS Enhanced User Interface (NetBEUI)

- Print device

- Print server

- Printer

- Protocol

70-073.03.05.001

You need to configure printing on your Windows NT network.

The required result is to install a network print server for use on your Windows NT Workstation–based computer.

The first optional result is to provide printing support for client computers running Windows NT. The second optional result is to provide printing support for client computers running Windows 95.

The proposed solution is to use the Add Printer Wizard to configure the printer, and use the Alternate Drivers section of the Sharing tab to install alternate drivers on the print server for Windows NT and Windows 95 clients.

What does the proposed solution provide?

A. The required result and all optional results.

B. The required result and one optional result.

C. The required result but none of the optional results.

D. The proposed solution does not provide the required result.

70-073.03.05.001

You need to configure printing on your Windows NT network.

The required result is to install a network print server for use on your Windows NT Workstation–based computer.

The first optional result is to provide printing support for client computers running Windows NT. The second optional result is to provide printing support for client computers running Windows 95.

The proposed solution is to use the Add Printer Wizard to configure the printer, and use the Alternate Drivers section of the Sharing tab to install alternate drivers on the print server for Windows NT and Windows 95 clients.

What does the proposed solution provide?

▶ **Correct Answer: A**

A. **Correct:** Using the Add Printer Wizard to configure the printer installs the network print server for use on your Windows NT Workstation–based computer. Using the Alternate Drivers section of the Sharing tab to install alternate drivers on the print server for Windows NT provides printing support for client computers running Windows NT. Using the Alternate Drivers section of the Sharing tab to install alternate drivers on the print server for Windows 95 provides printing support for client computers running Windows 95.

B. **Incorrect:** See the explanation for answer A.

C. **Incorrect:** See the explanation for answer A.

D. **Incorrect:** See the explanation for answer A.

70-073.03.05.002

Which protocol would you use to connect an HP JetDirect printer to your network?

A. Data Link Control (DLC)

B. Lightweight Directory Access Protocol (LDAP)

C. DECnet

D. NetBIOS Enhanced User Interface (NetBEUI)

70-073.03.05.002

Which protocol would you use to connect an HP JetDirect printer to your network?

▶ **Correct Answer: A**

    A. **Correct:** The DLC protocol is used to connect Hewlett-Packard LAN print devices, rather than a specific computer. To connect to and configure the print device, install the DLC protocol and the network port monitor on the Windows NT–based print server. Then use the Add Printer Wizard to install the network port and configure the print device.

    B. **Incorrect:** LDAP is a directory service implementation. LDAP has no specialized connectivity for Hewlett-Packard LAN print devices.

    C. **Incorrect:** DECnet is a protocol used by Digital Equipment Corp. network products. DECnet has no specialized connectivity for Hewlett-Packard LAN print devices.

    D. **Incorrect:** NetBEUI is a small, efficient, and fast protocol designed to support LANs with 20 to 200 workstations. NetBEUI has no specialized connectivity for Hewlett-Packard LAN print devices.

70-073.03.05.003

There are three HP LaserJet 4Si print devices attached to your Windows NT Workstation–based computer. There is a high volume of printing.

The required result is to configure one printer to route print jobs among the three print devices.

The first optional result is to decrease the time that documents wait in the print queue. The second optional result is to simplify administration of the three print devices.

The proposed solution is to create a printing pool by accessing the Printer Properties box, clicking on the Ports tab, clicking to select the Enable printer pooling checkbox, and selecting multiple ports in the Printer Properties box.

What does the proposed solution provide?

A. The required result and all optional results.

B. The required result and one optional result.

C. The required result but none of the optional results.

D. The proposed solution does not provide the required result.

70-073.03.05.003

There are three HP LaserJet 4Si print devices attached to your Windows NT Workstation–based computer. There is a high volume of printing.

The required result is to configure one printer to route print jobs among the three print devices.

The first optional result is to decrease the time that documents wait in the print queue. The second optional result is to simplify administration of the three print devices.

The proposed solution is to create a printing pool by accessing the Printer Properties box, clicking on the Ports tab, clicking to select the Enable printer pooling checkbox, and selecting multiple ports in the Printer Properties box.

What does the proposed solution provide?

▶ **Correct Answer: A**

A. **Correct:** You can create a printing pool by accessing the Printer Properties box, clicking on the Ports tab, clicking to select the Enable printer pooling checkbox, and selecting multiple ports in the Printer Properties box. Once the printing pool is created, it decreases the time that documents wait in the print queue and simplifies administration of the three print devices.

B. **Incorrect:** See the explanation for answer A.

C. **Incorrect:** See the explanation for answer A.

D. **Incorrect:** See the explanation for answer A.

Further Reading

  The *Microsoft Windows NT Network Administration* volume of the *Microsoft Windows NT Network Administration Training* kit Chapter 7, Lesson 2 contains detailed information on adding and sharing a new printer. Lesson 3 explains how to create a printing pool. Practice for both of these tasks is included on the CD provided in this kit.

 The *Microsoft Windows NT Server Networking Guide* Chapter 14 contains detailed information on using DLC to connect to Hewlett-Packard print devices.

Connectivity

The Connectivity domain examines the various services and protocols available for Windows NT Workstation.

Tested Skills and Suggested Practices

- Adding and configuring the network components of Windows NT Workstation. You must know how to add and configure network components using the Network program on the Control Panel.

    - Practice 1: Familiarize yourself with the Network program on the Control Panel. Learn the function of each tab in the Network program. Learn how to add and configure workgroups, domain and network services, protocols, adapters, and bindings.

- Using various methods to access network resources. Be able to set up access to network resources, including shared folders, network and printer connections, and remote access.

    - Practice 1: Learn how to map network drives and ensure access to a shared folder. Learn the various ways to map a network drive. Recognize the effects of mapping a network drive.

    - Practice 2: Learn the function of user profiles. Learn how to set up user profiles to provide network connections and printer connections. Differentiate between procedures for setting up a user profile and a roaming user profile.

    - Practice 3: Learn the function of Remote Access Service (RAS). Learn how to configure RAS to provide Windows NT Workstation users with remote access to their networks for services such as file and printer sharing.

    - Practice 4: Learn the function of hardware profiles. Learn to configure hardware profiles to provide the configuration(s) for a set of devices and services.

- Practice 5: Learn the function of Internet Protocol (IP) addresses. Learn to configure IP addresses to identify a node on a network and to specify routing information, allowing access to specific network resources.

- Implementing Windows NT Workstation as a client in a NetWare environment. You must be able to configure NetWare services for Windows NT Workstation clients.

  - Practice 1: Determine the function of NWLink protocol. Learn how NWLink works with various Microsoft NetWare tools to provide access to NetWare file and print resources.

  - Practice 2: Learn the purpose and availability of each of the following NetWare tools: Client Services for NetWare (CSNW), Gateway Service for NetWare (GSNW), Migration Tool for NetWare, File and Print Services for NetWare (FNPW), and Directory Service Manager for NetWare (DSMN). Determine the tool to use in a given situation.

- Using various configurations to install Windows NT Workstation as a TCP/IP client. Be able to configure Windows NT Workstation as a TCP/IP client.

  - Practice 1: Know the function, advantages, and disadvantages of the TCP/IP protocol. Learn the function of the IP address, subnet mask, and default gateway in setting up TCP/IP. Familiarize yourself with the purpose of various naming resolution methods and utilities for configuring TCP/IP.

  - Practice 2: Configure TCP/IP automatically using the Dynamic Host Configuration Protocol (DHCP) server service. Configure TCP/IP manually using the Protocols tab in the Network program in the Control Panel.

- Configuring and installing *Dial-Up Networking* in a given situation. Be able to set up Dial-Up Networking on a Windows NT Workstation client.

  - Practice 1: Learn the function of Dial-Up Networking. Know the function of the protocols used for remote access by Dial-Up Networking: Point-to-Point Protocol (PPP), Serial Line Internet Protocol (SLIP), and Point-to-Point Tunneling Protocol (PPTP). Recognize the various security features provided by RAS.

  - Practice 2: Configure Dial-Up Networking from the Dial-Up Networking icon in My Computer. Learn the purpose of Phonebook entries, logging on using a dial-in entry, and the AutoDial feature.

- Configuring Microsoft *Peer Web Services* (PWS) in a given situation. Be able to configure Peer Web Services on a Windows NT Workstation client.

    - Practice 1: Learn the function of Peer Web Services. Distinguish between the functions of the World Wide Web (WWW) service, File Transfer Protocol (FTP) service, and Gopher service.

    - Practice 2: Configure Peer Web Services using the Microsoft Internet Service Manager (ISM). Use the ISM to monitor Internet services on a Windows NT computer on the network.

OBJECTIVE 4.1

Add and configure the network components of the Windows NT Workstation.

Although the network components of the Windows NT Workstation are set up during the installation process, you can change the network configuration using the Network program on the Control Panel. The Network program has five tabs:

- **The Identification tab**—used to identify the computer to the network, using the computer name and workgroup or domain name. The computer name and workgroup/domain name can be changed by clicking the Change button.

- **The Services tab**—used to install and configure services for a computer running Windows NT Workstation with access to the network and its resources.

- **The Protocols tab**—used to install and configure protocols, which are the means for computers to connect and exchange information over the network.

- **The Adapters tab**—used to install and configure network adapter card drivers, which connect network cards to protocol drivers.

- **The Bindings tab**—used to install and configure bindings, which are connections between network cards, protocols, and services installed on the Windows NT Workstation.

Questions related to this objective are designed to determine if you have an awareness of these issues. To successfully answer the questions for this objective, you need a firm understanding of several key terms. For definitions of these terms, refer to the Glossary in this book.

Key Terms

- Bindings

- Frame type

- NetBIOS Enhanced User Interface (NetBEUI)

- Network adapter card

- Peer Web Services (PWS)

- Simple Network Management Protocol (SNMP)

- Transmission Control Protocol/Internet Protocol (TCP/IP)

- Trap messages

70-073.04.01.001

Which Windows NT service is needed to initiate a trap message to alert management systems to an extraordinary event?

A. SNMP

B. SMTP

C. SAM monitor

D. Network Monitor Agent

70-073.04.01.002

Which Network program tab should you select if you want to change the transceiver type for an Ethernet network interface adapter?

A. Services

B. Adapters

C. Protocols

D. Bindings

70-073.04.01.001

Which Windows NT service is needed to initiate a trap message to alert management systems to an extraordinary event?

▶ **Correct Answer: A**

A. **Correct:** SNMP is used to monitor and report on the activity of network devices, including hubs, routers, printers, workstations, and computers. When a change or error occurs on a computer in an SNMP-managed network, the agent program starts a trap operation to alert the SNMP management console. The agent program is a part of SNMP that is installed on each computer in an SNMP-managed network. To set trap messages, select SNMP service from the Services tab in the Network program window. Then select the Traps tab from the SNMP Properties window.

B. **Incorrect:** SMTP is a part of the TCP/IP suite of protocols that is used to send and receive mail over the Internet.

C. **Incorrect:** The Security Accounts Manager (SAM, also known as the *directory database*), contains information such as user account names, passwords, and security policy settings and is managed by the User Manager on a Windows NT workstation.

D. **Incorrect:** The Network Monitor Agent collects and displays statistics about packet-level activity detected by the network card in the computer. This data makes it easier to perform troubleshooting tasks and find network problems.

70-073.04.01.002

Which Network program tab should you select if you want to change the transceiver type for an Ethernet network interface adapter?

▶ **Correct Answer: B**

A. **Incorrect:** The Services tab installs network services, which provide a computer running Windows NT access to the network and its resources.

B. **Correct:** The Adapters tab is used to configure network adapter card drivers. To change the transceiver type, select the Ethernet adapter and click the Properties button. Use the Setup dialog box to configure the transceiver type.

C. **Incorrect:** The Protocols tab is used to install and configure protocols, which are a means for computers to connect with each other. While protocols communicate with adapter cards, you cannot change the transceiver type on the Protocols tab.

D. **Incorrect:** The Bindings tab is used to configure communication connections between network cards, protocols, and services installed on the computer. The tab shows the bindings of the installed network components from the upper-layer services and protocols to the lowest layer of network adapter card driver.

70-073.04.01.003

Which Network program tab should you select if you want to install Peer Web Services on a Windows NT Workstation computer?

A. Services

B. Adapters

C. Protocols

D. Bindings

70-073.04.01.004

Which Network program tab should you select if you want to temporarily disable NetBEUI?

A. Services

B. Adapters

C. Protocols

D. Bindings

70-073.04.01.003

Which Network program tab should you select if you want to install Peer Web Services on a Windows NT Workstation computer?

▶ **Correct Answer: A**

A. **Correct:** Peer Web Services is a collection of services that enable the user of a computer running Windows NT Workstation to publish a personal Web site from the desktop. Click Add on the Services tab to install PWS network services.

B. **Incorrect:** The Adapters tab is used to configure network adapter card drivers. Peer Web Services is a service; the Adapters tab is not used to add a service.

C. **Incorrect:** The Protocols tab is used to install and configure protocols, which are a means for computers to connect with each other. Peer Web Services is a service; the Protocols tab is not used to add a service.

D. **Incorrect:** The Bindings tab is used to configure communication connections between network cards, protocols, and services installed on the computer. The tab shows the bindings of the installed network components from the upper-layer services and protocols to the lowest layer of network adapter card driver. Peer Web Services is a service; the Bindings tab is not used to add a service.

70-073.04.01.004

Which Network program tab should you select if you want to temporarily disable NetBEUI?

▶ **Correct Answer: D**

A. **Incorrect:** The Services tab installs network services, which provide a computer running Windows NT access to the network and its resources. NetBEUI is a protocol; the Services tab is not used to add a protocol.

B. **Incorrect:** The Adapters tab is used to configure network adapter card drivers. NetBEUI is a protocol; the Adapters tab is not used to add a protocol.

C. **Incorrect:** The Protocols tab is used to install and configure protocols, which are a means for computers to connect with each other. Although NetBEUI is a protocol, the Protocols tab does not allow a protocol to be disabled.

D. **Correct:** The Bindings tab is used to configure communication connections between network cards, protocols, and services installed on the computer. Although NetBEUI is a protocol, you can temporarily disable NetBEUI from the Bindings tab by selecting NetBEUI and clicking the Disable button.

70-073.04.01.005

Which Network program tab should you select if you want to add TCP/IP to the system configuration?

A. Services

B. Adapters

C. Protocols

D. Bindings

70-073.04.01.006

You need to access an application on a NetWare server. NWLink is installed on your Windows NT Workstation 4.0 computer. You are unable to communicate with the NetWare server, and you suspect the frame type is set incorrectly. Which Network program tab should you select if you want to designate a different frame type for a network adapter card?

A. Services

B. Adapters

C. Protocols

D. Bindings

70-073.04.01.005

Which Network program tab should you select if you want to add TCP/IP to the system configuration?

▶ **Correct Answer: C**

A. **Incorrect:** The Services tab installs network services, which provide a computer running Windows NT access to the network and its resources. TCP/IP is a protocol; the Services tab is not used to add a protocol.

B. **Incorrect:** The Adapters tab is used to configure network adapter card drivers. TCP/IP is a protocol; the Adapters tab is not used to add a protocol.

C. **Correct:** The Protocols tab is used to install and configure protocols, which are a means for computers to connect with each other. To add TCP/IP to the system configuration, click Add from the Protocols tab, select TCP/IP protocol, and click OK.

D. **Incorrect:** The Bindings tab is used to configure communication connections between network cards, protocols, and services installed on the computer. The tab shows the bindings of the installed network components from the upper-layer services and protocols to the lowest layer of network adapter card driver. TCP/IP is a protocol; the Bindings tab is not used to add a protocol.

70-073.04.01.006

You need to access an application on a NetWare server. NWLink is installed on your Windows NT Workstation 4.0 computer. You are unable to communicate with the NetWare server, and you suspect the frame type is set incorrectly. Which Network program tab should you select if you want to designate a different frame type for a network adapter card?

▶ **Correct Answer: C**

A. **Incorrect:** The Services tab installs network services, which provide a computer running Windows NT access to the network and its resources. A frame type determines how the network adapter card formats data to be sent over the network and is not designated on the Services tab.

B. **Incorrect:** Although the Adapters tab is used to configure network adapter card drivers, this tab cannot be used to designate a network adapter card frame type. A frame type determines how the network adapter card formats data to be sent over the network and is set in the Protocols tab.

C. **Correct:** The Protocols tab is used to install and configure protocols, which are the means for computers to connect with each other. A frame type determines how the network adapter card formats data to be sent over the network and is also designated on the Protocols tab.

D. **Incorrect:** Although the Bindings tab is used to configure bindings, which are communication connections between network adapter card drivers, protocols, and services installed on the computer; this tab cannot be used to designate a network adapter card frame type. A frame type determines how the network adapter card formats data to be sent over the network and is set in the Protocols tab.

Further Reading

 The *Microsoft Windows NT Workstation 4.0 Resource Kit* Chapter 30 contains basic information about SNMP and TCP/IP.

 The *Microsoft Windows NT Server Networking Guide* volume of the *Microsoft Windows NT Server Resource Kit* Chapter 11 contains detailed information about using SNMP.

 Microsoft Windows NT Technical Support Self-Paced Training Chapter 10, Lesson 1 examines using the Adapters and Protocols tabs in the Network program. Lesson 2 explains setting up frame types. Lesson 4 covers the basics of TCP/IP installation and configuration, and also covers various TCP/IP utilities. Lesson 5 examines network bindings and the Bindings tab in the Network program. Chapter 11, Lesson 1 examines using the Services tab in the Network program.

O B J E C T I V E 4 . 2

Use various methods to access network resources.

The methods for accessing network resources examined in this objective are:

- **Mapping network drives**. To connect to shared folders, you must map to a network drive. If you do not have permissions to access the drive, you are not allowed to map to it. You must specify the path for the domain resource you want to access using the *universal naming convention* (UNC).

- **Configuring user profiles**. As discussed in Objective 3.2, user profiles allow users to select and store settings for the user environment, including network connections and printer connections.

- **Configuring Remote Access Service (RAS)**. RAS provides Windows NT Workstation users with remote access to their networks for services such as file and printer sharing.

- **Configuring hardware profiles**. Hardware profiles store the configuration(s) for a set of devices and services, depending on a user's needs.

- **Configuring IP addresses**. IP addresses are used to identify a node on a network and to specify routing information, allowing access to specific network resources.

Questions related to this objective are designed to determine if you have an awareness of these issues. To successfully answer the questions for this objective, you need a firm understanding of several key terms. For definitions of these terms, refer to the Glossary in this book.

Key Terms

- Hardware profile

- Internet Protocol (IP) address

- Line printer daemon (LPD)

- Line Printer Remote (LPR)

- Remote Access Service (RAS)

- Uniform Resource Locator (URL)

- Universal naming convention (UNC) name

70-073.04.02.001

A user needs access to a network application. The application is located in the DESIGN folder on a Windows NT Server named APP1. You have decided to map network drive H: to the Design folder and then use the mapping to create a Shortcut to the application.

How can you create the path to the folder?

A. By using the syntax \\APP1.DESIGN

B. By using the syntax H:APP1.DESIGN

C. By using the syntax \\APP1:DESIGN

D. By using the syntax \\APP1\DESIGN

E. By using the syntax H:\\APP1:DESIGN

F. By using the syntax H:\\APP1\DESIGN

70-073.04.02.002

You need to map network drive H: to a folder on the company intranet. The folder is named SHARED and is located at WWW.SALES.WIDGETSGALORE.COM. Which drive mapping path should you use?

A. \\SALES.WIDGETSGALORE.COM\SHARED

B. \\SALES\WIDGETSGALORE\COM\SHARED

C. H:\\SALES.WIDGETSGALORE.COM\SHARED

D. H:\\SALES\WIDGETSGALORE\COM\SHARED

70-073.04.02.001

A user needs access to a network application. The application is located in the DESIGN folder on a Windows NT Server named APP1. You have decided to map network drive H: to the Design folder and then use the mapping to create a Shortcut to the application.

How can you create the path to the folder?

▶ **Correct Answer: D**

    A. **Incorrect:** The universal naming convention path requires a backslash rather than a period between the server name and the shared folder name.

    B. **Incorrect:** The universal naming convention path does not require the drive letter and also requires a backslash rather than a period between the server name and the shared folder name.

    C. **Incorrect:** The universal naming convention path requires a backslash rather than a colon between the server name and the shared folder name.

    D. **Correct:** The universal naming convention path requires the \\SERVER_NAME\ SHARED_FOLDER_NAME syntax.

    E. **Incorrect:** The universal naming convention path does not require the drive letter and requires a backslash rather than a colon between the server name and the shared folder name.

    F. **Incorrect:** The universal naming convention path does not require the drive letter.

70-073.04.02.002

You need to map network drive H: to a folder on the company intranet. The folder is named SHARED and is located at WWW.SALES.WIDGETSGALORE.COM. Which drive mapping path should you use?

▶ **Correct Answer: A**

    A. **Correct:** The universal naming convention path requires the \\SERVER_NAME\ SHARED_FOLDER_NAME syntax.

    B. **Incorrect:** The universal naming convention path requires a period rather than a backslash between the parts of the URL.

    C. **Incorrect:** The universal naming convention path does not require the drive letter.

    D. **Incorrect:** The universal naming convention path does not require the drive letter and requires a period rather than a backslash between the parts of the URL.

70-073.04.02.003

A laptop user connects directly to the network at the office and uses RAS when traveling. The laptop must be configured differently depending upon which method is used to connect to the network.

The required result is to simplify the hardware configuration necessary to connect to the network using the two methods.

The first optional result is provide the user with the same desktop environment and the same access to network resources whether he attaches locally using the network adapter card or connects remotely using the modem. The second optional result is to run the laptop's video resolution at 640 × 480 when at home or traveling and 800 × 600 when at the office without manually configuring it each time the computer is restarted.

The proposed solution is to configure a roaming user profile for the user and create two hardware profiles: one that is used to connect locally and another to connect remotely.

What does the solution provide?

A. The required result and all optional results.

B. The required result and one optional result.

C. The required result and neither optional result.

D. The proposed solution does not provide the required result.

70-073.04.02.003

A laptop user connects directly to the network at the office and uses RAS when traveling. The laptop must be configured differently depending upon which method is used to connect to the network.

The required result is to simplify the hardware configuration necessary to connect to the network using the two methods.

The first optional result is provide the user with the same desktop environment and the same access to network resources whether he attaches locally using the network adapter card or connects remotely using the modem. The second optional result is to run the laptop's video resolution at 640 × 480 when at home or traveling and 800 × 600 when at the office without manually configuring it each time the computer is restarted.

The proposed solution is to configure a roaming user profile for the user and create two hardware profiles: one that is used to connect locally and another to connect remotely.

What does the solution provide?

▶ **Correct Answer: A**

A. **Correct:** By employing two hardware profiles, the hardware configuration necessary to connect to the network using the two methods has been simplified. Creating a roaming user profile provides the user with the same working environment and access to network resources regardless of whether he or she attaches locally with the network adapter card or remotely using the modem. Creating two hardware profiles allows the user to run the laptop's video resolution at 640 × 480 when traveling and 800 × 600 when at the office without manually configuring it each time. The user simply selects the appropriate configuration during startup.

B. **Incorrect:** See the explanation for answer A.

C. **Incorrect:** See the explanation for answer A.

D. **Incorrect:** See the explanation for answer A.

70-073.04.02.004

A laptop user connects directly to the network at the office and uses RAS when traveling. The laptop must be configured differently depending upon which device is used to connect to the network.

The required result is to simplify the hardware configuration necessary to connect to the network using the two methods.

The first optional result is provide the user with the same desktop environment and the same access to network resources whether he attaches locally using the network adapter card or connects remotely using the modem. The second optional result is to run the laptop's video resolution at 640×480 when at home or traveling and 800×600 when at the office without manually configuring it each time the computer is restarted.

The proposed solution is to configure logon scripts for the user and create two hardware profiles: one that is used to connect locally and another to connect remotely.

What does the solution provide?

A. The required result and all optional results.

B. The required result and one optional result.

C. The required result and neither optional result.

D. The proposed solution does not provide the required result.

70-073.04.02.004

A laptop user connects directly to the network at the office and uses RAS when traveling. The laptop must be configured differently depending upon which device is used to connect to the network.

The required result is to simplify the hardware configuration necessary to connect to the network using the two methods.

The first optional result is provide the user with the same desktop environment and the same access to network resources whether he attaches locally using the network adapter card or connects remotely using the modem. The second optional result is to run the laptop's video resolution at 640 × 480 when at home or traveling and 800 × 600 when at the office without manually configuring it each time the computer is restarted.

The proposed solution is to configure logon scripts for the user and create two hardware profiles: one that is used to connect locally and another to connect remotely.

What does the solution provide?

▶ **Correct Answer: B**

A. **Incorrect:** See the explanation for answer B.

B. **Correct:** By employing two hardware profiles, the hardware configuration necessary to connect to the network using the two methods has been simplified. Creating logon scripts for the user is unnecessary and does not provide the user with the same working environment and access to network resources regardless of whether he attaches locally with the network adapter card or remotely using the modem. Creating two hardware profiles allows the user to run the laptop's video resolution at 640 × 480 when traveling and 800 × 600 when at the office without manually configuring it each time. The user simply selects the appropriate configuration during startup.

C. **Incorrect:** See the explanation for answer B.

D. **Incorrect:** See the explanation for answer B.

70-073.04.02.005

A laptop user connects directly to the network at the office and uses RAS when traveling. The laptop must be configured differently depending upon which device is used to connect to the network.

The required result is to simplify the hardware configuration necessary to connect to the network using the two methods.

The first optional result is provide the user with the same desktop environment and the same access to network resources whether he attaches locally using the network adapter card or connects remotely using the modem. The second optional result is to run the laptop's video resolution at 640×480 when at home or traveling and 800×600 when at the office without manually configuring it each time the computer is restarted.

The proposed solution is to configure a roaming user profile for the user and create two logon scripts: one that runs when connecting locally and another that runs when connecting remotely.

What does the solution provide?

A. The required result and all optional results.

B. The required result and one optional result.

C. The required result and neither optional result.

D. The proposed solution does not provide the required result.

70-073.04.02.005

A laptop user connects directly to the network at the office and uses RAS when traveling. The laptop must be configured differently depending upon which device is used to connect to the network.

The required result is to simplify the hardware configuration necessary to connect to the network using the two methods.

The first optional result is provide the user with the same desktop environment and the same access to network resources whether he attaches locally using the network adapter card or connects remotely using the modem. The second optional result is to run the laptop's video resolution at 640 × 480 when at home or traveling and 800 × 600 when at the office without manually configuring it each time the computer is restarted.

The proposed solution is to configure a roaming user profile for the user and create two logon scripts: one that runs when connecting locally and another that runs when connecting remotely.

What does the solution provide?

▶ **Correct Answer: D**

A. **Incorrect:** See the explanation for answer D.

B. **Incorrect:** See the explanation for answer D.

C. **Incorrect:** See the explanation for answer D.

D. **Correct:** Since hardware profiles were not created, the hardware configuration necessary to connect to the network using the two methods has not been simplified. Roaming user profiles provide the user with the same desktop environment regardless of the Windows NT computer used to log on to the network; however, only one logon script may be used with each user account from any location. No action has been taken to allow the user to run the laptop's video resolution at 640 × 480 when traveling and 800 × 600 when at the office without manually configuring it each time.

70-073.04.02.006

You want to access a TCP/IP print device on your network from a computer running Windows NT Workstation. What must you know to access the printer? (Choose two.)

A. The name of the printer

B. The name of the printer driver

C. The IP address of the print server

D. The media access control (MAC) address of the print server

70-073.04.02.006

You want to access a TCP/IP print device on your network from a computer running Windows NT Workstation. What must you know to access the printer? (Choose two.)

▶ **Correct Answers: A and C**

    A. **Correct:** To access a TCP/IP print device, the LPR client needs the network address of the LPD print server and the name that the LPD service associates with the print device.

    B. **Incorrect:** It is not necessary to know the name of the printer driver to access a TCP/IP print device.

    C. **Correct:** To access a TCP/IP print device, the LPR client needs the network address of the LPD print server and the name that the LPD service associates with the print device.

    D. **Incorrect:** The MAC address is a unique 48-bit number assigned to the network interface card, not to the print server.

Further Reading

 Microsoft Windows NT Technical Support Self-Paced Training Chapter 2, Lesson 4 explains how to map a network drive, including creating a path using a universal naming convention address. Chapter 3, Lesson 3 examines creating hardware profiles. Practice for creating hardware profiles is included on the CD provided in this kit.

 Microsoft Windows NT Workstation Resource Kit Chapter 7 contains information about TCP/IP print service and the LPR printer protocol. Chapter 36 contains information on creating hardware profiles for laptop computers.

Microsoft Windows NT Network Administration Self-Paced Training Chapter 2, Lesson 4 contains information on creating roaming user profiles.

O B J E C T I V E   4 . 3

Implement Windows NT Workstation as a client in a NetWare environment.

To access and share resources with computers running Novell NetWare from Windows NT–based computers you must install some additional software.

NWLink

NetWare uses *Internetwork Packet Exchange/Sequenced Packet Exchange* (IPX/SPX), Novell's networking protocol. To allow Windows NT to communicate with NetWare servers and clients using this proprietary protocol, Microsoft developed NWLink. NWLink is provided with both Windows NT Server and Windows NT Workstation. However, NWLink alone does not provide access to NetWare file and print resources. You must use NWLink with additional software to provide Windows NT–based computers with access to NetWare resources or to provide NetWare clients with access to services on Windows NT servers.

NetWare Connectivity Components

Depending on your needs, the following software is available for NetWare connectivity with Windows NT:

Software included with Windows NT	Usage
Client Services for NetWare (CSNW)	Enables Windows NT Workstation to make direct connections to file and printer resources at NetWare servers.
Gateway Service for NetWare (GSNW)	Enables Windows NT Server to make direct connections to file and printer resources at NetWare servers and provide a gateway to these resources from Windows NT Workstation computers.
Migration Tool for NetWare	Allows easy transfer of user and group accounts, volumes, folders, and files from a NetWare server to a computer running Windows NT Server.

Add-on utilities for NetWare connectivity	Usage
File and Print Services for NetWare (FNPW)	Integrates NetWare clients into a Windows NT network and accesses resources on Windows NT Server.
Directory Service Manager for NetWare (DSMN)	Allows management of mixed Windows NT and NetWare environments as a single set of user and group accounts.

Questions related to this objective are designed to determine if you have an awareness of these issues. To successfully answer the questions for this objective, you need a firm understanding of several key terms. For definitions of these terms, refer to the Glossary in this book.

Key Terms

- Client

- Client Services for NetWare (CSNW)

- Distributed Component Object Model (DCOM)

- File and Print Services for NetWare (FPNW)

- Gateway Service for NetWare (GSNW)

- NetWare

- Novell Directory Services (NDS)

- NWLink

70-073.04.03.001

Your network consists of one NetWare 3.12 server, two Windows NT 4.0 servers, and 75 Windows client workstations, including Windows NT Workstation computers. All network print services are performed by the NetWare server.

Which component will allow Windows NT Workstation clients to send print jobs to network printers?

A. GSNW

B. CSNW

C. FPNW

D. DCOM

70-073.04.03.001

Your network consists of one NetWare 3.12 server, two Windows NT 4.0 servers, and 75 Windows client workstations, including Windows NT Workstation computers. All network print services are performed by the NetWare server.

Which component will allow Windows NT Workstation clients to send print jobs to network printers?

▶ **Correct Answer: B**

    A. **Incorrect:** Gateway Service for NetWare (GSNW) enables computers running Windows NT Server and using NWLink as a transport protocol to access files and printers at NetWare servers. To send print jobs, you need to access the NetWare server from a Windows NT Workstation.

    B. **Correct:** Client Services for NetWare (CSNW) enables computers running Windows NT Workstation to make direct connections to file and printer resources at NetWare servers running NetWare 2.x or later.

    C. **Incorrect:** File and Print Services for NetWare (FPNW) integrates NetWare clients into a Windows NT network and also allows them to access resources on computers running Windows NT Server. To send print jobs, you need to access the NetWare server from a Windows NT Workstation.

    D. **Incorrect:** Distributed Component Object Model (DCOM) is used to integrate client/server applications across multiple computers using reusable and replaceable objects. To send print jobs, you need to integrate platforms, not applications.

70-073.04.03.002

Your network consists of two NetWare 4 servers and 85 client workstations. Client workstations include Macintosh, UNIX, Windows 95, and Windows NT Workstation computers. All clients access network services through NetWare Directory Services (NDS).

Which component will allow Windows NT Workstation clients to access network services?

A. GSNW

B. CSNW

C. FPNW

D. DCOM

70-073.04.03.003

You are designing a new network that will consist of one NetWare 4 server and 30 Windows NT 4.0 Workstation clients. The network will use 10BaseT Ethernet. Which protocol should you implement for this network?

A. DECnet

B. TCP/IP

C. NWLink

D. NetBEUI

70-073.04.03.002

Your network consists of two NetWare 4 servers and 85 client workstations. Client workstations include Macintosh, UNIX, Windows 95, and Windows NT Workstation computers. All clients access network services through NetWare Directory Services (NDS).

Which component will allow Windows NT Workstation clients to access network services?

▶ **Correct Answer: B**

A. **Incorrect:** Gateway Service for NetWare (GSNW) enables computers running Windows NT Server and using NWLink as a transport protocol to access files and printers at NetWare servers. You need to access network services through the NetWare server from a Windows NT Workstation.

B. **Correct:** Client Services for NetWare (CSNW) enables computers running Windows NT Workstation to make direct connections to file and printer resources at NetWare servers running NetWare 2.x or later.

C. **Incorrect:** File and Print Services for NetWare (FPNW) integrates NetWare clients into a Windows NT network and also allows them to access resources on computers running Windows NT Server. To access network services, you need to access the NetWare server from a Windows NT Workstation.

D. **Incorrect:** Distributed Component Object Model (DCOM) is used to integrate client/server applications across multiple computers using reusable and replaceable objects. To access network services, you need to integrate platforms, not applications.

70-073.04.03.003

You are designing a new network that will consist of one NetWare 4 server and 30 Windows NT 4.0 Workstation clients. The network will use 10BaseT Ethernet. Which protocol should you implement for this network?

▶ **Correct Answer: C**

A. **Incorrect:** DECnet is a protocol used by DEC network products and has no specialized connectivity for NetWare.

B. **Incorrect:** Although TCP/IP is available for the NetWare operating system, this protocol is not the best choice. The configuration of clients and overall administration of TCP/IP can be difficult, requiring a multi-part naming scheme and identification of a default router for each station. NWLink protocol provides for a simple naming scheme and is more suited to this scenario.

C. **Correct:** NWLink provides computers running Windows NT Workstation with the ability to communicate with NetWare servers and clients, in addition to a simple means of configuration and administration.

D. **Incorrect:** NetBIOS Enhanced User Interface (NetBEUI) is a network protocol used in small, department-sized LANs of 1 to 200 clients. NetBEUI does not provide support for NetWare client/server applications.

70-073.04.03.004

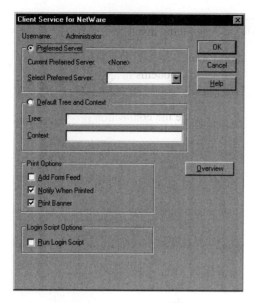

Examine the exhibit above to answer this question.

In which situation should you specify the default tree and context in the Client Services for NetWare dialog?

A. The client is in an Active Directory environment.

B. The client is in a bindery emulation environment.

C. The client is in a NetWare Directory Services environment.

D. The client is in a Windows NT Directory Services environment and accesses Novell servers through a Windows NT Server computer running GSNW.

70-073.04.03.004

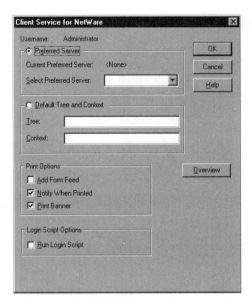

Examine the exhibit above to answer this question.

In which situation should you specify the default tree and context in the Client Services for NetWare dialog?

▶ **Correct Answer: C**

A. **Incorrect:** The Active Directory environment does not exist in Windows NT.

B. **Incorrect:** The bindery emulation environment uses a preferred server, which is queried for information about resources available on the NetWare network.

C. **Correct:** The NetWare Directory Services environment uses a default tree and context. The default tree defines the NDS name of the user name that is used for login. The default context is the position of the user name used for login. All resources in the default tree can then be accessed without requiring further prompts. NDS is supported by selecting the default tree and context when configuring CSNW or GSNW.

D. **Incorrect:** The default tree and context is only specified when setting up Client Services for NetWare (CSNW). When running Gateway Service for NetWare (GSNW), there is no need to specify the default tree and context.

70-073.04.03.005

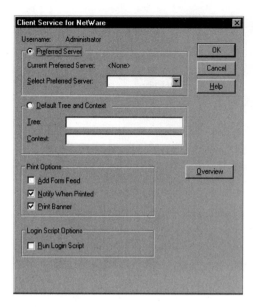

Examine the exhibit above to answer this question.

When should you specify a preferred server in the Client Services for NetWare dialog?

A. The client is in an Active Directory environment.

B. The client is in a bindery emulation environment.

C. The client is in a NetWare Directory Services environment.

D. The client is in a Windows NT Directory Services environment, and accesses Novell servers through a Windows NT Server computer running GSNW.

70-073.04.03.005

Examine the exhibit above to answer this question.

When should you specify a preferred server in the Client Services for NetWare dialog?

▶ **Correct Answer: B**

A. **Incorrect:** The Active Directory environment does not exist in Windows NT.

B. **Correct:** The bindery emulation environment uses a preferred server, which is queried for information about resources available on the NetWare network. Bindery emulation is supported by selecting the preferred server when configuring CSNW or GSNW.

C. **Incorrect:** The NetWare Directory Services environment uses a default tree and context. The default tree defines the NDS name of the user name that is used for login. The default context is the position of the user name used for login. All resources in the default tree can then be accessed without requiring further prompts.

D. **Incorrect:** The default tree and context is only specified when setting up Client Services for NetWare (CSNW). When running Gateway Service for NetWare (GSNW), there is no need to specify the default tree and context.

70-073.04.03.006

Your network consists of one NetWare 3.12 server, two Windows NT 4.0 servers, and 75 Windows client workstations. You would like to use NetWare utilities to administer user accounts located on the NetWare server from a Windows NT Workstation client.

Which component will allow you to administer NetWare 3.12 users from a Windows NT Workstation client?

A. GSNW

B. CSNW

C. FPNW

D. DCOM

70-073.04.03.006

Your network consists of one NetWare 3.12 server, two Windows NT 4.0 servers, and 75 Windows client workstations. You would like to use NetWare utilities to administer user accounts located on the NetWare server from a Windows NT Workstation client.

Which component will allow you to administer NetWare 3.12 users from a Windows NT Workstation client?

▶ **Correct Answer: B**

    A. **Incorrect:** Gateway Service for NetWare (GSNW) enables computers running Windows NT Server to act as a system console to administer NetWare servers. You need to administer a NetWare server from a Windows NT Workstation client.

    B. **Correct:** Client Services for NetWare (CSNW) enables computers running Windows NT Workstation to act as a system console to administer NetWare servers.

    C. **Incorrect:** File and Print Services for NetWare (FPNW) integrates NetWare clients into a Windows NT network and also allows them to access resources on computers running Windows NT Server. You need to administer a NetWare server from a Windows NT Workstation client.

    D. **Incorrect:** Distributed Component Object Model (DCOM) is used to integrate client/server applications across multiple computers using reusable and replaceable objects. To administer a NetWare server from a Windows NT Workstation client, you need to integrate platforms, not applications.

Further Reading

Microsoft Windows NT Technical Support Self-Paced Training Chapter 14, Lesson 1 discusses NWLink and Microsoft NetWare interoperability tools such as CSNW, GSNW, and FPNW. This lesson also covers the remote administration of Novell networks, Directory Service Manager for NetWare (DSMN), and the Windows NT Server Migration Tool for NetWare. Lesson 2 provides procedures for installing and configuring CSNW and GSNW. Practice for installing and configuring CSNW and GSNW is included on the CD provided in this kit.

Use Microsoft Technical Support Online (http://support.microsoft.com/) by searching for "Windows NT Workstation" and for "NetWare." Then click "Information on NWLink." Search for "NWLink" and view "How to: Install FPNW" and "How to: Install Gateway Service for NetWare."

Use Microsoft Technical Support Online (http://support.microsoft.com/) by searching for "Windows NT Workstation" and for "network protocols." Then click "Comparison of Windows NT Network Protocols."

O B J E C T I V E   4 . 4

Use various configurations to install Windows NT Workstation as a TCP/IP client.

TCP/IP is a suite of protocols that provides communication across interconnected networks of computers with diverse hardware architectures and platforms. Microsoft TCP/IP provides standards for how computers running Windows NT communicate in a network environment. You must be familiar with TCP/IP configuration options, name resolution, and utilities to install Windows NT Workstation as a TCP/IP client.

Configuration Options

There are two ways to configure TCP/IP: automatically and manually. Configuring TCP/IP automatically requires configuration of a Dynamic Host Configuration Protocol (DHCP) server service. Configuring TCP/IP manually requires use of the Protocols tab in the Network program in the Control Panel. When configuring TCP/IP, there are three parameters that are required for each network adapter card in the computer using TCP/IP:

- **IP address**—a logical 32-bit address used to identify a TCP/IP host. Each computer running TCP/IP requires a unique IP address.

- **Subnet mask**—used to block out a portion of the IP address so TCP/IP can find the network ID. Computers on the same network must have the same subnet mask to communicate.

- **Default gateway**—the intermediate network device (router) on the local network that has knowledge of the network IDs of the other networks on the Internet, so it can forward the packets to the other gateways until the packet is eventually delivered to a gateway connected to the specified destination. The default gateway is connected to the local subnet, and should be the same as other computers in the network.

When configuring automatically, the three required parameters are assigned by the DHCP server.

Name Resolution

Since TCP/IP allows interconnected networks of computers with diverse hardware architectures and platforms to communicate, there can be many ways of identifying the computers. However, TCP/IP uses only IP addresses to identify computers. Thus, TCP/IP relies on some of the following name resolution methods to match computer names to IP addresses and IP addresses to computer names:

- **Domain Name System (DNS)**—a TCP/IP protocol naming convention consisting of two parts: a host name and a domain name.

- **Windows Internet Naming Service (WINS)**—a name resolution service that resolves Windows networking computer names to IP addresses in a routed environment.

- **HOSTS file**—a local text file that maps remote host names to IP addresses.

- **LMHOSTS file**—a local text file that maps NetBIOS names to IP addresses.

Utilities

The following Windows NT utilities work with TCP/IP protocols to provide networking capabilities:

Utility	Function
Packet Internet Groper (PING)	Verifies configurations and tests connections.
File Transfer Protocol (FTP)	Provides bidirectional file transfers between a computer running Windows NT and any TCP/IP host running FTP.
Trivial File Transfer Protocol (TFTP)	Provides bidirectional file transfers between a computer running Windows NT and a TCP/IP host running TFTP.
TELNET	Provides terminal emulation to a TCP/IP host running Telnet.
Remote Copy Protocol (RCP)	Copies files between a computer running Windows NT and a UNIX host.
Remote Shell (RSH)	Runs commands on a UNIX host.
Remote Execution (REXEC)	Runs a process on a remote computer.
FINGER	Retrieves system information from a remote computer that supports TCP/IP and the finger service.
Microsoft Internet Explorer (IE)	Locates resources on the Internet.
Address Resolution Protocol (ARP)	Displays a cache of locally resolved IP addresses to physical addresses.
IPCONFIG	Displays current TCP/IP configuration.
NBTSTAT	Displays protocol statistics and connections using NetBIOS over TCP/IP.
NETSTAT	Displays TCP/IP protocol statistics and connections.
ROUTE	Displays or modifies the local routing table.
HOSTNAME	Returns the local computer's host name for authentication by the RCP, RSH, and REXEC utilities.
TRACERT	Checks the route to a remote system.

Questions related to this objective are designed to determine if you have an awareness of these issues. To successfully answer the questions for this objective, you need a firm understanding of several key terms. For definitions of these terms, refer to the Glossary in this book.

Key Terms

- Default gateway

- Domain Name System (DNS)

- Dynamic Host Configuration Protocol (DHCP)

- HOSTS file

- Internet Protocol (IP) address

- LMHOSTS file

- Network basic input/output system (NetBIOS)

- Router

- Subnet

- Subnet mask

- Wide area network (WAN)

- Windows Internet Naming Service (WINS)

70-073.04.04.001

You need to give each Windows NT Workstation client on your 10Base2 network access to the Internet through a WAN connection. In order to do so, you need to configure TCP/IP on each client. Since the network contains a large number of client workstations, the task of manually assigning IP address to each workstation would take an excessive amount of time to complete.

How should you configure each Windows NT 4.0 client if you want to avoid the task of manually assigning IP addresses for each of your Windows NT Workstations?

A. Configure each workstation to obtain an IP address from IIS.

B. Configure each workstation to obtain an IP address from the PDC.

C. Configure each workstation to obtain an IP address from a WINS server.

D. Configure each workstation to obtain an IP address from a DHCP server.

70-073.04.04.001

You need to give each Windows NT Workstation client on your 10Base2 network access to the Internet through a WAN connection. In order to do so, you need to configure TCP/IP on each client. Since the network contains a large number of client workstations, the task of manually assigning IP address to each workstation would take an excessive amount of time to complete.

How should you configure each Windows NT 4.0 client if you want to avoid the task of manually assigning IP addresses for each of your Windows NT Workstations?

▶ **Correct Answer: D**

 A. **Incorrect:** Internet Information Server (IIS) primarily transmits information in Hypertext Markup Language (HTML) by using Hypertext Transport Protocol (HTTP). You cannot obtain an IP address from IIS.

 B. **Incorrect:** The primary domain controller (PDC) contains the directory database for the domain and authenticates login requests. You cannot obtain an IP address from the PDC.

 C. **Incorrect:** The Windows Internet Name Service (WINS) server is a dynamic database that registers and resolves computer names (NetBIOS names) to IP addresses. You cannot obtain an IP address from a WINS server.

 D. **Correct:** The Dynamic Host Configuration Protocol (DHCP) server automatically assigns IP addresses to computers configured to use DHCP.

70-073.04.04.002

You need to connect the network at a remote office to your company intranet using an Integrated Services Digital Network (ISDN) WAN connection. You have decided to manually configure TCP/IP addresses so the clients at the remote site can access all services provided by the intranet. What information must be supplied for each Windows NT Workstation? (Choose all that apply.)

A. The RAS server

B. The IP address

C. The subnet mask

D. The DHCP relay

E. The default gateway

70-073.04.04.002

You need to connect the network at a remote office to your company intranet using an Integrated Services Digital Network (ISDN) WAN connection. You have decided to manually configure TCP/IP addresses so the clients at the remote site can access all services provided by the intranet. What information must be supplied for each Windows NT Workstation? (Choose all that apply.)

▶ **Correct Answers: B, C, and E**

   A. **Incorrect:** The RAS server provides remote dial-in access to internetworks, where a remote RAS-based client connects to a local RAS server. The RAS server is not required to manually configure TCP/IP.

   B. **Correct:** The IP address, a logical 32-bit address, is used to identify a TCP/IP host. An IP address is required for each network adapter card in the computer when manually configuring TCP/IP.

   C. **Correct:** The subnet mask blocks out a portion of the IP address so that TCP/IP can distinguish the network ID from the host ID. The subnet mask is required for each network adapter card in the computer when manually configuring TCP/IP. All computers on one network must have the same subnet mask to communicate.

   D. **Incorrect:** The DHCP relay is used to automatically and dynamically assign global and subnet TCP/IP parameters for an internetwork. These parameters include IP addresses, subnet masks, default gateway, and other configuration parameters optionally assigned to DHCP clients. If you use DHCP to assign IP addresses, you do not have to configure TCP/IP manually.

   E. **Correct:** If no other route is configured on the host to the destination network, TCP/IP sends packets to the default gateway, which is required for each network adapter card in the computer when manually configuring TCP/IP. A default gateway must be configured with an IP address. Communication may be limited to the local network if a default gateway is not configured.

70-073.04.04.003

You need to configure TCP/IP for a Windows NT Workstation client. The client is located on an Ethernet segment that is connected to the company backbone by a router. A Windows 95 client on the same network segment is assigned the IP address 208.15.208.87, subnet mask 255.255.255.0, and 208.15.208.81 for the default gateway. How should you configure TCP/IP on the client?

A. All three addresses should be identical to the Windows 95 client configuration.

B. All three addresses should be different from the Windows 95 client configuration.

C. The IP address should be different from the Windows 95 client, but the subnet mask and gateway should be the same as the Windows 95 client configuration.

D. The IP address and subnet mask should be different from the Windows 95 client, but the gateway should be the same as the Windows 95 client configuration.

70-073.04.04.003

You need to configure TCP/IP for a Windows NT Workstation client. The client is located on an Ethernet segment that is connected to the company backbone by a router. A Windows 95 client on the same network segment is assigned the IP address 208.15.208.87, subnet mask 255.255.255.0, and 208.15.208.81 for the default gateway. How should you configure TCP/IP on the client?

▶ **Correct Answer: C**

  A. **Incorrect:** Each computer running TCP/IP requires a unique IP address.

  B. **Incorrect:** Computers must have the same subnet mask to communicate on a network. In addition, the default gateway is connected to the local subnet, and should be the same as other computers in the network.

  C. **Correct:** Each computer running TCP/IP requires a unique IP address. However, computers must have the same subnet mask to communicate on a network. In addition, the default gateway is connected to the local subnet and should be the same as other computers in the network.

  D. **Incorrect:** Computers must have the same subnet mask to communicate on a network.

70-073.04.04.004

A company's intranet consists of two TCP/IP-only Ethernet segments connected by routers. Windows NT Workstation clients and Windows NT Servers are used exclusively. Also, two Windows NT Servers host the company's Internet Web site and four of the Windows NT Workstations host intranet sites for departments within the company.

The required result is to implement a method that allows all clients to access network services by using NetBIOS names.

The first optional result is to implement a method that allows departmental Web sites to be reached by their DNS names. The second optional result is to implement a method that automatically assigns an IP address to clients when they connect to the intranet.

The proposed solution is to configure HOSTS and LMHOSTS files on each Windows NT Workstation client.

What does this solution provide?

A. The required result and all optional results.

B. The required result and one optional result.

C. The required result and none of the optional results.

D. The proposed solution does not provide the required result.

70-073.04.04.004

A company's intranet consists of two TCP/IP-only Ethernet segments connected by routers. Windows NT Workstation clients and Windows NT Servers are used exclusively. Also, two Windows NT Servers host the company's Internet Web site and four of the Windows NT Workstations host intranet sites for departments within the company.

The required result is to implement a method that allows all clients to access network services by using NetBIOS names.

The first optional result is to implement a method that allows departmental Web sites to be reached by their DNS names. The second optional result is to implement a method that automatically assigns an IP address to clients when they connect to the intranet.

The proposed solution is to configure HOSTS and LMHOSTS files on each Windows NT Workstation client.

What does this solution provide?

▶ **Correct Answer: B**

A. **Incorrect:** See the explanation for answer B.

B. **Correct:** Configuring LMHOSTS files on each Windows NT Workstation client allows all clients access to network services through their NetBIOS names. Configuring HOSTS files on each Windows NT Workstation allows departmental web sites to be reached by their DNS names. However, the proposed solution does not include DHCP server service, which automatically assigns an IP address to clients when they connect to the intranet.

C. **Incorrect:** See the explanation for answer B.

D. **Incorrect:** See the explanation for answer B.

Further Reading

 Microsoft Windows NT Technical Support Self-Paced Training Chapter 10, Lesson 4 contains detailed information on configuring TCP/IP manually and automatically. Practice for configuring TCP/IP manually and automatically is included using the CD provided in this kit. In Chapter 11, Lesson 2 examines the Dynamic Host Configuration Protocol (DHCP) and its uses. Lesson 3 explains Windows Internet Service (WINS), including NetBIOS. Lesson 4 explains the function of the Domain Name System (DNS) Server Service. Practice for configuring DHCP, WINS, and DNS is included on the CD provided in this kit.

 Microsoft Windows NT Workstation Resource Kit Chapter 32 contains detailed information on using NetBIOS and DNS computer names, including HOSTS and LMHOSTS files.

OBJECTIVE 4.5

Configure and install Dial-Up Networking in a given situation.

Dial-up Networking works with a remote access server or *Internet service provider* (ISP) to extend network connectivity to remote clients. Remote clients can connect directly to a RAS server through:

- A *public-switched telephone network* (PSTN)

- An X.25 network

- An *Integrated Services Digital Network* (ISDN)

Protocols

Dial-up networking uses the following remote-access protocols:

Protocol	Description
Point-to-Point Tunneling Protocol (PPTP)	Provides secure remote access across the Internet. Benefits: Lower transmission costs, lower hardware costs, lower administrative overhead, security.
Serial Line Internet Protocol (SLIP)	Provides TCP/IP connections over serial lines. Disadvantages: Cannot utilize DHCP/WINS, relies on text-based logon sessions, does not support IPX/SPX or NetBEUI, authentication password issues.
Point-to-Point Protocol (PPP)	Provides dial-in to remote networks through any PPP server. Benefit: A means to increase transmission rates by combining multiple physical links.

Security Features

Windows NT RAS supports the following security measures:

- **Integrated domain security**. RAS server uses the same user account setup as the computer running Windows NT.

- **Encrypted authentication and logon process**. Authentication and logon information is encrypted using any authentication method when transmitted over RAS.

- **Auditing**. Audit information can be generated on all remote connections.

- **Intermediary security hosts**. A third-party intermediary security host can be added between the RAS client(s) and the RAS server(s). Clients must enter a password to establish a connection with the RAS server.

- **Callback security**. The RAS server can provide callbacks to ensure that the connection is made from a secure site.

- **PPTP filtering**. Filtering ensures that all protocols other than PPTP are disabled on the specified network adapter card.

Configuring a RAS Server

The RAS server is configured beginning at the Remote Access Setup dialog box, which is accessed from the Services tab in the Network program in the Control Panel. Configuring a RAS server requires you to know the following information:

- Modem type

- Communication port type

- Whether computer is used for dial in, dial out, or both

- Protocols used

- Modem settings (baud, kilobits per second)

- Security settings

Configuring Dial-up Networking

Dial-up networking is configured from the Dial-Up Networking icon in My Computer. There are many configuration options for Dial-Up Networking, including Phonebook entries, logging on using a dial-in entry, and the AutoDial feature. A *Phonebook* entry stores settings needed to connect to a specific remote network. A *dial-in entry* uses a Phonebook entry to establish a connection to the RAS server so that the domain controller can validate the logon request. *AutoDial* maps and maintains network addresses to Phonebook entries so they can be automatically dialed from an application or the command line.

Questions related to this objective are designed to determine if you have an awareness of these issues. To successfully answer the questions for this objective, you need a firm understanding of several key terms. For definitions of these terms, refer to the Glossary in this book.

Key Terms

- Callback

- Clear-text passwords

- Dial-Up Networking

- Encryption

- Integrated Services Digital Network (ISDN) line

- Multilink Protocol (MP)

- Phonebook entry

- Point-to-Point Protocol (PPP)

- Point-to-Point Tunneling Protocol (PPTP)

- PPP Multilink Protocol (MP)

- Public-switched telephone network (PSTN)

- Remote Access Service (RAS)

70-073.04.05.001

The Windows NT Workstation at your home office is configured with an ISDN modem. The modem is most often used to connect directly to the Remote Access Server at company headquarters. The ISDN-to-ISDN connection is made using two B-channels that share the same telephone number. In order to increase security, the RAS administrator is considering enabling callback.

If you use a Multilink-enabled Phonebook entry to call the server, how will enabling callback affect the connection?

A. It will function normally.

B. It will no longer function.

C. It will function much more slowly.

D. It will function much more quickly.

70-073.04.05.001

The Windows NT Workstation at your home office is configured with an ISDN modem. The modem is most often used to connect directly to the Remote Access Server at company headquarters. The ISDN-to-ISDN connection is made using two B-channels that share the same telephone number. In order to increase security, the RAS administrator is considering enabling callback.

If you use a Multilink-enabled Phonebook entry to call the server, how will enabling callback affect the connection?

▶ **Correct Answer: A**

A. **Correct:** Since the link between your home office and company headquarters is made using ISDN with two B-channels that share the same telephone number, then the Multilink-enabled Phonebook will work normally with callback.

B. **Incorrect:** Since the link between your home office and company headquarters is made using ISDN with two B-channels that share the same telephone number, then the Multilink-enabled Phonebook will work normally with callback.

C. **Incorrect:** Since the link between your home office and company headquarters is made using ISDN with two B-channels that share the same telephone number, then the Multilink-enabled Phonebook will work normally with callback and there will be no effect on speed.

D. **Incorrect:** Since the link between your home office and company headquarters is made using ISDN with two B-channels that share the same telephone number, then the Multilink-enabled Phonebook will work normally with callback and there will be no effect on speed.

70-073.04.05.002

You are working from home and want to access resources at the corporate office. However, directly dialing the RAS server would incur long-distance costs.

The required result is to configure Dial-Up Networking to establish a remote access session to a Windows NT RAS server computer at the corporate office from your Windows NT Workstation–based computer.

The first optional result is to maintain a high level of security. The second optional result is to minimize the cost of the communication session.

The proposed solution is to use PPTP over the Internet to access the RAS server.

What does the proposed solution provide?

A. The required result and all optional results.

B. The required result and one optional result.

C. The required result but none of the optional results.

D. The proposed solution does not provide the required result.

70-073.04.05.002

You are working from home and want to access resources at the corporate office. However, directly dialing the RAS server would incur long-distance costs.

The required result is to configure Dial-Up Networking to establish a remote access session to a Windows NT RAS server computer at the corporate office from your Windows NT Workstation–based computer.

The first optional result is to maintain a high level of security. The second optional result is to minimize the cost of the communication session.

The proposed solution is to use PPTP over the Internet to access the RAS server.

What does the proposed solution provide?

▶ **Correct Answer: A**

A. **Correct:** Using PPTP over the Internet allows you to establish a remote access session with the corporate office from your Windows NT Workstation computer. In addition, PPTP offers a higher level of security by encrypting data. PPTP also offers lower transmission costs, since local access through an Internet service provider (ISP) will be less than a long-distance call or using an 800 number.

B. **Incorrect:** See the explanation for answer A.

C. **Incorrect:** See the explanation for answer A.

D. **Incorrect:** See the explanation for answer A.

70-073.04.05.003

Your computer running Windows NT Workstation has two 28.8-Kbps modems installed, and each modem is connected to a dedicated PSTN line.

The required result is to establish a session with a RAS server that has two modems installed, each connected to a dedicated PSTN line, and MP enabled.

The first optional result is to use the Phonebook feature of RAS to configure the connection process. The second optional result is to minimize the RAS session time.

The proposed solution is to create one Phonebook entry for both modems with a separate RAS server phone number for each modem to dial. Use the PPP Multilink Protocol to establish a single 57.6-Kbps connection to the RAS server.

What does the proposed solution provide?

A. The required result and all optional results.

B. The required result and one optional result.

C. The required result but none of the optional results.

D. The proposed solution does not provide the required result.

70-073.04.05.003

Your computer running Windows NT Workstation has two 28.8-Kbps modems installed, and each modem is connected to a dedicated PSTN line.

The required result is to establish a session with a RAS server that has two modems installed, each connected to a dedicated PSTN line, and MP enabled.

The first optional result is to use the Phonebook feature of RAS to configure the connection process. The second optional result is to minimize the RAS session time.

The proposed solution is to create one Phonebook entry for both modems with a separate RAS server phone number for each modem to dial. Use the PPP Multilink Protocol to establish a single 57.6-Kbps connection to the RAS server.

What does the proposed solution provide?

▶ **Correct Answer: A**

A. **Correct:** By using the PPP Multilink Protocol to establish a single 57.6-Kbps connection to the RAS server, you have established a session with a RAS server that has both of your 28.8-Kbps modems installed, each connected to a dedicated PSTN line, which requires MP to be enabled. The PPP Multilink Protocol allows you to combine analog modem paths on both your computer and the server. In addition, session time and costs are reduced, since access speed is increased by combining modem paths. By creating one Phonebook entry for both modems with a separate RAS server phone number for each modem to dial, the connection is configured.

B. **Incorrect:** See the explanation for answer A.

C. **Incorrect:** See the explanation for answer A.

D. **Incorrect:** See the explanation for answer A.

70-073.04.05.004

You need to connect a Windows NT Workstation-based computer to a RAS server. Dial-Up Networking has been installed.

The required result is to configure Dial-Up Networking to establish a remote access session from a Windows NT Workstation-based computer.

The first optional result is to use a script with a PPP connection using RAS over TCP/IP. The second optional result is to use encryption. You do not want to transmit clear-text passwords on the phone line.

The proposed solution is to create a Phonebook entry by opening the Dial-Up Networking icon in My Computer, clicking New, and entering the name, area code, and phone number of the RAS server to be dialed. On the Server tab, ensure that PPP is selected, and ensure that the check box for TCP/IP is checked. On the Script tab, click the Run this script button, and specify a script. On the Security tab, verify that the Accept only encrypted authentication button is selected. Click OK.

What does the proposed solution provide?

A. The required result and all optional results.

B. The required result and one optional result.

C. The required result but none of the optional results.

D. The proposed solution does not provide the required result.

70-073.04.05.004

You need to connect a Windows NT Workstation-based computer to a RAS server. Dial-Up Networking has been installed.

The required result is to configure Dial-Up Networking to establish a remote access session from a Windows NT Workstation-based computer.

The first optional result is to use a script with a PPP connection using RAS over TCP/IP. The second optional result is to use encryption. You do not want to transmit clear-text passwords on the phone line.

The proposed solution is to create a Phonebook entry by opening the Dial-Up Networking icon in My Computer, clicking New, and entering the name, area code, and phone number of the RAS server to be dialed. On the Server tab, ensure that PPP is selected, and ensure that the check box for TCP/IP is checked. On the Script tab, click the Run this script button, and specify a script. On the Security tab, verify that the Accept only encrypted authentication button is selected. Click OK.

What does the proposed solution provide?

▶ **Correct Answer: A**

A. **Correct:** By creating a new Phonebook entry for the RAS server, you have configured Dial-Up Networking to establish a remote-access session from a Windows NT Workstation–based computer that already has Dial-Up Networking installed. By selecting PPP for the server type and TCP/IP for the network protocol on the Server tab, and specifying a script on the Script tab, you have configured a script with a PPP connection using RAS over TCP/IP. By selecting the Accept Only Encrypted Authentication Button on the Security tab, you have configured encryption, which does not transmit clear text passwords on the phone line.

B. **Incorrect:** See the explanation for answer A.

C. **Incorrect:** See the explanation for answer A.

D. **Incorrect:** See the explanation for answer A.

Further Reading

Microsoft Windows NT Technical Support Self-Paced Training Chapter 12, Lesson 1 includes basic information on Dial-Up Networking, including PPTP, PPP and RAS security features. Lesson 4 contains details on installing and configuring Dial-Up Networking, including Phonebook entries, logon options, and AutoDial. Practice for installing and configuring Dial-Up Networking, creating Phonebook entries, and configuring logon preferences is included on the CD provided in this kit. Lesson 5 lists some common errors that can occur when using Dial-Up Networking.

OBJECTIVE 4.6

Configure Microsoft Peer Web Services in a given situation.

Peer Web Services (PWS) are a collection of services that enable the user of a computer running Windows NT Workstation to publish a personal Web site from the desktop. The services include:

- **World Wide Web (WWW) service**—based on HTTP protocol, which allows you to link to and navigate Web documents and applications.

- **File Transfer Protocol (FTP) service**—used to transfer files between local and remote systems on a TCP/IP network and will allow users on a company intranet to be able to transfer files to and from the Web site.

- **Gopher service**—a hierarchical system for finding and retrieving files from Gopher servers on the Internet and will not allow users on a company intranet to navigate HTML documents.

Use the Microsoft Internet Service Manager (ISM) to configure PWS. You can access ISM from the Microsoft Peer Web Services Tools (Common) folder on the Windows NT Workstation. You can also use ISM to monitor Internet services on any Windows NT computer in the network.

Questions related to this objective are designed to determine if you have an awareness of these issues. To successfully answer the questions for this objective, you need a firm understanding of several key terms. For definitions of these terms, refer to the Glossary in this book.

Key Terms

- File Transfer Protocol (FTP)

- Gopher service

- Internet Information Server (IIS)

- Peer Web Services (PWS)

- World Wide Web service

70-073.04.06.001

A department wants to publish Web documents to the company intranet. However, the department does not have access to a server that can provide Web services. They do have a Window NT Workstation client computer that is no longer used and could be reconfigured to meet the department's needs.

What can you install on the Windows NT Workstation client computer to allow this department to publish Web documents to its own Web server?

A. IIS

B. DNS

C. RAS

D. PWS

70-073.04.06.001

A department wants to publish Web documents to the company intranet. However, the department does not have access to a server that can provide Web services. They do have a Window NT Workstation client computer that is no longer used and could be reconfigured to meet the department's needs.

What can you install on the Windows NT Workstation client computer to allow this department to publish Web documents to its own Web server?

▶ **Correct Answer: D**

A. **Incorrect:** Internet Information Server (IIS) provides Windows NT Servers with the ability to publish resources and services on the Internet and on private intranets. You need to provide this ability on Windows NT Workstation.

B. **Incorrect:** Domain Name System (DNS) is a database that provides a naming system for identifying hosts on the Internet. DNS will not allow the department to publish Web documents on its own Web server.

C. **Incorrect:** Remote Access Service (RAS) provides Windows NT–based computer users with remote access to their networks for services such as file and printer sharing, e-mail, scheduling, and SQL database access. RAS will not allow the department to publish Web documents on its own Web server.

D. **Correct:** Peer Web Services (PWS) provides Windows NT Workstation with the ability to publish resources and services on the Internet and on private intranets. You can install PWS on the Windows NT Workstation client computer to allow the department to publish Web documents on its own Web server.

70-073.04.06.002

Which PWS service should you enable if you want users on a company intranet to be able to navigate Hypertext Markup Language documents?

A. ODBC

B. FTP service

C. Gopher service

D. World Wide Web service

70-073.04.06.003

Which PWS service should you enable if you want users on a company intranet to be able to transfer files to and from the Web site?

A. ODBC

B. FTP service

C. Gopher service

D. World Wide Web service

70-073.04.06.002

Which PWS service should you enable if you want users on a company intranet to be able to navigate Hypertext Markup Language documents?

▶ **Correct Answer: D**

A. **Incorrect:** Open Database Connectivity (ODBC) is an application programming interface and will not allow users on a company intranet to navigate HTML documents.

B. **Incorrect:** File Transfer Protocol (FTP) is used to transfer files between local and remote systems on a TCP/IP network and will not allow users on a company intranet to navigate HTML documents.

C. **Incorrect:** The Gopher service is a hierarchical system for finding and retrieving files from Gopher servers on the Internet and will not allow users on a company intranet to navigate HTML documents.

D. **Correct:** The World Wide Web service uses Hypertext Transport Protocol (HTTP) to link to and navigate Hypertext Markup Language (HTML) documents.

70-073.04.06.003

Which PWS service should you enable if you want users on a company intranet to be able to transfer files to and from the Web site?

▶ **Correct Answer: B**

A. **Incorrect:** Open Database Connectivity (ODBC) is an application programming interface and will not allow users on a company intranet to be able to transfer files to and from the Web site.

B. **Correct:** File Transfer Protocol (FTP) is used to transfer files between local and remote systems on a TCP/IP network and will allow users on a company intranet to be able to transfer files to and from the Web site.

C. **Incorrect:** The Gopher service is a hierarchical system for finding and retrieving files from Gopher servers on the Internet and will not allow users on a company intranet to be able to transfer files to and from the Web site.

D. **Incorrect:** The World Wide Web service uses Hypertext Transport Protocol (HTTP) to link to and navigate Hypertext Markup Language (HTML) documents and will not allow users on a company intranet to be able to transfer files to and from the Web site.

Further Reading

 Microsoft Windows NT Technical Support Self-Paced Training Chapter 13, Lesson 2 details the networking components of Peer Web Services (PWS) and PWS installation.

 Microsoft Windows NT Server Internet Guide Chapter 1 contains detailed information on Internet services provided with the Internet Information Server and Peer Web Services, including World Wide Web service, FTP service, and Gopher service.

Running Applications

The Running Applications domain covers how to administer applications in Windows NT. The support of MS-DOS– and Win16 (Windows 3.1)–based applications on the Windows NT platform is explored in this Objective Domain, including the advantages and disadvantages of various configuration strategies. The setting of *application base priorities*, which control the way applications are processed, is also discussed.

Tested Skills and Suggested Practices

- Starting applications on Intel and RISC platforms in various operating system environments. You must be able to configure Windows NT to run both MS-DOS– and Win16-based applications on Intel and RISC platforms.

  - Practice 1: Read about the Windows NT Architecture and learn the three subsystems used to emulate the other operating system environments.

  - Practice 2: Read about *NT Virtual DOS Machine* (NTVDM) and WOW (Win16 on Win32 [Windows 95/NT]) and the advantages and disadvantages of running applications in multiple NTVDM environments and in the WOW environment.

  - Practice 3: Start a Win16-based application in its own NTVDM using both the command prompt (START/SEPARATE [PATH] APPLICATION_EXECUTABLE) and the Start menu (specify "Run in Separate Memory Space").

  - Practice 4: Read about Intel and RISC platform capabilities for supporting various applications. Determine the application compatibility for each platform.

- Starting applications at various priorities. You must be able to differentiate between the four priority levels that can be assigned to applications and know how to set priority levels for applications.

  - Practice 1: Learn the four priority levels that can be set for applications. Read about how a system can be affected when the Real-time priority is used.

  - Practice 2: Set priorities for applications using the Start command and for processes using the Task Manager.

Start applications on Intel and RISC platforms in various operating system environments.

Windows NT is designed to run existing applications that require the following operating systems:

- MS-DOS

- OS/2

- Portable Operating System Interface for Unix (POSIX)

- Windows 3.1 (Win16)

- Windows 95/NT (Win32)

Since Windows NT is a 32-bit operating system, it uses one of three environment subsystems to emulate the other operating system environments, which enable the applications to run. An *environment subsystem* acts as an intermediary between the kernel mode of Windows NT and an application designed for another environment.

The three environment subsystems in Windows NT are as follows:

Subsystem	Function
Win32	Supports Win32–, MS-DOS–, and Windows 3.x–based applications.
OS/2	Supports OS/2 1.x, character-based applications on Intel platforms.
POSIX	Supports POSIX applications that meet the U.S. Federal Information Processing Standard 151.

The Win32 subsystem supports Win32-, MS-DOS–, and Windows 3.x–based applications. Win32-based applications employ the reliability of Windows NT along with multithreading, object linking and embedding (OLE)/ActiveX and OpenGL support, and DirectX application programming interfaces (APIs).

MS-DOS–based applications run inside an NT Virtual DOS Machine (NTVDM) application to provide a simulated MS-DOS environment in Windows NT. Each MS-DOS–based application requires its own NTVDM application, which is configured in the MS-DOS–based application's program information file.

Windows 3.x–based applications use Win16 on Win32 (WOW) Windows NT program inside an NTVDM application to allow 16-bit programs to run in a simulated MS-DOS environment in Windows NT. WOW is a 32-bit Windows NT program that allows Win16-based applications to run in a Win32 environment. If a Win16-based application fails, it can halt other Win16-based applications running in the same NTVDM. However, depending on your system needs, you can set up Win16-based applications to run in separate NTVDMs, increasing reliability.

Questions related to this objective are designed to determine if you have an awareness of these issues. To successfully answer the questions for this objective, you need a firm understanding of the following key terms. For definitions of these terms, refer to the Glossary in this book.

Key Terms

- NT Virtual DOS Machine (NTVDM)

- Preemptive multitasking

- Thunk

- Win16 on Win32 (WOW)

70-073.05.01.001

In which environment do MS-DOS–based applications run when launched on Windows NT Workstation computers?

A. DOS

B. WOW

C. DCOM

D. NTVDM

70-073.05.01.002

What is the main disadvantage of running multiple Windows 16-bit applications in the same NTVDM?

A. Windows 16-bit applications cannot share memory with other 16-bit Windows applications that may be running in the NTVDM.

B. If one Windows 16-bit application fails, it can adversely affect all other Windows 16-bit applications running in the NTVDM.

C. When the single thread shared by Windows 16-bit applications is preempted, all Windows 16-bit applications running in the NTVDM can become unavailable.

D. The WOW thunking process grows exponentially with each additional Windows 16-bit application running in the NTVDM, which can adversely affect performance for other applications running on the machine.

70-073.05.01.001

In which environment do MS-DOS–based applications run when launched on Windows NT Workstation computers?

▶ **Correct Answer: D**

A. **Incorrect:** Windows NT does not run the Disk Operating System (DOS) environment.

B. **Incorrect:** Win16 on Win32 (WOW) allows Win16-based applications to run in a Win32 environment. You want to run MS-DOS–based applications.

C. **Incorrect:** Distributed Component Object Model (DCOM, also known as *Networked OLE*) is a tool used to integrate client/server applications across multiple computers using reusable and replaceable objects.

D. **Correct:** NT Virtual DOS Machine (NTVDM), a special Win32-based application, supports MS-DOS–based applications when launched on Windows NT Workstation computers.

70-073.05.01.002

What is the main disadvantage of running multiple Windows 16-bit applications in the same NTVDM?

▶ **Correct Answer: B**

A. **Incorrect:** Windows 16-bit applications *do* share memory with other Windows 16-bit applications running in the same NTVDM. Windows 16-bit applications running in NTVDM cannot share memory with 32-bit applications running in Windows NT, and the two applications cannot call each other's dynamic-link libraries (DLLs).

B. **Correct:** If one 16-bit application running in NTVDM fails it must be closed before another 16-bit application can gain access to the processor.

C. **Incorrect:** If the single thread shared by Windows 16-bit applications is preempted (interrupted by a higher-priority thread), the other 16-bit applications running in NTVDM may be slowed, but they do not become unavailable.

D. **Incorrect:** Since all of the Win16-based applications are running in a shared memory space, only one Win16-based application is running at a time. Therefore, the thunking process cannot grow exponentially, nor can it affect performance for applications running on the machine.

70-073.05.01.003

What are the advantages of running Windows 16-bit applications in separate NTVDMs? (Choose all that apply.)

A. If a single Windows application is preempted, all other applications continue to run.

B. A single faulty Windows 16-bit application does not affect other Windows 16-bit applications.

C. The system moves subsequent NTVDMs to a higher priority level that improves application performance.

D. Fewer thunking processes are necessary to provide translation from 16-bit to 32-bit, which reduces system overhead.

70-073.05.01.003

What are the advantages of running Windows 16-bit applications in separate NTVDMs? (Choose all that apply.)

▶ **Correct Answers: A and B**

   A. **Correct:** Since each 16-bit application is running in its own memory space, all applications continue to run, even when one is busy.

   B. **Correct:** Since each 16-bit application is running in its own memory space, all applications continue to run, even when one is faulty.

   C. **Incorrect:** There are no priority levels for NTVDMs. You can set priority levels for applications using the Task Manager.

   D. **Incorrect:** The same number of thunking processes are necessary whether running in one or separate NTVDMs.

Further Reading

 Microsoft Windows NT Technical Support Self-Paced Training Chapter 2, Lesson 2 explains the three subsystems used to support various applications in Windows NT. Lesson 5 contains information on supporting MS-DOS and Win16-based applications on Windows NT using NTVDM and WOW, including running multiple NTVDMs. Lesson 6 explains the platform capabilities of Intel and RISC computers.

 Microsoft Windows NT Workstation Resource Kit Chapter 5 contains information on the environment subsystems and details on running MS-DOS–based applications and Win16-based applications in Windows NT.

OBJECTIVE 5.2

Start applications at various priorities.

Windows NT prioritizes applications, determining how processing takes place. This processing is determined by *preemptive multitasking*, where the system schedules threads for the processor based on the priority level of the thread, processing the highest-priority threads first. Thus, any one program is prevented from monopolizing the system. However, you can increase or decrease the priority level of an application or process.

Priorities are set in a range from 0–31, with 0 as lowest priority. Priority levels 0–15 are used by dynamic applications such as user applications and most non-critical operating system functions. Priority levels 16–31 are used by real-time applications such as the kernel, which cannot be written to the page file. Eight is the normal priority. You can set four priority levels using the Start command or the Task Manager as follows:

Priority option	Priority level
Real-time	24
High	13
Normal	8
Low	4

Questions related to this objective are designed to determine if you have an awareness of these issues. To successfully answer the questions for this objective, you need a firm understanding of the following key terms. For definitions of these terms, refer to the Glossary in this book.

Key Terms

- Base priority levels

- Preemptive multitasking

70-073.05.02.001

Which command should you use to launch a program in Windows NT Workstation and specify a base priority level?

A. Run

B. Start

C. Launch

D. Execute

70-073.05.02.002

You need to run a Windows 32–based application on your Windows NT Workstation. The application should run at the highest base priority level possible, but it should not interfere with the operating system kernel. What priority level should you specify when launching the application?

A. Low

B. High

C. Normal

D. Real-time

70-073.05.02.001

Which command should you use to launch a program in Windows NT Workstation and specify a base priority level?

▶ **Correct Answer: B**

    A. **Incorrect:** In Windows NT, the Run command is no longer a command but is accessed by clicking Run from the Start button. Clicking Run allows you to launch a program, but not to specify a base priority level.

    B. **Correct:** Using the Start command at the Command Prompt allows you to specify a base priority level for an application by adding one of the following options: /LOW, /NORMAL, /HIGH, /REALTIME.

    C. **Incorrect:** The Launch command is not recognized in Windows NT.

    D. **Incorrect:** The Execute command is not recognized in Windows NT.

70-073.05.02.002

You need to run a Windows 32–based application on your Windows NT Workstation. The application should run at the highest base priority level possible, but it should not interfere with the operating system kernel. What priority level should you specify when launching the application?

▶ **Correct Answer: B**

    A. **Incorrect:** Low priority sets the base priority to 4, which is too low for the specified need.

    B. **Correct:** High priority sets the base priority to 13, which is the highest possible to meet the specified need without preventing other processes and services from running.

    C. **Incorrect:** Normal priority sets the base priority to 8, which is too low for the specified need.

    D. **Incorrect:** Real-time priority sets the base priority to 24, which can destabilize your system and prevent other processes from running.

70-073.05.02.003

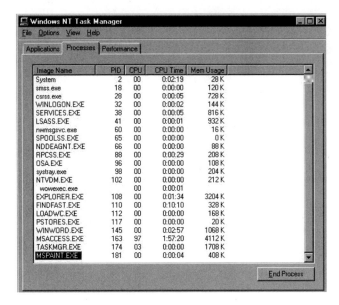

Examine the exhibit above to answer this question.

How should you change the priority level for MSACCESS.EXE?

A. Right-click MSACCESS.EXE, select the Set Priority option, and select the appropriate base priority level.

B. Double-click MSACCESS.EXE, select the Set Priority option, and select the appropriate base priority level.

C. Highlight MSACCESS.EXE, select the Performance tab, select the Set Priority option, and select the appropriate base priority level.

D. Highlight MSACCESS.EXE, select the Applications tab, select the Set Priority option, and select the appropriate base priority level.

70-073.05.02.003

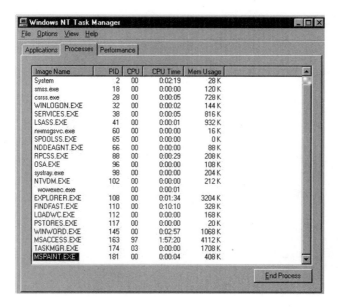

Examine the exhibit above to answer this question.

How should you change the priority level for MSACCESS.EXE?

▶ **Correct Answer: A**

A. **Correct:** To change the priority level for MSACCESS.EXE, right-click MSACCESS.EXE on the Task Manager Processes tab, select the set priority option, and then select the appropriate base priority level.

B. **Incorrect:** Double-clicking MSACCESS.EXE on the Task Manager Processes tab does not allow you to set a priority level.

C. **Incorrect:** Highlighting MSACCESS.EXE and selecting the Task Manager Performance tab shows a dynamic overview of the computer's performance but does not allow you to set a priority level.

D. **Incorrect:** Highlighting MSACCESS.EXE and selecting the Task Manager Applications tab shows the status of the programs (tasks) that are currently running on the computer but does not allow you to set a priority level.

70-073.05.02.004

You want to increase the base priority for an application running on your Windows NT Workstation computer to Real-time, but the system will not let you. What is wrong?

A. You do not have Administrator privileges.

B. The application is not a kernel application.

C. Another process is already running at Real-time priority.

D. The application does not support preemptive multitasking.

70-073.05.02.004

You want to increase the base priority for an application running on your Windows NT Workstation computer to Real-time, but the system will not let you. What is wrong?

▶ **Correct Answer: A**

A. **Correct:** Only users with Administrator privileges are allowed to set the /REALTIME option, since running an application at high priority from the Start command may slow performance.

B. **Incorrect:** Although it is not recommended, less critical dynamic applications can use the /REALTIME base priority.

C. **Incorrect:** Although it is not recommended, more than one process can use the /REALTIME base priority.

D. **Incorrect:** Applications running in Windows NT are affected by preemptive multitasking based on their assigned priority levels. The ability to set a priority level is not affected by preemptive multitasking, which is used in Windows NT.

Further Reading

 The *Microsoft Windows NT Technical Support* volume of the *Microsoft Windows NT Technical Support Training* kit Chapter 2, Lesson 8 explains base priority levels and how they are set for applications.

Monitoring and Optimization

The Monitoring and Optimization domain examines how you can monitor system performance and optimize system resources for Windows NT Workstation. You can use Task Manager and Performance Monitor to monitor system performance and determine whether performance problems exist. If problems exist, you can resolve them by optimizing existing system resources or taking steps to add resources.

Tested Skills and Suggested Practices

- Monitoring system performance using various tools. You must be able to use Task Manager and Performance Monitor to monitor various system components and to distinguish between the purpose of Task Manager and the purpose of Performance Manager.

    - Practice 1: Use Task Manager to monitor performance of a computer. Learn the purpose of the Applications, Processes, and Performance tabs. Examine the various column settings on the Processes tab.

    - Practice 2: Use Performance Monitor to monitor performance of a computer. Learn the purpose of objects, object instances, and counters. Add various counters to the Performance Monitor chart, and view the results on the chart.

- Identifying and resolving a given performance problem. You must be able to identify memory, processor, and disk bottlenecks and be able to resolve them using Task Manager and Performance Monitor.

    - Practice 1: Distinguish between memory, processor, and disk bottlenecks. Learn the counters typically used to identify each type of bottleneck.

- Optimizing system performance in various areas. Learn ways to optimize system performance without adding costly resources.

    - Practice 1: Recognize the difference between optimizing system performance and adding resources. Learn the ways to optimize memory, processor, and disk performance.

    - Practice 2: Learn the purpose of *volume sets* and *stripe sets*. Read about when to use volume sets and stripe sets.

O B J E C T I V E   6 . 1

Monitor system performance by using various tools.

Windows NT provides two main tools for monitoring system performance: Task Manager and Performance Monitor. In addition, many other general-purpose monitoring tools (which are not supported by Microsoft) are included on the *Windows NT Resource Kit* CD. However, you should use Task Manager and Performance Monitor whenever possible. Task Manager provides a snapshot view of key performance areas on your computer. Performance Monitor provides detailed information about selectable performance areas on your computer or other computers on a network, with the added capabilities of reporting and logging.

Task Manager

Task Manager allows you to monitor, start, and stop the active applications and processes on your computer. Unlike Performance Monitor, Task Manager does not allow data logging or remote monitoring. You can view three tabs in Task Manager: Applications, Processes, and Performance.

The Applications Tab

The applications tab displays the status of active applications on the computer. From this tab you can end a task, switch to another task you specify, or start a new task.

The Processes Tab

The Processes tab displays a list of running processes and process measures, including percentage of CPU time, amount of CPU time, and amount of memory used by the process.

Using Select Columns in the View menu, you can change the process measures to include any of the following: memory usage delta, page faults, page faults delta, virtual memory size, paged pool, nonpaged pool, base priority, handle count, and thread count. From the Processes tab you can end a process, change the base priority of a process, or start a debugger (if installed).

The Performance Tab

The Performance tab displays a dynamic, real-time overview of system performance, including graphic and numeric displays of processor and memory usage.

Performance Monitor

Performance Monitor is a dynamic, real-time display for measuring the performance of your computer or other computers on a network. Specifically, the performance of *objects* is being measured. Objects are system components such as processors, memory, cache, threads, and processes.

The following is a complete list of objects measured by Performance Monitor:

Object name	Description
Cache	Area of physical memory that holds recently used data
Logical disk	Disk partitions and other logical views of disk space
Memory	Random-access memory used to store code and data
Objects	Certain system software objects
Paging file	File used to back up virtual memory applications
Physical disk	Hardware disk unit
Process	A running program
Processor	Hardware unit that executes program instructions
Redirector	File system that diverts file requests to network servers
System	All system hardware and software
Thread	The part of a process that uses the processor

Objects may have *instances*, which are specific examples of an object. Object instances are measured by *counters,* which provide information about device usage, queue lengths, and other information used to measure system traffic. Many counters are available for each object. For example, physical disk objects are the various disks that exist on a computer. To add items to the Performance Monitor graph, use the Add to Chart dialog box to specify the object, counter, and instance for display.

Performance Monitor allows you to chart and log current activity and set alerts. In addition, you can create reports and work with input from log files to determine a more thorough analysis of the behavior of your system over time.

Questions related to this objective are designed to determine if you have an awareness of these issues. To successfully answer the questions for this objective, you need a firm understanding of several key terms. For definitions of these terms, refer to the Glossary in this book.

Key Terms

- Event

- Paging file

- Process

- Service

70-073.06.01.001

Which utilities can you use to monitor CPU use on your Windows NT Workstation computer? (Choose all that apply.)

A. Explorer

B. Event Viewer

C. Task Manager

D. Response Probe

E. Performance Monitor

70-073.06.01.002

Which utility can you use to log CPU use over time?

A. SC utility

B. Task Manager

C. Process Monitor

D. Performance Monitor

70-073.06.01.001

Which utilities can you use to monitor CPU use on your Windows NT Workstation computer? (Choose all that apply.)

▶ **Correct Answers: C and E**

A. **Incorrect:** The Explorer enables you to view and manage files and folders. It replaces Program Manager and File Manager, which were available in earlier versions of Windows NT.

B. **Incorrect:** The Event Viewer monitors *events* in your system. Events are any significant occurrence in the system or in an application that requires either users to be notified or an entry added to a log. Use Event Viewer to manage system, security, and application event logs.

C. **Correct:** Task Manager displays information about the processes running on your computer. Task Manager also allows you to end processes and to monitor how each process is using CPU and memory resources through a real-time display.

D. **Incorrect:** The Response Probe is a utility that enables you to test the performance of hardware and software configurations through simulated workloads. You can test each component in your configuration and how it responds to variances in the workload or to changes in equipment.

E. **Correct:** Performance Monitor is a graphical tool that monitors the performance of Windows NT servers and workstations. You can view the behavior of objects you select, including processors, memory, and processes on your computer or other computers on a network. Each object has a set of counters allowing you to track data; you can also set up alarms or trigger programs or procedures when certain thresholds are reached or exceeded.

70-073.06.01.002

Which utility can you use to log CPU use over time?

▶ **Correct Answer: D**

A. **Incorrect:** The service controller (SC) utility allows you to display the configuration of services and drivers on the system in the command prompt window.

B. **Incorrect:** Task Manager displays information about the processes running on your computer. You can also end processes and monitor how each process is using CPU and memory resources via a real-time display. Although Task Manager includes a CPU usage history graph, CPU usage data is not logged.

C. **Incorrect:** Process Monitor is a utility that displays process statistics in the command prompt window. The statistics are updated every 5 seconds.

D. **Correct:** Performance Monitor is a graphical tool that monitors the performance of Windows NT servers and workstations. You can view the behavior of objects you select, including processors, memory, and processes on your computer or other computers on a network. Each object has a set of counters allowing you to log data, including CPU usage, over a time period you specify.

70-073.06.01.003

Which utility can present memory use data in line graphs?

A. SC utility

B. Task Manager

C. Process Monitor

D. Performance Monitor

70-073.06.01.003

Which utility can present memory use data in line graphs?

▶ **Correct Answer: D**

A. **Incorrect:** The service controller (SC) utility allows you to display the configuration of services and drivers on the system in the command prompt window.

B. **Incorrect:** Task Manager displays information about the processes running on your computer. You can also end processes and monitor how each process is using CPU and memory resources via a real-time display. Although Task Manager includes a memory usage history graph, the graph shows only real-time memory usage and does not retain memory usage data for presentation.

C. **Incorrect:** Process Monitor is a utility that displays process statistics in the command prompt window. The statistics are updated every 5 seconds.

D. **Correct:** Performance Monitor is a graphical tool that monitors the performance of Windows NT servers and workstations. You can view the behavior of objects you select, including processors, memory, and processes on your computer or other computers on a network. Each object has a set of counters allowing you to track data, including memory usage, over a time period you specify and to display that data in line graphs for presentation.

70-073.06.01.004

You need to make a tool available so power users can monitor, start, and stop basic Windows NT processes. You do not want to give them access to performance log files.

Which tool should you use in this situation?

A. Task Manager

B. Network Monitor

C. Performance Monitor

D. Network Monitor Agent

E. Windows NT Diagnostics

70-073.06.01.004

You need to make a tool available so power users can monitor, start, and stop basic Windows NT processes. You do not want to give them access to performance log files.

Which tool should you use in this situation?

▶ **Correct Answer: A**

A. **Correct:** Task Manager displays information about the processes running on your computer. You can also end processes and monitor how each process is using CPU and memory resources through a real-time display. Unlike Performance Monitor, Task Manager does not create performance log files.

B. **Incorrect:** The Network Monitor is a service in the Network program on the Control Panel that is used to monitor network traffic to and from the local computer at a specific time. You cannot start and stop basic Windows NT processes using the Network Monitor.

C. **Incorrect:** Performance Monitor is a graphical tool that monitors the performance of Windows NT servers and workstations. You can view the behavior of objects you select, including processors, memory, and processes on your computer or other computers on a network. Each object has a set of counters allowing you to create performance log files. Since Performance Monitor allows access to performance log files, this is not the tool for your power users.

D. **Incorrect:** The Network Monitor Agent monitors activity detected by the network card in the computer. The Network Monitor can attach to computers running the Network Agent to monitor remote computers. You cannot start and stop basic Windows NT processes using the Network Monitor Agent.

E. **Incorrect:** Windows NT Diagnostics is a tool that allows you to view Registry information, including computer hardware and operating system data. You cannot start and stop basic Windows NT processes using Windows NT Diagnostics.

70-073.06.01.005

You are using Task Manager to monitor how much of the paging file is being used by a particular process. You want to monitor the same statistic on a remote computer. Which Performance Monitor counter should you use to monitor this statistic?

A. Page File Bytes

B. Page Faults/sec

C. Pool Paged Bytes

D. Pool Nonpaged Bytes

70-073.06.01.005

You are using Task Manager to monitor how much of the paging file is being used by a particular process. You want to monitor the same statistic on a remote computer. Which Performance Monitor counter should you use to monitor this statistic?

▶ **Correct Answer: A**

    A. **Correct:** The Page File Bytes counter in Performance Monitor displays how much of the paging file is being used by a process. Note that Performance Monitor is the tool to use when monitoring statistics on remote computers.

    B. **Incorrect:** The Page Faults/sec counter in Performance Monitor shows the rate of page faults over time. Page faults are the number of times data for the process had to be retrieved from disk because it could not be found in memory.

    C. **Incorrect:** The Pool Paged Bytes counter in Performance Monitor shows the amount of virtual memory available to be paged to disk, including all user memory and a portion of system memory.

    D. **Incorrect:** The Pool Nonpaged Bytes counter in Performance Monitor shows the amount of operating system memory that is never paged to disk.

Further Reading

 The *Microsoft Windows NT Technical Support* volume of the *Microsoft Windows NT Technical Support Training* kit Chapter 18, Lesson 1 contains detailed information on Event Viewer, Windows NT Diagnostics, Performance Monitor, and Network Monitor.

 The *Microsoft Windows NT Workstation Resource Kit* Chapter 9 compares the function and purpose of Task Manager and Performance Monitor. Chapter 10 covers the operation of Performance Monitor's administrative tools and data interpretation. Chapter 11 describes the tools that work with Performance Monitor.

O B J E C T I V E   6 . 2

Identify and resolve a given performance problem.

Detecting and resolving performance problems is a task requiring knowledge about and skill in the use of performance monitoring tools. While the design of Windows NT has eliminated many performance issues, you should know details about the three main areas where performance bottlenecks occur: memory, processor, and disk.

Memory Bottlenecks

Memory bottlenecks are the most common performance bottlenecks, and they often masquerade as processor bottlenecks. The best indicator of a memory bottleneck is a sustained high rate of hard page faults. Page faults occur when a program requests a page of code not in its working set (the portion of the physical memory used by a particular application). A hard page fault occurs when the requested page must be accessed from disk. A soft page fault occurs when the requested page is accessed elsewhere in physical memory. The most commonly used memory counters are:

Counter	Description
Page Faults/sec	How often is data not found in a process's working set?
Pages Input/sec	How many pages are being retrieved from disk to satisfy page faults?
Pages Output/sec	How many pages are being written to disk to free up space in the working set for faulted pages?
Pages/sec	Sum of Pages Input/sec and Pages Output/sec
Page Reads/sec	How often is the system reading from disk because of page faults? How much is page faulting affecting the disk?
Page Writes/sec	How often is the system writing to disk because of page faults?
Available bytes	How much memory is left for processes to allocate?

Processor Bottlenecks

Processor bottlenecks occur when the processor is so busy that it can no longer handle processing requests. Not only is processing time high, but queues are long and application response is poor.

▶ **If you suspect a processor bottleneck, you should:**

1. Determine the processes using excessive processor time.

2. Monitor the threads for processor-intensive processes.

3. Examine the priority level for the processor-intensive processes and threads.

The most commonly used processor counters are:

Counter	Description
System: % Total Processor Time	For what proportion of the sample interval were all processors busy?
System: Processor Queue Length	How many threads are ready but have to wait for a processor?
Processor: % Processor Time	For what proportion of the sample interval was each processor busy?
Process: % Processor Time	For what proportion of the sample interval was the processor running the threads of this process?
Process, Thread: Priority Base	What is the base priority of the process or thread?

Disk Bottlenecks

Disk bottlenecks involve time, not disk space. Disk bottlenecks occur when system components performing read/write (input/output) functions cannot keep up with the rest of the system. Determining a disk bottleneck involves first ruling out memory and processor bottlenecks. Check the Memory: Paging counters first to rule out a memory bottleneck. Then check the Processor and System: Interrupt counters to rule out a processor bottleneck. The most commonly used processor counters are:

Counter	Description
% Disk time	How often is the disk busy (percentage of time)?
Avg. Disk Queue Length	How often is the disk busy (decimal with no defined maximum)?
Current Disk Queue Length	How many disk requests waiting?
Avg. Disk sec/Transfer	How fast is data being moved (in seconds)?
Disk Bytes/sec	How fast is data being moved (in bytes)?

Questions related to this objective are designed to determine if you have an awareness of these issues. To successfully answer the questions for this objective, you need a firm understanding of several key terms. For definitions of these terms, refer to the Glossary in this book.

Key Terms

- Bottleneck
- Cache
- Page faults
- Working set

70-073.06.02.001

You are investigating a performance problem on a computer running Windows NT Workstation. Using Performance Monitor, you discover a sustained high rate of hard page faults. What should you do to solve this performance problem?

A. Add more RAM.

B. Tune the cache.

C. Install a faster disk channel or hard disk.

D. Upgrade the CPU or install a second CPU.

70-073.06.02.002

Which Performance Monitor memory counter should you use to determine how often the system is reading data from the hard disk drive because of page faults?

A. Page Reads/sec

B. Page Faults/sec

C. Pages Input/sec

D. Pages Output/sec

70-073.06.02.001

You are investigating a performance problem on a computer running Windows NT Workstation. Using Performance Monitor, you discover a sustained high rate of hard page faults. What should you do to solve this performance problem?

▶ **Correct Answer: A**

A. **Correct:** When the requested data is repeatedly not found, the rate of hard page faults increases because memory is limited. If no single application is causing the memory shortage, the high number of page faults is best resolved by adding more RAM.

B. **Incorrect:** Cache problems are generally indicated by irregular cache counter readings. A high rate of page faults does not indicate a problem with cache. Cache activity generally has an insignificant effect on the system, disks, and memory, so tuning does not solve the performance problem.

C. **Incorrect:** Although sustained paging can look like a disk bottleneck, disk problems are generally indicated by irregular disk counter readings. A high rate of page faults does not indicate a problem with a disk, so installing a faster disk channel or hard disk does not solve the performance problem.

D. **Incorrect:** Processor problems are generally indicated by irregular process and thread counter readings. A high rate of page faults does not indicate a problem with a processor, so upgrading the CPU or installing a second CPU does not solve the performance problem.

70-073.06.02.002

Which Performance Monitor memory counter should you use to determine how often the system is reading data from the hard disk drive because of page faults?

▶ **Correct Answer: A**

A. **Correct:** Page Reads/sec indicates how often the system is reading from disk because of page faults, a primary indicator of memory shortage.

B. **Incorrect:** Page Faults/sec indicates how often data is not found in a process's working set, an indicator that the working set is too small due to limited memory.

C. **Incorrect:** Pages Input/sec indicates how many pages are being retrieved from disk to satisfy page faults. This data should be compared with Page Faults/sec to see how many faults are satisfied by reading from disk.

D. **Incorrect:** Pages Output/sec indicates how many pages are being written to disk to free up space in the working set for faulted pages. A high rate indicates that memory is becoming scarce.

70-073.06.02.003

You are investigating a performance problem on a network client computer running Windows NT Workstation. The computer is a Pentium-based PC with 32 MB of RAM, two 4.2-GB SCSI hard disk drives, one 24-speed CD-ROM drive, and a PCI network card.

You suspect the CPU is causing a system bottleneck, since Performance Monitor indicates %Processor Time often exceeds 90 percent.

Which other potential bottlenecks should you rule out before upgrading or installing a second processor? (Choose two.)

A. Disk

B. Cache

C. Network

D. Memory

E. Process or processes

70-073.06.02.003

You are investigating a performance problem on a network client computer running Windows NT Workstation. The computer is a Pentium-based PC with 32 MB of RAM, two 4.2-GB SCSI hard disk drives, one 24-speed CD-ROM drive, and a PCI network card.

You suspect the CPU is causing a system bottleneck, since Performance Monitor indicates %Processor Time often exceeds 90 percent.

Which other potential bottlenecks should you rule out before upgrading or installing a second processor? (Choose two.)

▶ **Correct Answers: D and E**

A. **Incorrect:** % Processor Time exceeding 90 percent does not indicate a problem with a disk bottleneck. Disk bottlenecks are generally indicated by irregular disk counter readings.

B. **Incorrect:** % Processor Time exceeding 90 percent does not indicate a problem with a cache bottleneck. Cache bottlenecks are generally indicated by irregular cache counter readings.

C. **Incorrect:** Performance Monitor and % Processor Time measure performance of processor objects on the Windows NT Workstation, not the network.

D. **Correct:** Memory bottlenecks are the most common bottleneck and can often look like high processor use. A sustained, high rate of hard page faults is the best indicator of a memory bottleneck. A hard page fault occurs when the data that a program needs is not available in its working set and must be retrieved from and written to disk, resulting in increased processing time.

E. **Correct:** Once a processor bottleneck has been identified you should determine whether a process or processes are consuming the processor. If so, you can replace or tune the inefficient application. Upgrading or installing a new processor should be a last resort.

70-073.06.02.004

Over the last several days, there have been an increasing number of complaints about system performance. Users tell you that they must wait longer for applications to start and that more time is spent waiting for data transfers than in the past.

Which action should you take first to resolve this problem?

A. Check for sufficient memory.

B. Monitor system processor counters.

C. Check for sufficient available disk space.

D. Check network cards and interface cables.

70-073.06.02.004

Over the last several days, there have been an increasing number of complaints about system performance. Users tell you that they must wait longer for applications to start and that more time is spent waiting for data transfers than in the past.

Which action should you take first to resolve this problem?

▶ **Correct Answer: A**

A. **Correct:** Since lack of memory is the most common cause of system performance problems, you should check for sufficient memory first.

B. **Incorrect:** Processor counter symptoms do not always indicate processor problems. Check for memory shortages first, since memory shortages often look like processor problems.

C. **Incorrect:** Disk counter symptoms like sustained paging do not always indicate disk problems. Check for memory shortages first, since memory shortages can look like a disk bottleneck.

D. **Incorrect:** Network cards and interface cables are used to connect computers to a LAN and could indicate a problem for a specific Windows NT Workstation. However, since there has been an increase in the number of complaints about system performance in general, it is unlikely that network cards and interface cables are the problem, and they should not be checked first.

70-073.06.02.005

Response time on your Windows NT network has degraded substantially for applications running on the network. Using Performance Monitor, you notice that the % Total Processor Time counter is close to 100 percent. The Processor Queue Length counter has not been decreasing as it should.

Using Task Manager, you notice that a particular process, called Proc1, could be the source of the problem.

Which action should you take to resolve the problem?

A. Stop and restart process Proc1.

B. Add more memory to the computer.

C. Increase the size of the paging file.

D. Adjust the base priority of process Proc1.

E. Configure an additional processor on the computer.

70-073.06.02.005

Response time on your Windows NT network has degraded substantially for applications running on the network. Using Performance Monitor, you notice that the % Total Processor Time counter is close to 100 percent. The Processor Queue Length counter has not been decreasing as it should.

Using Task Manager, you notice that a particular process, called Proc1, could be the source of the problem.

Which action should you take to resolve the problem?

▶ **Correct Answer: D**

   A. **Incorrect:** Stopping and restarting Proc1 will not resolve the high % Total Processor Time. However, you can determine if Proc1 is the source of the problem by stopping Proc1 and seeing if the bottleneck continues.

   B. **Incorrect:** Since you have determined that Proc1, a single process, is probably responsible for the bottleneck, adding memory will not resolve the problem. The scenario suggests a processor bottleneck, not a memory bottleneck.

   C. **Incorrect:** Since you have determined that Proc1, a single process, is probably responsible for the bottleneck, increasing paging file size will not resolve the problem. The scenario suggests a processor bottleneck, not a memory bottleneck.

   D. **Correct:** By changing the base priority of Proc1, you may be able to reduce the number of threads contending for the processor and reduce the Processor Queue Length.

   E. **Incorrect:** In addition to changing the base priority of Proc1, you could consider replacing the process or trying to tune the process to resolve the problem before configuring an additional processor. Configuring an additional processor is a last resort.

Further Reading

 The *Microsoft Windows NT Technical Support* volume of the *Microsoft Windows NT Technical Support Training* kit Chapter 18, Lesson 1 contains details on the Processor: % Processor Time and System: Processor Queue Length counters in Performance Monitor.

 The *Microsoft Windows NT Workstation Resource Kit* Chapter 10 covers the operation of the Performance Monitor administrative tool and data interpretation. Chapter 12 helps you detect memory bottlenecks, the most common type of bottleneck. Chapters 13, 14, and 15 examine the characteristics of processor, disk, and cache bottlenecks, respectively.

 Windows NT Workstation 4.0 Study Guide. Osborne McGraw-Hill, Berkeley, CA, 1998. ISBN 0-07-882492-3. Chapter 14 contains detailed information on performance tuning, including bottlenecks and troubleshooting memory, processor, and disk drive performance.

OBJECTIVE 6.3

Optimize system performance in various areas.

Although Windows NT was designed to optimize system performance, there are still areas you can tune for memory performance, processor performance, and disk performance.

Before adding memory, you should optimize memory performance. To optimize memory performance, you can:

- Replace or correct applications that leak memory or use it inefficiently.

- Free up space on hard drives to allow the paging file to expand, or increase the size of the paging file if possible.

- If you have added memory, increase the secondary memory cache.

- Remove unnecessary protocols and drivers.

Before adding processors, you should optimize processor performance. To optimize processor performance, you can:

- Replace or try to fix the application using excessive processor time.

- Upgrade network or disk adapter cards to 16-bit or 32-bit cards that use bus-mastering *direct memory access* (DMA).

- Increase processor clock speed.

- If you have added memory, increase the secondary memory cache.

Before adding a disk, you should optimize disk performance. To optimize disk performance, you can partition unformatted free space on a Windows NT Workstation using *volume sets* or *stripe sets*. Volume sets allow you to combine available space on up to 32 areas on one or more hard drives into one volume with one drive letter. In a volume set, data is written to one member of a set at a time until the set is filled. Stripe sets allow you to combine available space on up to 32 areas on at least two hard drives into one volume with one drive letter. In a stripe set, data is written evenly across all of the disks, one row at a time. System and boot partitions cannot be used in either a volume or a stripe set. Fault tolerance is not provided in either a volume or a stripe set.

To optimize disk performance you can also:

- Upgrade your disk controller card.

- Upgrade the device bus.

- Upgrade disk adapter cards to 16-bit or 32-bit cards that use bus-mastering direct memory access (DMA).

- Place a new disk on a separate I/O bus.

Questions related to this objective are designed to determine if you have an awareness of these issues. To successfully answer the questions for this objective, you need a firm understanding of several key terms. For definitions of these terms, refer to the Glossary in this book.

Key Terms

- Bus-mastering DMA

- Direct memory access (DMA)

- Disk controller

- Fault tolerance

- Input/output (I/O)

- Mirror set

- Parallel

- Redundant array of inexpensive disks (RAID)

- Serial

- Stripe set

- Throughput

- Volume set

70-073.06.03.001

You have determined that the disk channel in your Windows NT Workstation computer needs to be reconfigured to optimally support read/write intensive applications. The computer is equipped with a single IDE hard drive containing the boot partition and four SCSI 4.3 GB hard disks for data.

The required result is to optimize the read performance of the SCSI hard disk drives.

The first optional result is to optimize the write performance of the SCSI hard disks. The second optional result is to provide fault tolerance for data stored on hard disks.

You propose to configure the new SCSI disks to use RAID 0.

What does the proposed solution provide?

A. The required result and both optional results.

B. The required result and one optional result.

C. The required result but none of the optional results.

D. The proposed solution does not provide the required result.

70-073.06.03.001

You have determined that the disk channel in your Windows NT Workstation computer needs to be reconfigured to optimally support read/write intensive applications. The computer is equipped with a single IDE hard drive containing the boot partition and four SCSI 4.3 GB hard disks for data.

The required result is to optimize the read performance of the SCSI hard disk drives.

The first optional result is to optimize the write performance of the SCSI hard disks. The second optional result is to provide fault tolerance for data stored on hard disks.

You propose to configure the new SCSI disks to use RAID 0.

What does the proposed solution provide?

▶ **Correct Answer: B**

A. **Incorrect**: See the explanation for answer B.

B. **Correct**: RAID 0 implements striping without any drive redundancy. Reading and writing is performed in parallel on each of the disks in the array, which optimizes performance for optimum throughput. However, stripe sets do not provide fault tolerance, so if one disk fails you lose all the data in the stripe set.

C. **Incorrect**: See the explanation for answer B.

D. **Incorrect**: See the explanation for answer B.

70-073.06.03.002

You have determined that the disk channel in your Windows NT Workstation computer needs to be reconfigured to optimally support read/write intensive applications. The computer's original disk configuration consists of a single 5-GB IDE hard disk and IDE controller. This will be enhanced by the addition of three SCSI 4.3-GB hard disks and a single SCSI controller.

The required result is to optimize performance for optimum throughput for files stored on the local hard disk drives.

The first optional result is to provide fault tolerance for data stored on hard disks. The second optional result is to optimize disk storage space.

You propose to configure the IDE hard disk as the boot partition, and configure the new SCSI hard disks as a volume set.

What does the proposed solution provide?

A. The required result and both optional results.

B. The required result and one optional result.

C. The required result but none of the optional results.

D. The proposed solution does not provide the required result.

70-073.06.03.002

You have determined that the disk channel in your Windows NT Workstation computer needs to be reconfigured to optimally support read/write intensive applications. The computer's original disk configuration consists of a single 5-GB IDE hard disk and IDE controller. This will be enhanced by the addition of three SCSI 4.3-GB hard disks and a single SCSI controller.

The required result is to optimize performance for optimum throughput for files stored on the local hard disk drives.

The first optional result is to provide fault tolerance for data stored on hard disks. The second optional result is to optimize disk storage space.

You propose to configure the IDE hard disk as the boot partition, and configure the new SCSI hard disks as a volume set.

What does the proposed solution provide?

▶ **Correct Answer: D**

A. **Incorrect:** See the explanation for answer D.

B. **Incorrect:** See the explanation for answer D.

C. **Incorrect:** See the explanation for answer D.

D. **Correct:** One of the advantages of using a volume set is the ability to combine free disk space from several areas, including different types of hard disks. Since you have not combined the disks into one volume set, you have not optimized performance for optimum throughput, which is the required result to the problem.

70-073.06.03.003

You have determined that the disk channel in your Windows NT Workstation computer needs to be reconfigured to optimally support read/write-intensive applications. The computer's original disk configuration consists of a single 5-GB IDE hard disk and IDE controller. This will be enhanced by the addition of a second 5-GB hard disk drive attached to the existing IDE chain.

The required result is to optimize performance for optimum throughput for files stored on the local hard disk drives.

The first optional result is to provide fault tolerance for data stored on hard disks. The second optional result is to optimize disk storage space.

You propose to mirror the two disks.

What does the proposed solution provide?

A. The required result and both optional results.

B. The required result and one optional result.

C. The required result but none of the optional results.

D. The proposed solution does not provide the required result.

70-073.06.03.003

You have determined that the disk channel in your Windows NT Workstation computer needs to be reconfigured to optimally support read/write-intensive applications. The computer's original disk configuration consists of a single 5-GB IDE hard disk and IDE controller. This will be enhanced by the addition of a second 5-GB hard disk drive attached to the existing IDE chain.

The required result is to optimize performance for optimum throughput for files stored on the local hard disk drives.

The first optional result is to provide fault tolerance for data stored on hard disks. The second optional result is to optimize disk storage space.

You propose to mirror the two disks.

What does the proposed solution provide?

▶ **Correct Answer: D**

A. **Incorrect:** See the explanation for answer D.

B. **Incorrect:** See the explanation for answer D.

C. **Incorrect:** See the explanation for answer D.

D. **Correct:** Mirroring disks is not supported in Windows NT Workstation, therefore optimizing performance for optimum throughput, fault tolerance, and optimizing disk storage space are not accomplished in this scenario.

70-073.06.03.004

You have installed and set up several new applications on your Windows NT Workstation. After running these applications for several days, you notice an increase in system response time. You suspect that one of these applications may be failing to release memory properly.

Which Performance Monitor counter will help you isolate the process that may be causing the problem?

A. Page Faults/sec

B. % Total Processor Time

C. Processor Queue Length

D. Average Disk Queue Length

70-073.06.03.004

You have installed and set up several new applications on your Windows NT Workstation. After running these applications for several days, you notice an increase in system response time. You suspect that one of these applications may be failing to release memory properly.

Which Performance Monitor counter will help you isolate the process that may be causing the problem?

▶ **Correct Answer: A**

A. **Correct:** The best indicator of memory problems is a high rate of hard page faults. Viewing the Page Faults/sec counter displays all page faults for the system and the page faults for each application, helping you isolate the process that is causing the problem.

B. **Incorrect:** % Total Processor Time displays the proportion of time when all processors are busy, a key indicator of a processor problem. Since you suspect a memory problem with a specific application, the % Total Processor Time display will not help you isolate the application.

C. **Incorrect:** Processor Queue Length displays the number of threads ready and waiting for a processor, a key indicator of a processor problem. Since you suspect a memory problem with a specific application, the Processor Queue Length display will not help you isolate the application.

D. **Incorrect:** Average Disk Queue Length displays how often the disk is busy, a key indicator of a disk problem. Since you suspect a memory problem with a specific application, the Average Disk Queue Length display will not help you isolate the application.

70-073.06.03.005

Which technique can increase disk I/O speed?

A. Use a longer disk cable.

B. Add an additional disk drive on the same I/O bus.

C. Use bus-mastering DMA instead of programmed I/O.

D. Switch from a serial bus configuration to a parallel bus configuration for disk I/O.

70-073.06.03.005

Which technique can increase disk I/O speed?

▶ **Correct Answer: C**

A. **Incorrect:** Cable length does not measurably affect disk I/O speed. Cable length is a consideration that can affect signal degradation when connecting PC hard drives.

B. **Incorrect:** You could add a disk to increase disk I/O speed. However, when adding a disk, you should place it on a *separate* I/O bus. Otherwise, the benefit of extra disk space is limited by the already crowded bus.

C. **Correct:** By upgrading your disk adapter to use bus-mastering DMA instead of programmed I/O, you can increase disk I/O speed. Programmed I/O uses the processor for transfers, while bus-mastering DMA uses the disk controller to manage the I/O bus and the DMA controller to manage DMA operation. Bus-mastering DMA frees the processor for other operations.

D. **Incorrect:** Since all disk interfaces used in personal computers are parallel, you could not switch from a serial bus configuration to a parallel bus configuration.

Further Reading

 The *Microsoft Windows NT Technical Support* volume of the *Microsoft Windows NT Technical Support Training* kit Chapter 6, Lesson 1 defines and includes guidelines for using volume and stripe sets.

 The *Microsoft Windows NT Workstation Resource Kit* Chapter 12 includes information on using Page Faults/sec to determine memory use by applications. Chapter 13 includes information on detecting and eliminating processor bottlenecks. Chapter 14 includes information on detecting and removing disk bottlenecks.

 Windows NT Workstation 4.0 Study Guide. Osborne McGraw-Hill, Berkeley, CA, 1998. ISBN 0-07-882492-3. Chapter 5 contains detailed information on using volume and stripe sets with Windows NT Workstation, including a table showing when to use each set.

 Windows NT Workstation 4.0 Study Guide. Sybex, Alameda, CA, 1998. ISBN 0-7821-2223-X. Chapter 5 contains detailed information using volume and stripe sets with Windows NT Workstation, including procedures for creating each set and for extending a volume set.

 Use Microsoft Technical Support Online (http://support.microsoft.com) by searching for "Windows NT Server" and for "RAID." Then click "Overview of Redundant Arrays of Inexpensive Disks (RAID)."

 Use Microsoft Technical Support Online (http://support.microsoft.com) by searching for "Windows NT Workstation" and for "volume set." Then click "Overview of Disk Volume Sets in Windows NT" and "Mirroring of Software Fault Tolerant Solutions."

Troubleshooting

The Troubleshooting domain covers problem resolution for various areas in Windows NT Workstation using a variety of tools. The problems and troubleshooting options discussed are:

Problem	Troubleshooting options
Boot process failure	Use the emergency repair process.
	Use the Last Known Good Configuration option.
Print job failure	Control the printer using the Printer folder.
	Use resources such as the *Microsoft Windows NT Workstation 4.0 Resource Kit* or the *Windows NT Server Reference Guide* to determine problems and tests.
Installation failure	Use references to determine problems and tests.
Application failure	Check STATUS messages. Use Event Viewer.
User access failure	Use the permissions checklist in this chapter. Use troubleshooting tools for Remote Access Service.

This domain also covers the following advanced troubleshooting tools:

Tool	Description
Registry	Tool used to edit system configuration via remote access.
Memory dump file	Tool used to create a file for analysis by technical support.

Tested Skills and Suggested Practices

- Choosing the appropriate course of action to take when the boot process fails. You must be able to distinguish between a missing or corrupted boot file and an incorrect configuration, and use the appropriate tools for recovery.

  - Practice 1: Learn the steps in the boot process. Recognize the files needed for booting in your operating system and their functions.

  - Practice 2: Determine when to use the emergency repair process. Learn to recognize the common boot process error messages. Read about the procedure and materials necessary for restoring missing or corrupted boot files.

  - Practice 3: Determine when to use the Last Known Good Configuration option. Learn to recognize the symptoms of an incorrect configuration. Read about the procedure for using the Last Known Good Configuration option.

- Choosing the appropriate course of action to take when a print job fails. You must be able to resolve local and network printing problems.

  - Practice 1: Control a print job from the Printers folder. Use the Printer menu to pause printing on a printer and purge documents. Use the Document menu to pause, resume, and restart a print job.

  - Practice 2: Learn the seven processes involved in a network printing job. Using references, familiarize yourself with the symptoms and tests for each process. Using resources such as the *Microsoft Windows NT Workstation 4.0 Resource Kit* or the *Windows NT Server Resource Guide*, view the series of troubleshooting steps for printing.

- Choosing the appropriate course of action to take when the installation process fails. You must be able to resolve installation process problems.

  - Practice 1: Learn the installation process. Using references, familiarize yourself with the typical problems encountered while installing Windows NT Workstation and their solutions.

- Choosing the appropriate course of action to take when an application fails. You must be able to resolve application problems.

  - Practice 1: Learn the symptoms of an application failure. Read about the three types of STATUS messages that detect conditions in an application. Familiarize yourself with the various STATUS messages.

- Practice 2: Use the Event Viewer to view events for an application. View detail for an event. Familiarize yourself with the Message Database help file on the *Microsoft Windows NT Workstation 4.0 Resource Kit* CD.

- Choosing the appropriate course of action to take when a user cannot access a resource. You must be able to resolve resource access problems.

  - Practice 1: Distinguish between share permissions and NT File System (NTFS) permissions. Analyze how each type of permission affects users, groups, folders, and files using the Permissions Checklist. Learn how combining share permissions and NTFS permissions can secure resources. Learn how moving and copying folders and files within or between NTFS and file allocation table (FAT) file systems affects permissions.

  - Practice 2: Identify troubleshooting tools for Remote Access Service (RAS). Determine which tool to use in a given situation.

- Modifying the Registry using the appropriate tool in a given situation. You must be able to resolve basic configuration problems using the Registry Editor.

  - Practice 1: Familiarize yourself with Registry tools. Distinguish between the capabilities of REGEDT32 and REGEDIT. Learn which Registry-management tools are provided with Windows NT. Learn which Registry-management tools are provided on the *Microsoft Windows NT Workstation 4.0 Resource Kit* CD.

  - Practice 2: Learn the Registry structure. Know the five subkeys and the areas they control. Determine which subkey to modify in a given situation.

- Implementing advanced techniques to resolve various problems. You must be able to create a memory dump file for use in system troubleshooting.

  - Practice 1: Learn the procedure for creating a memory dump file. Learn the three utilities for processing memory dump files. Know which utility to use in a given situation.

O B J E C T I V E 7 . 1

Choose the appropriate course of action to take when the boot process fails.

You must understand the boot process to be able to effectively troubleshoot boot failures. The boot process is divided into two parts:

- **Initialization steps**. These steps occur prior to the boot sequence, initializing and locating the boot portion of the hard disk.

- **Boot sequence steps**. These steps gather information about hardware and drivers in preparation for the Windows NT load phases.

Initialization Steps

The following initialization steps are performed prior to the boot sequence on Intel computers:

1. Power on self-test (POST) routines run.

2. The *Master Boot Record* (MBR) is loaded and the program in MBR runs.

3. The Master Boot Record locates the active partition and loads the boot sector into memory.

4. The NTLDR file, the system file that loads the operating system, is loaded and initialized.

Boot Sequence Steps

The following boot sequence steps are performed on Intel computers after the initialization steps:

1. NTLDR changes processor to 32-bit flat memory mode.

2. NTLDR starts mini–file system drivers for finding and loading file system formats (FAT or NTFS).

3. NTLDR reads BOOT.INI file and displays Boot Loader Operating System Selection menu.

4. NTLDR loads the default or user-selected operating system. If an operating system other than Windows NT is selected, BOOTSECT.DOS is loaded to pass control to the selected operating system, and the Windows NT boot process ends.

5. NTLDR runs NTDETECT.COM to detect hardware.

6. NTLDR loads NTOSKRNL.EXE, HAL.DLL, and the System hive, which contains information about the devices and services on the system. NTLDR loads device drivers that start during the boot process. NTLDR starts NTOSKRNL.EXE. Loading and initializing of Windows NT begins.

Troubleshooting

The two main causes of problems that occur during the boot process are as follows:

- Missing or corrupted files.

- Incorrect configuration changes.

Missing or Corrupted Files

The following table lists the files used during the boot process on an Intel platform, their functions, and the error messages generated when the file is missing or corrupted:

Intel x86-based file	Function/Error message
NTLDR	A hidden, read-only system file that loads the operating system. "BOOT: Couldn't find NTDLR Please insert another disk."
BOOT.INI	A read-only system file read by NTLDR to build the Boot Loader Operating System Selection menu. "Windows NT could not start because the following file is missing or corrupt: <winnt root>\system32\ntoskrnl.exe Please reinstall a copy of the above file."
BOOTSECT.DOS	A hidden system file loaded by NTLDR in dual-boot systems if an operating system other than Windows NT is selected by the user. "I/O Error accessing boot sector file multi(0)disk(0)rdisk(0)partition(1):\bootss"

(continued)

NTDETECT.COM	A hidden, read-only system file run by NTLDR to determine available hardware.
	      "NTDETECT V4.0 Checking Hardware…
	      NTDETECT failed"

NTOSKRNL.EXE	The Windows NT kernel file.
	      "Windows NT could not start because the following
	      file is missing or corrupt:
	      \winnt root\system32\ntoskrnl.exe
	      Please re-install a copy of the above file."

Files that are missing or corrupted should be recovered using the *emergency repair process*. This process requires use of the *emergency repair disk* and the Windows NT Setup disks. The emergency repair disk is created using the RDISK utility and contains information for:

- Inspecting Registry files.

- Inspecting the startup environment.

- Verifying Windows NT system files.

- Inspecting the boot sector.

The emergency repair disk is useful only when it is maintained. The repair disk should be updated whenever a change is made to the system configuration or security setup and when users are added. Otherwise you may be restoring an outdated configuration.

To perform the emergency repair process, you must start Setup using the Windows NT Setup disks, indicate that you want to repair files, and then insert the emergency repair disk. The system prompts you through the repair process. When the process finishes, remove the emergency repair disk and restart your computer.

Incorrect Configuration Changes

If you have problems with startup after you have changed or installed a new device driver, your configuration is probably incorrect. The symptoms of an incorrect configuration are the message "One or more services failed to start" or a sudden lack of system response.

Incorrect configurations can be returned to the last successful configuration settings by using the Last Known Good Configuration option. The Last Known Good control set, stored in the Registry, contains the configuration saved when you last successfully logged on to your computer. If you have problems with startup you can always return to the Last Known Good configuration *as long as you haven't logged on*. If you believe the startup problems may be caused by an incorrect configuration, shut down your computer and restart. Select Last Known Good from the Hardware Profile/Last Known Good menu, and the previous configuration will be restored when you log on. The Last Known Good Configuration option does not restore corrupted or missing drivers or files.

Questions related to this objective are designed to determine if you have an awareness of these issues. To successfully answer the questions for this objective, you need a firm understanding of several key terms. For definitions of these terms, refer to the Glossary in this book.

Key Terms

- Control set

- Default configuration

- Emergency repair process

- Emergency repair disk

- Hive

- Last Known Good configuration

- Master Boot Record (MBR)

- NTLDR file

70-073.07.01.001

While booting your Windows NT Workstation computer, you receive this message:

"BOOT: Couldn't find NTLDR
Please insert another disk."

What should you do to solve this problem?

A. Restart the computer in MS-DOS and repair the Master Boot Record using the DiskSave utility.

B. Restart the computer and select Use the Last Known Good Configuration option when presented.

C. Insert the Windows NT Workstation Installation CD-ROM or installation floppy disk #1 into the appropriate local drive and press Enter.

D. Insert the Windows NT Workstation Setup boot disk, restart the computer, and repair the installation using the emergency repair process.

70-073.07.01.001

While booting your Windows NT Workstation computer, you receive this message:

> "BOOT: Couldn't find NTLDR
> Please insert another disk."

What should you do to solve this problem?

▶ **Correct Answer: D**

A. **Incorrect:** The message you received means the NTLDR file is missing or corrupt. DiskSave restores the Master Boot Record (MBR). Since the MBR does not contain the NTLDR file, DiskSave cannot restore the file.

B. **Incorrect:** The message you received means the NTLDR file is missing or corrupt. Booting from the Last Known Good Configuration option provides a way to recover from configuration problems. The option is not used to recover from problems caused by missing drivers or files and will not restore the NTLDR file.

C. **Incorrect:** The message you received means the NTLDR file is missing or corrupt. Inserting the Windows NT Workstation installation CD-ROM or floppy and pressing Enter will not restore the NTLDR file. However, if the NTLDR file is located on the installation CD-ROM or floppy disk you can restore the file by *copying* it from the disk to the corresponding location on your system partition.

D. **Correct:** The message you received means the NTLDR file is missing or corrupt. The emergency repair process is used to restore the missing NTLDR file. This process requires you to use the Windows NT Workstation Setup boot disk and the emergency repair disk to restore the file.

70-073.07.01.002

While booting your Windows NT Workstation computer, you receive this message:

"NTDETECT V4.0 Checking Hardware...
NTDETECT failed."

What should you do to solve this problem?

A. Restart the computer in MS-DOS and repair the Master Boot Record using the DiskSave utility.

B. Restart the computer and select Use the Last Known Good Configuration option when presented.

C. Insert the Windows NT Workstation Installation CD-ROM or installation floppy disk #1 into the appropriate local drive and press Enter.

D. Insert the Windows NT Workstation Setup boot disk, restart the computer, and repair the installation using the emergency repair process.

70-073.07.01.002

While booting your Windows NT Workstation computer, you receive this message:

"NTDETECT V4.0 Checking Hardware...
NTDETECT failed."

What should you do to solve this problem?

▶ **Correct Answer: D**

A. **Incorrect:** The message you received means the NTDETECT.COM file is missing or corrupt. DiskSave restores the Master Boot Record (MBR). Since the MBR does not contain the NTDETECT.COM file, DiskSave cannot restore the file.

B. **Incorrect:** The message you received means the NTDETECT.COM file is missing or corrupt. Booting from the Last Known Good Configuration option provides a way to recover from configuration problems. The option is not used to recover from problems caused by missing drivers or files and will not restore the NTDETECT.COM file.

C. **Incorrect:** The message you received means the NTDETECT.COM file is missing or corrupt. Inserting the Windows NT Workstation installation CD-ROM or floppy and pressing enter will not restore the NTDETECT.COM file. However, if the NTDETECT.COM file is located on the installation CD-ROM or floppy disk, you can restore the file by copying it from the disk to the corresponding location on your system partition.

D. **Correct:** The message you received means the NTDETECT.COM file is missing or corrupt. The emergency repair process is used to restore the missing NTDETECT.COM file. This process requires you to use the Windows NT Workstation Setup boot disk and the emergency repair disk to restore the file.

70-073.07.01.003

While booting your Windows NT Workstation computer, you receive this message:

> "Windows NT could not start because the following file is missing or corrupt:
> \winnt root\system32\ntoskrnl.exe
> Please re-install a copy of the above file."

What should you do solve this problem?

A. Restart the computer in MS-DOS and repair the Master Boot Record using the DiskSave utility.

B. Restart the computer and select Use the Last Known Good Configuration option when presented.

C. Insert the Windows NT Workstation Installation CD-ROM or installation floppy disk #1 into the appropriate local drive and press Enter.

D. Insert the Windows NT Workstation Setup boot disk, restart the computer, and repair the installation using the emergency repair process.

70-073.07.01.003

While booting your Windows NT Workstation computer, you receive this message:

> "Windows NT could not start because the following file is missing or corrupt:
> \winnt root\system32\ntoskrnl.exe
> Please re-install a copy of the above file."

What should you do solve this problem?

▶ **Correct Answer: D**

A. **Incorrect:** The message you received means the NTOSKRNL.EXE file is missing or corrupt. DiskSave restores the Master Boot Record (MBR). Since the MBR does not contain the NTOSKRNL.EXE file, DiskSave cannot restore the file.

B. **Incorrect:** The message you received means the NTOSKRNL.EXE file is missing or corrupt. Booting from the Last Known Good Configuration option provides a way to recover from configuration problems. The option is not used to recover from problems caused by missing drivers or files and will not restore the NTOSKRNL.EXE file.

C. **Incorrect:** The message you received means the NTOSKRNL.EXE file is missing or corrupt. Inserting the Windows NT Workstation installation CD-ROM or floppy and pressing enter will not restore the NTDETECT.COM file. However, if the NTOSKRNL.EXE file is located on the installation CD-ROM or floppy disk you can restore the file by copying it from the disk to the corresponding location on your system partition.

D. **Correct:** The message you received means the NTOSKRNL.EXE file is missing or corrupt. The emergency repair process is used to restore the missing NTOSKRNL.EXE file. This process requires you to use the Windows NT Workstation Setup boot disk and the emergency repair disk to restore the file.

70-073.07.01.004

You have a computer that dual-boots into either MS-DOS or Windows NT Workstation. While booting the computer into Windows NT Workstation, you receive this message:

"I/O Error accessing boot sector file
multi (0) disk(0) rdisk (0) partition (1):\bootss"

What should you do to solve this problem?

A. Restart the computer in MS-DOS and repair the Master Boot Record using the DiskSave utility.

B. Restart the computer and select Use the Last Known Good Configuration option when presented.

C. Insert the Windows NT Workstation Installation CD-ROM or installation floppy disk #1 into the appropriate local drive and press enter.

D. Insert the Windows NT Workstation Setup boot disk, restart the computer, and repair the installation using the emergency repair process.

70-073.07.01.004

You have a computer that dual-boots into either MS-DOS or Windows NT Workstation. While booting the computer into Windows NT Workstation, you receive this message:

"I/O Error accessing boot sector file
multi (0) disk(0) rdisk (0) partition (1):\bootss"

What should you do to solve this problem?

▶ **Correct Answer: D**

   A. **Incorrect:** The message you received means the BOOTSECT.DOS file is missing or corrupt. DiskSave restores the Master Boot Record (MBR). Since the MBR does not contain the BOOTSECT.DOS file, DiskSave cannot restore the file.

   B. **Incorrect:** The message you received means the BOOTSECT.DOS file is missing or corrupt. Booting from the Last Known Good Configuration option provides a way to recover from configuration problems. The option is not used to recover from problems caused by missing drivers or files and will not restore the BOOTSECT.DOS file.

   C. **Incorrect:** The message you received means the BOOTSECT.DOS file is missing or corrupt. Inserting the Windows NT Workstation installation CD-ROM or floppy and pressing Enter will not restore the BOOTSECT.DOS file. However, if the BOOTSECT.DOS file is located on the installation CD-ROM or floppy disk you can restore the file by copying it from the disk to the corresponding location on your system partition.

   D. **Correct:** The message you received means the BOOTSECT.DOS file is missing or corrupt. The emergency repair process is used to restore the missing BOOTSECT.DOS file. This process requires you to use the Windows NT Workstation Setup boot disk and the emergency repair disk to restore the file.

70-073.07.01.005

You update the device drivers for the SCSI tape backup on a computer running Windows NT Workstation. When you attempt to restart after installing the new drivers, the system stops responding.

What should you do solve this problem?

A. Restart the computer in MS-DOS and repair the Master Boot Record using the DiskSave utility.

B. Restart the computer and select Use the Last Known Good Configuration option when presented.

C. Insert the Windows NT Workstation Installation CD-ROM or installation floppy disk #1 into the appropriate local drive and press Enter.

D. Insert the Windows NT Workstation Setup boot disk, restart the computer, and repair the installation using the emergency repair process.

70-073.07.01.005

You update the device drivers for the SCSI tape backup on a computer running Windows NT Workstation. When you attempt to restart after installing the new drivers, the system stops responding.

What should you do solve this problem?

▶ **Correct Answer: B**

A. **Incorrect:** The system stopped responding because there is a problem with the new device driver configuration. DiskSave restores the Master Boot Record (MBR). Since the MBR does not contain the configuration for device drivers, DiskSave cannot restore the configuration.

B. **Correct:** The system stopped responding because there is a problem with the new device driver configuration (used in the default configuration). When you encounter this problem, it is important that you do not log on, but shut down the computer and restart using the Last Known Good Configuration option. Booting from the Last Known Good Configuration option allows you to start Windows NT because it does not contain the new device driver settings.

C. **Incorrect:** The system stopped responding because there is a problem with the new device driver configuration. Inserting the Windows NT Workstation installation CD-ROM or floppy and pressing Enter will not restore the device driver configuration.

D. **Incorrect:** The system stopped responding because there is a problem with the new device driver configuration. The emergency repair process is used to restore missing or corrupted drivers. Since you only need to return to the previously used device driver configuration, it is not necessary to use the emergency repair process.

70-073.07.01.006

The last time you were logged on to your Windows NT Workstation computer, you installed a new video device driver. Now the computer hangs during startup.

Which action should you take to resolve the problem?

A. Use FDISK to set the system partition.

B. Reboot the computer with the Windows NT Emergency Repair Disk.

C. Shut down the computer and restart with the Last Known Good Configuration option.

D. Reboot the computer with a DOS diskette and delete the video driver from the hard drive.

70-073.07.01.006

The last time you were logged on to your Windows NT Workstation computer, you installed a new video device driver. Now the computer hangs during startup.

Which action should you take to resolve the problem?

► **Correct Answer: C**

A. **Incorrect:** Since you installed a new video device driver the last time you were logged on to your Windows NT Workstation, it is likely that your configuration is incorrect. FDISK is used to check for and set the system partition, not to recover from an incorrect configuration.

B. **Incorrect:** Since you installed a new video device driver the last time you were logged on to your Windows NT Workstation, it is likely that your configuration is incorrect. The emergency repair process is used to restore missing or corrupted drivers. Since you only need to return to the previously used device driver configuration, it is not necessary to use the emergency repair process.

C. **Correct:** The system hangs during setup because there is a problem with the new video device driver configuration (used in the default configuration). When you encounter this problem, it is important that you do not log on, but shut down the computer and restart using the Last Known Good Configuration option. Booting from the Last Known Good Configuration option allows you to start Windows NT because it does not contain the new device driver settings.

D. **Incorrect:** You need to return to the previously used video device driver configuration, which cannot be reset by rebooting with a DOS diskette and deleting the video driver. This action only removes your screen display.

70-073.07.01.007

Your Pentium-based computer dual-boots MS-DOS and Windows NT Workstation. Windows NT Workstation successfully starts each time, but when starting MS-DOS the message below is displayed.

"Couldn't open boot sector file
multi(0)disk(0)rdisk(0)partition(1):\Bootsect.dos"

Which two steps should you complete to resolve this problem? (Choose two.)

A. Start the computer using a DOS floppy disk and issue the SYS C: command.

B. Start the computer and use the DiskSave utility to restore the Master Boot Record.

C. Start the computer, boot into Windows NT Workstation, and edit the boot sector values.

D. Start the computer using the Windows NT Setup disks and repair using the emergency repair disk.

70-073.07.01.007

Your Pentium-based computer dual-boots MS-DOS and Windows NT Workstation. Windows NT Workstation successfully starts each time, but when starting MS-DOS the message below is displayed.

"Couldn't open boot sector file
multi(0)disk(0)rdisk(0)partition(1):\Bootsect.dos"

Which two steps should you complete to resolve this problem? (Choose two.)

▶ **Correct Answers: A and D**

A. **Correct:** The message you received means the BOOTSECT.DOS file is missing or corrupt. To restore the BOOTSECT.DOS file you must use the MS-DOS Sys.com program SYS C: command to replace the partition boot sector along with the emergency repair disk to repair the boot sector.

B. **Incorrect:** The message you received means the BOOTSECT.DOS file is missing or corrupt. DiskSave restores the Master Boot Record (MBR). Since the MBR does not contain the BOOTSECT.DOS file, DiskSave cannot restore the file.

C. **Incorrect:** The message you received means the BOOTSECT.DOS file is missing or corrupt. Editing boot sector values will not allow you to restore the BOOTSECT.DOS file.

D. **Correct:** The message you received means the BOOTSECT.DOS file is missing or corrupt. To restore the BOOTSECT.DOS file you must use the SYS C: command to replace the partition boot sector along with the emergency repair disk to repair the boot sector.

Further Reading

 The *Microsoft Windows NT Technical Support* volume of the *Microsoft Windows NT Technical Support Training* kit Chapter 17, Lesson 1 contains an overview of the Windows NT boot process, including file descriptions of boot sequence files. Lesson 2 explains the common boot process errors and troubleshooting recommendations. Lesson 3 explains the purpose of and how to use the Last Known Good Configuration option to recover from incorrect configurations. Practice for using the Last Known Good Configuration is included on the CD provided with this kit. Lesson 4 explains the purpose of and how to use the emergency repair process to recover missing or damaged boot files. Practice for updating an emergency repair disk is included on the CD provided with this kit.

 The *Microsoft Windows NT Workstation 4.0 Resource Kit* Chapter 20 contains detailed information on backing up the Master Boot Record and on restoring Windows NT files. Chapter 21 explains how to use FDISK to check for and set the system partition and how to use SYS C: command and the emergency repair disk to replace the BOOTSECT.DOS file.

 Use Microsoft Technical Support Online (http://support.microsoft.com/) by searching for "Windows NT Workstation" and for "emergency repair disk." Then click "Description of Windows NT Emergency Repair Disk."

OBJECTIVE 7.2

Choose the appropriate course of action to take when a print job fails.

You must understand the network printing processes to be able to effectively trouble-shoot print job failures. The steps below describe a network printing job:

1. An administrator creates a print share on the print server.

2. A client system connects to that share.

3. The client system creates a print job.

4. The client system sends the print job to the print share on the print server.

5. The print server receives, spools, and sometimes modifies the print job.

6. The print server sends the job to the print device.

7. The print device interprets the job and produces hardcopy output.

▶ **To troubleshoot printing problems:**

1. Identify which process is causing the problem, using the list of symptoms provided for each process in the *Microsoft Windows NT Workstation 4.0 Resource Kit* or the *Windows NT Server Resource Guide*.

2. Reconfigure the process using suggestions in the references.

3. Test the print job. If the print job is not successful, you must try other suggestions from the references.

You can also control print jobs from the Printers folder. You can control a specific printer by selecting it from the Printers folder and using the Printer menu. From the Printer menu you can pause printing or purge print documents *for the printer*. You can control a specific print job by selecting it from the list of print jobs and using the Document menu. From the Document menu you can pause, resume, or restart the specified *print job*.

Questions related to this objective are designed to determine if you have an awareness of these issues. To successfully answer the questions for this objective, you need a firm understanding of several key terms. For definitions of these terms, refer to the Glossary in this book.

Key Terms

- Despooling
- Parallel
- PostScript files
- Print device
- Print driver
- Print job
- Print monitor
- Print server
- Print spooler
- Printer
- Protocol
- Serial
- Spool file
- Spooling

70-073.07.02.001

A user is printing a lengthy report from an application running on her Windows NT Workstation computer to a locally attached printer. A paper jam occurs, so she pauses the printer, clears the jam, and reinitializes the printer. Since the jam occurred near the end of the print job, she wants to print only those pages that have not yet printed.

What should she do to finish printing the report?

A. Select the printer from the Printers folder and double-click the print job.

B. Select the printer from the Printers folder and choose the Restart option from the Document menu.

C. Select the printer from the Printers folder and choose the Resume option from the Document menu.

D. Select the printer from the Printers folder and modify the print job properties to print only the remaining pages.

70-073.07.02.001

A user is printing a lengthy report from an application running on her Windows NT Workstation computer to a locally attached printer. A paper jam occurs, so she pauses the printer, clears the jam, and reinitializes the printer. Since the jam occurred near the end of the print job, she wants to print only those pages that have not yet printed.

What should she do to finish printing the report?

▶ **Correct Answer: C**

A. **Incorrect:** Selecting the printer from the Printers folder and double-clicking the print job shows the properties for the job and does not print the pages of the report that have not yet printed.

B. **Incorrect:** Selecting the printer from the Printers folder and choosing the Restart option from the Document menu will print the entire report.

C. **Correct:** Selecting the printer from the Printers folder and choosing the Resume option from the document menu will print the pages of the report that have not yet printed.

D. **Incorrect:** Since there is no way to request specific page numbers in the print job properties (Notification, Priority, and Scheduling), you cannot use print job properties to print only the remaining pages.

70-073.07.02.002

A user is having trouble with garbled printing when printing documents from a word processing application running on her Windows NT Workstation client computer. This problem consistently occurs when printing PostScript files to the department's HP laser printer.

Other users in the department are also having the same printing troubles, but only those who are running the Window NT Workstation operating system. Windows 3.1 and Windows 95 clients are able to print PostScript files to the HP laser printer without encountering any problems.

What should you do to solve this printing problem?

A. Install new print drivers.

B. Create more free disk space.

C. Install a compatible network protocol.

D. Replace the parallel cable or parallel port.

70-073.07.02.002

A user is having trouble with garbled printing when printing documents from a word processing application running on her Windows NT Workstation client computer. This problem consistently occurs when printing PostScript files to the department's HP laser printer.

Other users in the department are also having the same printing troubles, but only those who are running the Window NT Workstation operating system. Windows 3.1 and Windows 95 clients are able to print PostScript files to the HP laser printer without encountering any problems.

What should you do to solve this printing problem?

▶ **Correct Answer: A**

    A. **Correct:** Installing new print drivers will solve the problem of a client application printing garbled results for all Windows NT Workstation clients when sending PostScript files to the printer. This is a solution when there is a problem with the client application creating a print job.

    B. **Incorrect:** You would create more free disk space if there were problems with the printer server spooler processing the print job. Symptoms of printer server spooler problems are: extra form feeds or no form feeds and the job sticking in the printer.

    C. **Incorrect:** You would install a compatible network protocol if there were problems with the client sending the job to the spooler. You may have problems with the client sending jobs to the spooler if the job is not started until the application is exited, the pages come out incomplete, or the print server has run out of disk space.

    D. **Incorrect:** You would replace the parallel cable or parallel port if there were problems with the print server spooler sending a job to a print device. You may have printer spooler problems if trying a different parallel cable or sending the job to the same device using another protocol, serial, or parallel port produces a successful print.

70-073.07.02.003

A user is having trouble with garbled printing when printing documents from any application running on his Windows NT Workstation computer. This problem consistently occurs when he prints to the printer attached locally to his workstation, but does not occur when he prints to an identical shared printer on the network.

What is the most likely cause of this printing problem?

A. Incompatible print drivers

B. Not enough free disk space

C. Incompatible network protocol

D. Defective parallel cable or parallel port

70-073.07.02.003

A user is having trouble with garbled printing when printing documents from any application running on his Windows NT Workstation computer. This problem consistently occurs when he prints to the printer attached locally to his workstation, but does not occur when he prints to an identical shared printer on the network.

What is the most likely cause of this printing problem?

▶ **Correct Answer: D**

A. **Incorrect:** Since the user does not have the garbled printing problem when printing to an identical shared printer, print drivers cannot be incompatible. There is not a problem with the client application creating a print job.

B. **Incorrect:** Since the user is the only one reporting a problem and he does not have the garbled printing problem when printing to an identical shared printer, there must be enough free disk space. There is not a problem with the receiving and spooling of the print job.

C. **Incorrect:** Since the user has not experienced a problem with a particular protocol and he does not have the garbled printing problem when printing to an identical shared printer, incompatible network protocol cannot be the problem. There is not a problem with the client sending the print job to the spooler.

D. **Correct:** Since the user experiences a problem with garbled printing only on the printer attached locally, the problem is a defective parallel cable or port. The print server cannot correctly send the job to the print device.

70-073.07.02.004

One of the users on your Windows NT network attempts to print a document to a printer that is attached to a print server. The pages of this document are coming out incomplete.

Which network print process is most likely the source of the problem?

A. The client application

B. The process that sends the print job to the spooler

C. The printer server process that handles the print job

D. The process that interprets the print job at the print device

70-073.07.02.004

One of the users on your Windows NT network attempts to print a document to a printer that is attached to a print server. The pages of this document are coming out incomplete.

Which network print process is most likely the source of the problem?

▶ **Correct Answer: B**

A. **Incorrect:** The "client application" print process is responsible for running the application and interacting with the print driver to create output. Incomplete pages are not a symptom of a problem with the "client application" print process.

B. **Correct:** The "client sends job to spooler" print process is responsible for sending the job to the client's transport protocol, to the network adapter, over the network hardware, to the transport software on the print server, and to the appropriate print server service on the print server. Pages coming out incomplete are a symptom of a problem with the "client sends job to spooler" print process.

C. **Incorrect:** The "print server spooler processes print job" print process receives, spools, and sometimes modifies the print job. Incomplete pages are not a symptom of a problem with the "print server spooler processes print job" print process.

D. **Incorrect:** The "print server spooler sends job to print device" print process includes the print monitor receiving the job from the print spooler and interacting with the local hardware and transport drivers to send the job to its destination. Incomplete pages are not a symptom of a problem with the "print server spooler sends job to print device" print process.

70-073.07.02.005

You are a Windows NT administrator and have been receiving calls from users on the network who are having trouble printing to one particular network printer. All print jobs are coming out with extra form feeds.

Which network print process is most likely the source of the problem?

A. The client application

B. The process that sends the print job to the spooler

C. The process that interprets the print job at the print device

D. The process in which the Print Server spooler processes the print job

70-073.07.02.006

When a user tries to print to a network printer, the system accesses the local hard disk but the document never reaches the print server. What should you do to solve this problem?

A. Select a default printer.

B. Install new printer drivers.

C. Change the user's permissions to the printer.

D. Create more free hard disk space on the local client.

70-073.07.02.005

You are a Windows NT administrator and have been receiving calls from users on the network who are having trouble printing to one particular network printer. All print jobs are coming out with extra form feeds.

Which network print process is most likely the source of the problem?

▶ **Correct Answer: D**

A. **Incorrect:** The "client application" print process is responsible for running the application and interacting with the print driver to create output. Extra form feeds are not a symptom of a problem with the "client application" print process.

B. **Incorrect:** The "client sends job to spooler" print process is responsible for sending the job to the client's transport protocol, to the network adapter, over the network hardware, to the transport software on the print server, and to the appropriate print server service on the print server. Extra form feeds are not a symptom of a problem with the "client sends job to spooler" print process.

C. **Incorrect:** The "print server spooler processes print job" print process receives, spools, and sometimes modifies the print job. Extra form feeds are not a symptom of a problem with the "print server spooler processes print job" print process.

D. **Correct:** The "print server spooler sends job to print device" print process includes the print monitor receiving the job from the print spooler and interacting with the local hardware and transport drivers to send the job to its destination. Extra form feeds are a symptom of a problem with the "print server spooler sends job to print device" print process.

70-073.07.02.006

When a user tries to print to a network printer, the system accesses the local hard disk but the document never reaches the print server. What should you do to solve this problem?

▶ **Correct Answer: D**

A. **Incorrect:** You would select a default printer if a 16-bit Windows–based program displayed an out-of-memory error on startup.

B. **Incorrect:** You would install new print drivers if the document did not print completely or was garbled, if you could not connect to a printer, or if you sent a document from an MS-DOS–based program on a Windows NT–based client to the printer and it never printed.

C. **Incorrect:** You would change a user's printer permissions if he received an access-denied message when trying to configure a printer from within a program.

D. **Correct:** If the document does not reach the print server, you should create more free hard disk space on the local client for spooling the document.

70-073.07.02.007

A user working in Word receives an access-denied message when she tries to configure a printer connected to a Windows NT Workstation in the workgroup. What should you do to solve this problem?

A. Select a default printer.

B. Install new print drivers.

C. Change the user's permissions to the printer.

D. Create more free hard disk space on the local client.

70-073.07.02.007

A user working in Word receives an access-denied message when she tries to configure a printer connected to a Windows NT Workstation in the workgroup. What should you do to solve this problem?

▶ **Correct Answer: C**

A. **Incorrect:** You would select a default printer if a 16-bit Windows–based program displayed an out-of-memory error on startup.

B. **Incorrect:** You would install new print drivers if the document did not print completely or was garbled, if you could not connect to a printer, or if you sent a document from an MS-DOS–based program on a Windows NT–based client to the printer and it never printed.

C. **Correct:** If a user received an access-denied message when trying to configure a printer from within a program, you should change the user's printer permissions.

D. **Incorrect:** You would create more free hard disk space on the local client for spooling the document if the document did not reach the print server.

Further Reading

  The *Microsoft Windows NT Network Administration* volume of the *Microsoft Windows NT Network Administration Training* kit Chapter 8, Lesson 2 explains how to control document printing. Lesson 3 explains how to control the printer, including pausing, resuming, and purging. Practice for controlling the printer is included on the CD provided with this kit. Lesson 4 contains a high-level printer troubleshooting checklist and a table of printer problems and solutions.

 The *Microsoft Windows NT Workstation 4.0 Resource Kit* Chapter 7 contains detailed information on troubleshooting printer problems using the Windows NT modular printing architecture, including a list of symptoms and tests.

 Use Microsoft Technical Support Online (http://support.microsoft.com) by searching for "Windows NT Workstation" and for "printer problems." Then click "Isolating General Printing Problems."

 Use Microsoft Technical Support Online (http://support.microsoft.com) by searching for "Windows NT Workstation" and for "printing." Then click "Popular Topics for Windows NT Workstation," "Help with Common Windows NT Issues," "Microsoft Technical Support Troubleshooting Wizards," and "Windows NT 4.0 General Application Troubleshooter" to proceed through a series of troubleshooting steps for printing.

 Use Microsoft Technical Support Online (http://support.microsoft.com) by searching for "Windows NT Workstation" and for "printing." Then click "Windows NT Server and Workstation 4.0 Printing Frequently Asked Questions." Select from various printer troubleshooting topics.

O B J E C T I V E   7 . 3

Choose the appropriate course of action to take when the installation process fails.

You must understand the Windows NT Workstation installation process and the various installation methods to be able to effectively troubleshoot installation failures. You can install Windows NT Workstation using the CD-ROM drive, the hard disk, or the network. The steps below outline the installation process and the actions required for each step:

1. **Installation begins**. Start Setup using setup disks, CD-ROM, or a network connection.

2. **Hardware detection occurs**. Configure a mass storage device, configure disk partitions, choose a file system for the Windows NT partition, choose a directory for Windows NT Workstation files.

3. **Computer restarts; graphical user interface starts**. Enter personal information and password and indicate that you want to create an emergency repair disk during setup.

4. **Networking information is requested**. Indicate network type, detect, select, and configure network adapters. Select network protocols and network services. Confirm network component settings. Adjust the network bindings. Join a workgroup or domain.

5. **Emergency repair disk is made**.

6. **Installation is complete**. Review and approve date, time, and video display settings. Remove disks and reboot to start Windows NT Workstation.

▶   **To troubleshoot installation problems:**

1. Identify the step in which you are experiencing the installation problem. Use references to find solutions to your installation problems.

2. Begin the installation process again, using suggestions in the references.

3. If the installation is not successful you must try other suggestions from the references.

Questions related to this objective are designed to determine if you have an awareness of these issues. To successfully answer the questions for this objective, you need a firm understanding of several key terms. For definitions of these terms, refer to the Glossary in this book.

Key Terms

- Extended memory

- Kernel STOP errors

- Shared directory

70-073.07.03.001

You are installing Windows NT Workstation on a Pentium-based computer using source installation files stored on a directory on a Windows NT server. The server is located on an Ethernet segment that is connected to the local segment by a router. During the installation process, you receive this error message:

"The specified shared directory cannot be found."

What should you do to solve this problem?

A. Disable routing.

B. Share the source directory.

C. Map a drive to the source directory.

D. Configure NetBEUI on the client workstation.

70-073.07.03.002

You are installing Windows NT Workstation on a Pentium-based computer using source installation files stored on a shared directory on a Windows NT server. Both the client and source server are located on a 10BaseT Ethernet segment running TCP/IP and NetBEUI. During the installation process, you receive an error message indicating a lack of extended memory.

Which two methods could you use at the client to solve this problem?

A. Add more RAM.

B. Disable TCP/IP.

C. Enable virtual memory.

D. Use EMM386.EXE and HIMEM.SYS to provide extended memory.

70-073.07.03.001

You are installing Windows NT Workstation on a Pentium-based computer using source installation files stored on a directory on a Windows NT server. The server is located on an Ethernet segment that is connected to the local segment by a router. During the installation process, you receive this error message:

"The specified shared directory cannot be found."

What should you do to solve this problem?

▶ **Correct Answer: B**

   A. **Incorrect:** Disabling the router would also disable the network connection, which would not help you access the shared directory.

   B. **Correct:** If you receive an error message stating that the specified shared directory cannot be found, you must make sure that the directory containing the Windows NT installation files is shared on the Windows NT Server computer.

   C. **Incorrect:** It is not necessary to map a drive on your Windows NT Workstation computer to the source directory containing installation files on the Windows NT Server. Installation is a task that is performed rarely; mapping a drive provides a connection to the installation program that is retained until disconnected.

   D. **Incorrect:** NetBEUI does not support traffic across routers and cannot be used to connect to the source directory containing installation files on the Windows NT Server.

70-073.07.03.002

You are installing Windows NT Workstation on a Pentium-based computer using source installation files stored on a shared directory on a Windows NT server. Both the client and source server are located on a 10BaseT Ethernet segment running TCP/IP and NetBEUI. During the installation process, you receive an error message indicating a lack of extended memory.

Which two methods could you use at the client to solve this problem?

▶ **Correct Answers: B and D**

   A. **Incorrect:** RAM is used for running software processes, not for storing the operating system. Adding more RAM will not provide more extended memory.

   B. **Correct:** If the computer displays an extended memory error message, you can disable TCP/IP and run the installation using the faster NetBEUI protocol.

   C. **Incorrect:** Virtual memory is used by paging files, not for storing the operating system. Enabling virtual memory will not provide more extended memory.

   D. **Correct:** If the computer displays an extended memory error message you can modify the CONFIG.SYS file to use extended memory provided by EMM386.EXE and HIMEM.SYS.

70-073.07.03.003

What should you do if you encounter a STOP screen during the Windows NT Workstation installation process?

A. Clean or reset the Master Boot Record.

B. Reformat the boot partition to NTFS and restart the install.

C. Check compatibility of the computer and its components in the Windows NT Hardware Compatibility List.

D. Reboot the computer into DOS 5.0 or above, and use EMM386.EXE and HIMEM.SYS to provide extended memory.

E. Run the SYSDIFF utility with the /INF parameter to discover any unqualified filenames in the system INF directory.

70-073.07.03.003

What should you do if you encounter a STOP screen during the Windows NT Workstation installation process?

▶ **Correct Answer: C**

    A. **Incorrect:** Resetting the Master Boot Record is not necessary if you encounter a STOP screen during the Windows NT Workstation installation process. If the Master Boot Record is not performing properly, it displays the error message "Missing operating system" or "Invalid Partition Table" during startup.

    B. **Incorrect:** There is no need to reformat the boot partition to NTFS if you encounter a STOP screen during the Windows NT installation process. Windows NT 4.0 supports both FAT and NTFS file systems.

    C. **Correct:** When a STOP screen appears during installation, you should check the compatibility of the computer and its peripheral hardware with Windows NT by using the Windows NT Hardware Compatibility List (HCL). The HCL is available in the *Windows NT Server Resource Kit* and on the Web.

    D. **Incorrect:** There is no need to reboot the computer into DOS 5.0 or above and use EMM386.EXE and HIMEM.SYS to provide extended memory if you encounter a STOP screen during the Windows NT installation process. Extended memory is needed only if the computer displays an extended memory error message during installation.

    E. **Incorrect:** Running the SYSDIFF utility with the /INF parameter is not necessary if you encounter a STOP screen during the Windows NT Workstation installation process. The SYSDIFF utility with the /INF parameter is used to preinstall applications.

70-073.07.03.004

You are deploying Windows NT Workstation on 25 computers by using Network Installation Startup disks. During the first installation, you receive an error message stating

"The specified shared directory cannot be found."

Which action should you take to resolve the problem?

A. Reconfigure the appropriate answer file on the distribution share.

B. Modify the CONFIG.SYS file on the Network Installation Startup disk to use extended memory.

C. Make sure the directory containing the Windows NT installation files is shared on the Windows NT Server computer.

D. Reconfigure the appropriate Windows NT Server .INF file and share it with the appropriate permissions on the network.

70-073.07.03.004

You are deploying Windows NT Workstation on 25 computers by using Network Installation Startup disks. During the first installation, you receive an error message stating

"The specified shared directory cannot be found."

Which action should you take to resolve the problem?

▶ **Correct Answer: C**

A. **Incorrect:** Reconfiguring the answer file is not necessary, since you were unable to connect to the distribution sharepoint to begin the installation process. You must connect to the distribution sharepoint before the answer file is accessed.

B. **Incorrect:** There is no need to modify the CONFIG.SYS file on the Network Installation Startup disk to use extended memory. Extended memory is needed only if the computer displays an extended memory error message during installation.

C. **Correct:** If you receive an error message stating that the specified shared directory cannot be found, you must make sure that the directory containing the Windows NT installation files is shared on the Windows NT Server computer.

D. **Incorrect:** Device information (INF) files are used to install applications and other components into Windows NT. Reconfiguring and sharing an .INF file would not locate or share the directory containing the Windows NT installation files.

Further Reading

 The *Microsoft Windows NT Workstation 4.0 Resource Kit* Chapter 2 provides details on troubleshooting an installation using network installation startup disks. Solutions for the error message "The specified shared directory cannot be found" and lack of memory error messages are provided. Chapter 38 includes a section on STOP screens encountered during the installation process and referring to the Windows NT Hardware Compatibility List as a means to a solution.

 Microsoft Windows NT Workstation Start Here. Microsoft Press. 1997. ISBN 1-57231-522-9. Chapters 5 through 8 cover the installation process in detail. Appendix A covers Windows NT Setup troubleshooting, including using the Hardware Compatibility List and a list of frequently asked questions.

 Use Microsoft Technical Support Online (http://support.microsoft.com/) by searching for "Windows NT Workstation" and for "installation." Then click "View Windows NT 4.0 Setup Troubleshooting Guide."

 Use Microsoft Technical Support Online (http://support.microsoft.com/) by searching for "Windows NT Workstation" and for "STOP screens." Then click "Debugging Windows NT Setup STOP Screens."

OBJECTIVE 7.4

Choose the appropriate course of action to take when an application fails.

When an application fails on Windows NT Workstation, you may receive a message, the system may lock, or application performance may be impaired. If you can identify messages or system actions and use resources to interpret them, you can begin to troubleshoot application problems.

Messages

Windows NT displays a STATUS message box to inform you of conditions occurring within an application. There are three types of STATUS messages:

- System-information messages—Provide information on conditions in an application that should be noted, but do not stop the application from running.

- Warning messages—Advise you to take action on a condition to keep running the application. Also warn you that results from a running application may not be correct.

- Application-termination messages—Warn you that the application or thread will be terminated.

Interpretation Resources

The Event Viewer provides information about events, including error and warning messages. The Event Viewer records events in three types of logs: system, security, and application. You can use the application log to see events logged by an application.

By looking at the detail for an event, you can view the date and time of the event, an event ID, and a text description, all of which can help you interpret an error or warning message.

The Message Database help file on the *Windows NT Workstation Resource Kit 4.0* CD contains information on error and system information messages, some application or device messages, and an online database of event log messages. Use the help file to interpret messages you may receive for an application.

If you are running a 16-bit application and have problems, you may want to consider the configuration of the NT Virtual DOS Machine (NTVDM) and Win16 on Win32 (WOW) environment. Changing the configuration to use either single or multiple NTVDMs or to use or not use WOW provides advantages and disadvantages for each situation.

Questions related to this objective are designed to determine if you have an awareness of these issues. To successfully answer the questions for this objective, you need a firm understanding of several key terms. For definitions of these terms, refer to the Glossary in this book.

Key Terms

- Application-termination message

- Default printer

- Event Viewer

- NT Virtual DOS Machine (NTVDM)

- Warning message

70-073.07.04.001

You have installed Windows NT Workstation on a Pentium-based computer and are in the process of setting up applications. You are having problems running a 16-bit accounting application on the computer. It always gives an out-of-memory error when launched.

Other applications start and operate properly on the computer. Also, other Windows NT Workstation users report no similar errors using the accounting application.

What should you do to solve this problem?

A. Start the application in its own separate NTVDM.

B. Make sure you have the proper permissions to run the application.

C. Make sure printing is properly configured and a default printer is defined.

D. Check the computer and its components for compatibility in the Windows NT Hardware Compatibility List.

70-073.07.04.001

You have installed Windows NT Workstation on a Pentium-based computer and are in the process of setting up applications. You are having problems running a 16-bit accounting application on the computer. It always gives an out-of-memory error when launched.

Other applications start and operate properly on the computer. Also, other Windows NT Workstation users report no similar errors using the accounting application.

What should you do to solve this problem?

▶ **Correct Answer: C**

A. **Incorrect:** Starting the application in its own NTVDM causes additional memory to be used and is not a solution to an out-of-memory error.

B. **Incorrect:** If you did not have the proper permissions to run the application, you would receive an access-denied error message when the application is launched. Changing permissions is not a solution to an out-of-memory error.

C. **Correct:** Receiving an out-of-memory error message is a problem encountered when a default printer is not selected on a computer. You must create a printer and set it as the default printer.

D. **Incorrect:** Since other applications start and operate properly on the computer and the 16-bit accounting application runs properly on other Windows NT Workstation computers, hardware compatibility is not the problem.

70-073.07.04.002

You are running a 32-bit Windows based application on a Windows NT Workstation client computer and this message is displayed:

"The application or DLL <VSPELL> is not a valid Windows NT image.
Please check against your installation disk."

What should you do to solve this problem?

A. Reinstall the application.

B. Start the application in its own separate NTVDM.

C. Make sure printing is properly configured and a default printer is defined.

D. Check the computer and its components for incompatibility in the Windows NT Hardware Compatibility List.

70-073.07.04.002

You are running a 32-bit Windows based application on a Windows NT Workstation client computer and this message is displayed:

> "The application or DLL <VSPELL> is not a valid Windows NT image.
> Please check against your installation disk."

What should you do to solve this problem?

▶ **Correct Answer: A**

A. **Correct:** The application-termination message you are receiving advises you to reinstall before restarting the application. You might also contact the supplier of the application for more information.

B. **Incorrect:** The application is a 32-bit application and does not need to run in NTVDM. NTVDM is a special Win32-based application that supports MS-DOS–based applications when launched on Windows NT Workstation computers.

C. **Incorrect:** If there was a problem with printer configuration or a default printer you would receive an out-of-memory error message. The application-termination message you are receiving cannot be solved by changing the printer configuration or defining a default printer.

D. **Incorrect:** Since the application-termination message indicates a problem with software, hardware compatibility is not the problem. Check on hardware compatibility using the Windows NT Hardware Compatibility List (HCL) when a STOP screen appears during installation.

70-073.07.04.003

All Windows for Workgroups computers in a peer-to-peer network were replaced with new Windows NT Workstation computers. However, a frequently used 16-bit application suite was not replaced or upgraded to the 32-bit version. Users are complaining that they are not able to share data between the various applications within the suite as they did before the computer upgrade.

What should you do to solve this problem?

A. Reinstall the application.

B. Start each application in its own separate NTVDM.

C. Make sure printing is properly configured and a default printer is defined.

D. Check the computer and its components for incompatibility in the Windows NT Hardware Compatibility List.

70-073.07.04.004

You are running a new application on your Windows NT Workstation computer and receive a "Page Locked" message. Which Windows NT tool should you use to determine the cause of this warning?

A. Task Manager

B. Performance Monitor

C. Event Viewer System Log

D. Event Viewer Application Log

70-073.07.04.003

All Windows for Workgroups computers in a peer-to-peer network were replaced with new Windows NT Workstation computers. However, a frequently used 16-bit application suite was not replaced or upgraded to the 32-bit version. Users are complaining that they are not able to share data between the various applications within the suite as they did before the computer upgrade.

What should you do to solve this problem?

▶ **Correct Answer: B**

A. **Incorrect:** It is not necessary to reinstall the application suite. When installed, the applications run one at a time and cannot interoperate; you need to configure them so they can share data.

B. **Correct:** By running each of the applications in the suite in a separate NTVDM, each application is provided with its own memory space. Since each application has its own memory space, all of the applications can interoperate and share data.

C. **Incorrect:** If there was a problem with printer configuration or a default printer, you would receive an out-of-memory error message. The lack of interoperability between applications in the suite cannot be solved by changing the printer configuration or defining a default printer.

D. **Incorrect:** Since the applications in the suite are all working individually and there are no other reported problems, hardware compatibility is not the problem. You need to configure the applications so they can share data.

70-073.07.04.004

You are running a new application on your Windows NT Workstation computer and receive a "Page Locked" message. Which Windows NT tool should you use to determine the cause of this warning?

▶ **Correct Answer: D**

A. **Incorrect:** Task Manager is used to monitor, start, and stop active applications and processes on your computer. Task Manager does not monitor events such as errors and warnings and cannot tell you the cause of the "Page Locked" warning message.

B. **Incorrect:** Performance Monitor is used to measure your computer's efficiency, identify and troubleshoot possible performance problems, and plan for hardware needs. Performance Monitor does not monitor events such as errors and warnings and cannot tell you the cause of the "Page Locked" warning message.

C. **Incorrect:** The Event Viewer System Log contains information about events logged by the Windows NT *system* components and device drivers. The System Log cannot determine the cause of the warning message, because the "Page Locked" warning message is an event generated about a condition within an *application*.

D. **Correct:** The Event Viewer Application Log contains information about events logged by applications, including errors, warnings, and the success or failure of tasks. Application developers determine which events are monitored. Event Detail provides the date and time of the event, an event ID, and a text description.

Further Reading

 The *Microsoft Windows NT Network Administration* volume of the *Microsoft Windows NT Network Administration Training* kit Chapter 8, Lesson 4 provides information on problems encountered when a default printer is not selected.

 The *Microsoft Windows NT Technical Support* volume of the *Microsoft Windows NT Technical Support Training* kit Chapter 8, Lesson 5 covers the advantages and disadvantages of multiple NTVDMs. Chapter 18, Lesson 1 provides details on the purpose of the Event Viewer and interpreting an event. Practice for viewing events is included on the CD provided with this kit.

 The *Microsoft Windows NT Workstation 4.0 Resource Kit* Chapter 37 provides detailed information on monitoring events, including error and warning messages, using the Event Viewer. Chapter 38 includes detailed information on Windows-mode STATUS messages, including system information, warning, and application-termination messages.

OBJECTIVE 7.5

Choose the appropriate course of action to take when a user cannot access a resource.

Typically, users cannot access a resource because of inadequate access permissions. The following permissions checklist is a list of items to consider when troubleshooting a situation that involves access and permissions:

Permissions Checklist

- What is the permission assigned to the user? Is the permission a share permission or an NTFS permission?

- To which group(s) is the user assigned? What is the permission assigned to the group(s)? Is the permission a share permission or an NTFS permission?

- What is the permission assigned to the folder? Is the permission a share permission or an NTFS permission?

- What is the permission assigned to the file? Is the permission a share permission or an NTFS permission?

- What rules for combining share permissions and NTFS permissions apply to this situation?

- Is the resource you want to access on a FAT or an NTFS partition?

- Have files or folders recently been copied or moved within NTFS volumes or between NTFS or FAT volumes? How has this move affected the permissions on the files or folders?

If you have problems with Remote Access Service (RAS) access, you can use the following tools:

- **Event Viewer**—Used to view RAS events in the system log.

- **Dial-up Networking Monitor**—Used to show the status of a session in progress, including the duration of the call, amount of data being transmitted and received, number of errors, and lines being used for Multilink sessions.

- **PPP.LOG file**—Can be created to provide debugging information for PPP connections.

- **Authentication settings**—Used to provide a range of encryption levels. Authentication settings can be set low to start and increased to the highest level that can be used successfully between two systems.

Questions related to this objective are designed to determine if you have an awareness of these issues. To successfully answer the questions for this objective, you need a firm understanding of several key terms. For definitions of these terms, refer to the Glossary in this book.

Key Terms

- Access token

- Dial-Up Networking

- Multilink Protocol (MP)

- NTFS permissions

- Permissions

- Remote Access Service (RAS)

- Share permissions

70-073.07.05.001

A user on a Windows NT Workstation client computer has No Access permissions to a shared folder on a Windows NT server. She needs Read and Change permissions to the folder. The permissions were granted directly to the user's Windows NT user account, but she is still not able to access the folder.

What should you do to solve this problem?

A. Grant the user ownership of the share.

B. Have the user log off and then back on.

C. Map a drive to the share using the UNC path.

D. Make sure NetBEUI is configured on the client computer.

70-073.07.05.002

An application directory was moved from one NTFS partition to another NTFS partition on the same Windows NT Server. Users that were able to access the application directory before the move are not able to access it now.

What should you do first to solve this problem?

A. Check for inherited permissions.

B. Have users log off and then back on.

C. Map a network drive to the new location.

D. Make sure there is adequate free disk space at the new location.

70-073.07.05.001

A user on a Windows NT Workstation client computer has No Access permissions to a shared folder on a Windows NT server. She needs Read and Change permissions to the folder. The permissions were granted directly to the user's Windows NT user account, but she is still not able to access the folder.

What should you do to solve this problem?

▶ **Correct Answer: B**

    A. **Incorrect:** Granting ownership of the share will allow the user to share the folder or assign permissions to the folder, which is not necessary.

    B. **Correct:** Since the permissions were granted directly to the user's account, the user must log off and log back on for the permissions to take effect. An access token that contains permissions information is created for a user every time he logs on. To update the access token, a user must log off and log on again; a remote user must disconnect and then reconnect.

    C. **Incorrect:** Mapping a drive to the shared folder will not provide access to the folder. In order to map a drive, you must first have the appropriate permission.

    D. **Incorrect:** NetBEUI is a protocol and will not affect the permission assigned for the shared folder.

70-073.07.05.002

An application directory was moved from one NTFS partition to another NTFS partition on the same Windows NT Server. Users that were able to access the application directory before the move are not able to access it now.

What should you do first to solve this problem?

▶ **Correct Answer: A**

    A. **Correct:** Since the directory was moved to another NTFS partition, the directory has inherited the permissions of the destination folder. By changing the permissions on the destination folder, you can restore access to the users.

    B. **Incorrect:** Since the user's permissions were not changed, logging off and then logging back on is not necessary.

    C. **Incorrect:** Mapping a drive to the application directory will not provide access to the directory. In order to map a drive, you must first have the appropriate permission.

    D. **Incorrect:** There is no indication that users are encountering a memory problem; adding free disk space will not solve a permission problem.

70-073.07.05.003

Your computer running Windows NT Workstation has two modems. You are having trouble establishing a RAS session to a remote server using the PPP Multilink Protocol (MP). Each time you attempt to dial the RAS server, the session lasts only a few seconds before disconnecting.

The required result is to monitor the status of a dial-up networking session that is in progress.

The first optional result is to monitor the number of errors occurring during the dial-up networking session. The second optional result is to determine which lines are being used for Multilink sessions.

The proposed solution is to attempt the RAS session again, and view the connection status using Dial-Up Networking Monitor.

What does the proposed solution provide?

A. The required result and all optional results.

B. The required result and one optional result.

C. The required result but none of the optional results.

D. The proposed solution does not provide the required result.

70-073.07.05.004

You need to grant Read and Write access to a user on a file located in the shared folder \MKTG. You assign the Read and Write NTFS permissions to this file. The user complains that he still cannot save changes to that file. He has already logged off and back on again and still has the problem.

Which condition could be the cause of the problem?

A. The NTFS permission on the \MKTG folder is set to Read Only.

B. The NTFS permission on the \MKTG folder is set to Read, Write, and Execute.

C. The user is not a member of the Everyone group which has Full Control permissions on this folder.

D. The user is a member of the Everyone group, which has Full Control permissions on the \MKTG folder.

70-073.07.05.003

Your computer running Windows NT Workstation has two modems. You are having trouble establishing a RAS session to a remote server using the PPP Multilink Protocol (MP). Each time you attempt to dial the RAS server, the session lasts only a few seconds before disconnecting.

The required result is to monitor the status of a dial-up networking session that is in progress.

The first optional result is to monitor the number of errors occurring during the dial-up networking session. The second optional result is to determine which lines are being used for Multilink sessions.

The proposed solution is to attempt the RAS session again, and view the connection status using Dial-Up Networking Monitor.

What does the proposed solution provide?

▶ **Correct Answer: A**

A. **Correct:** The Dial-Up Networking Monitor is used to troubleshoot RAS, and monitors the status of a dial-up networking session in progress. In addition, the Dial-Up Networking Monitor provides the number of errors that occur during the dial-up session and can also show which lines are used for Multilink sessions.

B. **Incorrect:** See the explanation for answer A.

C. **Incorrect:** See the explanation for answer A.

D. **Incorrect:** See the explanation for answer A.

70-073.07.05.004

You need to grant Read and Write access to a user on a file located in the shared folder \MKTG. You assign the Read and Write NTFS permissions to this file. The user complains that he still cannot save changes to that file. He has already logged off and back on again and still has the problem.

Which condition could be the cause of the problem?

▶ **Correct Answer: A**

A. **Correct:** You provided Read and Write NTFS permissions to the user for the file. The NTFS permission for the /MKTG folder is Read, which prohibits the user from accessing the file. Set the share permission for the /MKTG folder to Change and the user will be able to save changes to the file.

B. **Incorrect:** If the NTFS permission for the \MKTG folder is Read, Write, and Execute, the user would be able to save changes to the file.

C. **Incorrect:** Being a member of the Everyone group, which has Full Control, has no effect on the NTFS permissions set for the /MKTG folder or for the file within the folder.

D. **Incorrect:** Being a member of the Everyone group, which has Full Control, has no effect on the NTFS permissions set for the /MKTG folder or for the file within the folder.

Further Reading

The *Microsoft Windows NT Network Administration* volume of the *Microsoft Windows NT Network Administration Training* kit Chapter 6, Lesson 2 provides details on combining share permissions and NTFS permissions and includes a short video and exercises explaining how the two types of permissions work together. Lesson 7 provides information on troubleshooting permission-related problems. Practice for troubleshooting permission problems is included on the CD provided with this kit.

The *Microsoft Windows NT Technical Support* volume of the *Microsoft Windows NT Technical Support Training* kit Chapter 12, Lesson 5 provides information on troubleshooting Remote Access Service.

Windows NT Workstation 4.0 Study Guide. Osborne McGraw-Hill, Berkeley, CA, 1998. ISBN 0-07-882492-3. Chapter 6 contains detailed information on access tokens, file and directory security using NTFS, share permissions, and moving and copying files and folders. There is also a discussion of using share permissions with NTFS permissions.

O B J E C T I V E   7 . 6

Modify the Registry using the appropriate tool in a given situation.

The Registry is a database where Windows NT stores the hardware and software configuration for a computer and the initialization information to load device drivers and network protocols. The following information is contained in the Registry:

- Hardware information.
- Installed device drivers.
- Installed applications.
- Installed network protocols.
- Network adapter card settings.
- User account information.

The Control Panel, User Manager, and System Policy Editor are provided in Windows NT to assist you in adding and changing the entries in the Registry. These applications are easier to use than the Registry and are the preferred interface for adding and changing configuration information. You should modify the Registry only if changes cannot be made using these applications. When viewing the Registry, you can select Read Only mode from the Options menu to avoid making inadvertent changes.

Registry Tools

The Registry provides two Registry Editors, REGEDT32 and REGEDIT, which allow you to make changes to the Registry. REGEDT32 is the 32-bit editor designed for Windows NT. REGEDIT is designed for Windows 95, but included with Windows NT. While both editors are similar, only REGEDT32 supports the security functions provided with the Registry and provides secondary mouse-click support. Only REGEDIT can search for specific values in the Registry (REGEDT32 can search for keys only).

The Registry Editors contain no checks for invalid entries. A change made to a configuration using the Registry is final.

In addition to the Registry Editors, the following administrative tools for managing the Registry are provided in Windows NT.

Tool	Description
Backup	Backs up the Registry hives in a tape backup routine.
Emergency repair disk	Restores hives to the system.
Repair Disk utility	Updates the emergency repair disk with a current backup of Registry hives.
Windows NT Explorer	Applies access controls to Registry Editor and hive files on NTFS partitions.

The following administrative tools for managing the Registry are provided on the *Microsoft Windows NT Workstation 4.0 Resource Kit* CD:

Tool	Description
REGBACK.EXE	Creates backups of Registry files.
REGENTRY.HLP	Documents Windows NT Registry entries.
REGINI.EXE	Makes Registry changes using script files.
REGREST.EXE	Restores Registry hives.

The Registry Structure

Five databases make up the Registry. You access Registry information through these databases, known as *subtrees*. The following table lists and briefly defines each subtree:

Subtree	Description
HKEY_LOCAL_MACHINE	Contains configuration data about the computer.
HKEY_USERS	Contains system default settings and the security ID (SID) of the user currently logged on to the computer.
HKEY_CURRENT_USER	Contains data about the user currently logged on interactively.
HKEY_CLASSES_ROOT	Contains information about file associations and data associated with COM objects.
HKEY_CURRENT_CONFIG	Contains data about the active hardware profile.

Questions related to this objective are designed to determine if you have an awareness of these issues. To successfully answer the questions for this objective, you need a firm understanding of several key terms. For definitions of these terms, refer to the Glossary in this book.

Key Terms

- Control set

- Hive

- Key

- Registry

- Registry Editor

- Subkey

- Subtree

70-073.07.06.001

Which tool should you use to search the entire Windows NT Workstation Registry for a key value?

A. SYSDIFF

B. REGEDIT

C. REGSVR32

D. REGEDT32

E. Event Viewer

70-073.07.06.002

Which tools can you use to modify the network settings in the Windows NT Workstation Registry? (Choose all that apply.)

A. REGINI

B. REGEDIT

C. REGEDT32

D. Event Viewer

E. Control Panel

F. Windows NT Diagnostics

70-073.07.06.001

Which tool should you use to search the entire Windows NT Workstation Registry for a key value?

▶ **Correct Answer: B**

A. **Incorrect:** The SYSDIFF utility is used to preinstall applications and cannot be used to search the entire Windows NT Workstation Registry for a key value.

B. **Correct:** REGEDIT, the Windows 95 Registry Editor included in the Windows NT Setup, contains a more powerful search engine than REGEDT32. REGEDIT allows you to find keys, values, and data in the Registry.

C. **Incorrect:** REGSVR32 is an application that registers dynamic-link libraries (DLLs) and ActiveX controls (formerly called *OLE Custom Controls*) in the Registry and cannot be used to search the entire Windows NT Workstation Registry for a key value.

D. **Incorrect:** REGEDT32 allows you to search only for keys and subkeys in the Registry and cannot be used to search the entire Windows NT Workstation Registry for a key value.

E. **Incorrect:** The Event Viewer provides information about events, including error and warning messages, and cannot be used to search the entire Windows NT Workstation Registry for a key value.

70-073.07.06.002

Which tools can you use to modify the network settings in the Windows NT Workstation Registry? (Choose all that apply.)

▶ **Correct Answers: B, C, and E**

A. **Incorrect:** REGINI makes Registry changes using script files and cannot be used to modify network settings in the Windows NT Workstation Registry.

B. **Correct:** The REGEDIT Registry Editor can be used to modify network settings in the Windows NT Workstation Registry under the HKEY_LOCAL_MACHINE\Software and HKEY_LOCAL_MACHINE\System keys.

C. **Correct:** The REGEDT32 Registry Editor can be used to modify network settings in the Windows NT Workstation Registry under the HKEY_LOCAL_MACHINE\Software and HKEY_LOCAL_MACHINE\System keys.

D. **Incorrect:** The Event Viewer provides information about events, including error and warning messages, and cannot be used to modify network settings in the Windows NT Workstation Registry.

E. **Correct:** The Network Adapters tab in the Network program on the Control Panel can be used to modify network settings in the Windows NT Workstation Registry.

F. **Incorrect:** Windows NT Diagnostics are used to display Registry information in an easily readable format and cannot be used to modify network settings in the Windows NT Workstation Registry.

70-073.07.06.003

Which tool should you use to modify Windows NT Workstation Registry settings using script files?

A. SYSDIFF

B. REGINI

C. REGSVR32

D. REGEDT32

E. Event Viewer

70-073.07.06.004

Which Windows NT Registry key should you modify if you want to modify the way a device driver behaves during system startup?

A. HKEY_LOCAL_MACHINE\System

B. HKEY_LOCAL_MACHINE\Hardware

C. HKEY_LOCAL_MACHINE\System\CurrentControlSet\Control

D. HKEY_LOCAL_MACHINE\System\CurrentControlSet\Services\DriverName

70-073.07.06.003

Which tool should you use to modify Windows NT Workstation Registry settings using script files?

▶ **Correct Answer: B**

A. **Incorrect:** The SYSDIFF utility is used to preinstall applications and cannot be used to modify Windows NT Workstation Registry settings using script files.

B. **Correct:** REGINI is a character-based batch file utility that you can use to make changes to the Windows NT Workstation Registry using script files.

C. **Incorrect:** REGSVR32 is an application that registers dynamic-link libraries (DLLs) and ActiveX controls (formerly called *OLE Custom Controls*) in the Registry and cannot be used to modify Windows NT Workstation Registry settings using script files.

D. **Incorrect:** REGEDT32 is a Registry Editor and cannot be used to modify Windows NT Workstation Registry settings using script files.

E. **Incorrect:** The Event Viewer provides information about events, including error and warning messages, and cannot be used to modify Windows NT Workstation Registry settings using script files.

70-073.07.06.004

Which Windows NT Registry key should you modify if you want to modify the way a device driver behaves during system startup?

▶ **Correct Answer: D**

A. **Incorrect:** The Local Machine subtree contains configuration data about the local computer. The System hive contains information about devices and services. However, you need to specify the key, subkey, and value to identify the device driver you want to modify.

B. **Incorrect:** The Local Machine subtree contains configuration data about the local computer. The Hardware key contains information collected each time the computer is started about the physical devices attached to the computer. Because this key is used to tell the computer how to react to hardware components, it cannot be used to modify the way a device driver behaves during system startup.

C. **Incorrect:** The Local Machine subtree contains configuration data about the local computer. The System hive contains information about devices and services. The CurrentControlSet subkey is used to link to the control set indicated by the value of *Current*. The Control subkey contains configuration data used to control the system, such as the computer name and subsystems to start. This is not the correct subkey; you require a subkey that contains drivers used in the system.

D. **Correct:** The Local Machine subtree contains configuration data about the local computer. The System hive contains information about devices and services. The CurrentControlSet subkey is used to link to the control set indicated by the value of *Current*. The Services subkey in each control set lists all device drivers, file system drivers, and Win32 service drivers. The DriverName value identifies the device driver you want to modify.

Further Reading

The *Microsoft Windows NT Technical Support* volume of the *Microsoft Windows NT Technical Support Training* kit Chapter 3, Lesson 1 provides basic information on the Registry structure. Lesson 4 contains information on using the Registry Editor. Practice for using the Registry Editor is included on the CD provided in this kit.

The *Microsoft Windows NT Workstation 4.0 Resource Kit* Chapter 23 provides an in-depth analysis of the Registry structure, including subtrees, keys, and subkeys. Chapter 24 provides detailed information on using the Registry Editors and a summary of administrative tools used for the Registry.

Windows NT Workstation 4.0 Study Guide. Osborne McGraw-Hill, Berkeley, CA, 1998. ISBN 0-07-882492-3. Chapter 3 contains information on the Registry structure and a comparison of the REGEDIT and REGEDT32 Registry Editors.

Use Microsoft Technical Support Online (http://support.microsoft.com/) by searching for "All Products" and for "REGSV32A.EXE." Then click "ACC:Regsv32a.exe Available on MSL" for a description of the REGSV32 program.

Implement advanced techniques to resolve various problems.

Windows NT provides the opportunity to debug kernel STOP errors using a memory dump file. You can configure your system to write a memory dump file to a location you specify every time a kernel STOP error occurs. The memory dump file provides all error information to troubleshoot a kernel STOP error as if you were connected to the computer experiencing the problem. The main purpose for creating a memory dump file is to generate a text file recreating the error for technical support personnel.

There are three utilities for processing memory dump files:

- **DUMPFLOP**—Writes a memory dump file to floppy disks.

- **DUMPCHK**—Verifies that a memory dump file has been created correctly.

- **DUMPEXAM**—Examines a memory dump file, extracts information from it, and writes the information to a text file.

You can set up this debugging action by accessing System Properties in the Control Panel. In the System Properties dialog box, select the Startup/Shutdown tab. Then click the checkbox labeled "Write debugging information to:" and specify the location where the file should be written. To overwrite existing memory dump files (file size is the same size as the computer's RAM) check the box labeled "Overwrite any existing file."

Questions related to this objective are designed to determine if you have an awareness of these issues. To successfully answer the questions for this objective, you need a firm understanding of several key terms. For definitions of these terms, refer to the Glossary in this book.

Key Terms

- DUMPCHK utility

- DUMPEXAM utility

- DUMPFLOP utility

- Kernel STOP errors

- Memory dump file

70-073.07.07.001

A Pentium-based Windows NT Workstation computer is experiencing frequent STOP errors. You are unable to determine the source of the problem because the workstation is located at a remote site.

The required result is to have the workstation user create a file that contains adequate debugging information to allow an analysis of the STOP errors.

The first optional result is to have the workstation user verify that a memory dump file has been created correctly. The second optional result is to have the workstation user create a text file from the memory dump file to send to support personnel.

The proposed solution is to create a memory dump file by having the workstation user access System Properties in Control Panel, select the "Write debugging information to:" recovery option, and specify a path and filename. Have the user copy the DUMPCHK.EXE, DUMPEXAM.EXE, IMAGEHLP.DLL, and KDEXTX86.DLL files from the Windows NT Workstation compact disc to a folder on the local hard drive. Have the user recreate the condition that caused the STOP error, run DUMPCHK, and then DUMPEXAM.

What does the solution provide?

A. The required result and both optional results.

B. The required result and one optional result.

C. The required result and neither optional result.

D. The proposed solution does not provide the optional result.

70-073.07.07.001

A Pentium-based Windows NT Workstation computer is experiencing frequent STOP errors. You are unable to determine the source of the problem because the workstation is located at a remote site.

The required result is to have the workstation user create a file that contains adequate debugging information to allow an analysis of the STOP errors.

The first optional result is to have the workstation user verify that a memory dump file has been created correctly. The second optional result is to have the workstation user create a text file from the memory dump file to send to support personnel.

The proposed solution is to create a memory dump file by having the workstation user access System Properties in Control Panel, select the "Write debugging information to:" recovery option, and specify a path and filename. Have the user copy the DUMPCHK.EXE, DUMPEXAM.EXE, IMAGEHLP.DLL, and KDEXTX86.DLL files from the Windows NT Workstation compact disc to a folder on the local hard drive. Have the user recreate the condition that caused the STOP error, run DUMPCHK, and then DUMPEXAM.

What does the solution provide?

▶ **Correct Answer: A**

A. **Correct:** Selecting the "Write debugging information to:" recovery option when a STOP error is generated creates a memory dump file the next time a STOP error is encountered. This file contains adequate debugging information to allow an analysis of the STOP error. Copying the listed files from the Windows NT Workstation CD allows the workstation user to use the utilities for processing memory dump files. The DUMPCHK utility is used to verify that the memory dump file has been created correctly. Then the memory dump file is examined by the DUMPEXAM utility, which extracts information and writes it to a text file that can be sent to support personnel.

B. **Incorrect:** See the explanation for answer A.

C. **Incorrect:** See the explanation for answer A.

D. **Incorrect:** See the explanation for answer A.

70-073.07.07.002

A Pentium-based Windows NT Workstation computer is experiencing frequent STOP errors. You are unable to determine the source of the problem because the workstation is located at a remote site.

The required result is to have the workstation user create a file that contains adequate debugging information to allow an analysis of the STOP errors.

The first optional result is to have the workstation user verify that a memory dump file has been created correctly. The second optional result is to have the workstation user create a text file from the memory dump file to send to support personnel.

The proposed solution is to create a memory dump file by having the workstation user access System Properties in the Control Panel, and select the "Write an event to the system log" recovery option. Have the user copy the DUMPCHK.EXE, DUMPEXAM.EXE, IMAGEHLP.DLL, and KDEXTX86.DLL files from the Windows NT Workstation compact disc to a folder on the local hard drive. Have the user recreate the condition that caused the STOP error, and run the DUMPCHK and DUMPEXAM utilities.

What does the solution provide?

A. The required result and both optional results.

B. The required result and one optional result.

C. The required result and neither optional result.

D. The proposed solution does not provide the required result.

70-073.07.07.002

A Pentium-based Windows NT Workstation computer is experiencing frequent STOP errors. You are unable to determine the source of the problem because the workstation is located at a remote site.

The required result is to have the workstation user create a file that contains adequate debugging information to allow an analysis of the STOP errors.

The first optional result is to have the workstation user verify that a memory dump file has been created correctly. The second optional result is to have the workstation user create a text file from the memory dump file to send to support personnel.

The proposed solution is to create a memory dump file by having the workstation user access System Properties in the Control Panel, and select the "Write an event to the system log" recovery option. Have the user copy the DUMPCHK.EXE, DUMPEXAM.EXE, IMAGEHLP.DLL, and KDEXTX86.DLL files from the Windows NT Workstation compact disc to a folder on the local hard drive. Have the user recreate the condition that caused the STOP error, and run the DUMPCHK and DUMPEXAM utilities.

What does the solution provide?

▶ **Correct Answer: D**

A. **Incorrect:** See the explanation for answer D.

B. **Incorrect:** See the explanation for answer D.

C. **Incorrect:** See the explanation for answer D.

D. **Correct:** Selecting the "Write an event to the system log" Recovery option when a STOP error is generated allows you only to use the Event Viewer for troubleshooting. This action does not create the memory dump file that contains the debugging information for the STOP errors. Since the DUMPCHK and DUMPEXAM utilities require a memory dump file, these utilities cannot verify that a memory dump file has been created correctly or create a text file to send to support personnel.

70-073.07.07.003

A Pentium-based Windows NT Workstation computer is experiencing frequent STOP errors. You are unable to determine the source of the problem because the workstation is located at a remote site.

The required result is to have the workstation user create a file that contains adequate debugging information to allow an analysis of the STOP errors.

The first optional result is to have the workstation user verify that a memory dump file has been created correctly. The second optional result is to have the workstation user create a text file from the memory dump file to send to support personnel.

The proposed solution is to create a memory dump file by having the workstation user access System Properties in the Control Panel, select the "Write debugging information to:" recovery option, and specify a path and filename. Have the user copy the DUMPCHK.EXE, DUMPFLOP.EXE, IMAGEHLP.DLL, and KDEXTX86.DLL files from the Windows NT Workstation compact disc to a folder on the local hard drive. Have the user recreate the condition that caused the STOP error, and run the DUMPCHK and DUMPFLOP utilities.

What does the solution provide?

A. The required result and both optional results.

B. The required result and one optional result.

C. The required result but none of the optional results.

D. The proposed solution does not provide the optional result.

70-073.07.07.003

A Pentium-based Windows NT Workstation computer is experiencing frequent STOP errors. You are unable to determine the source of the problem because the workstation is located at a remote site.

The required result is to have the workstation user create a file that contains adequate debugging information to allow an analysis of the STOP errors.

The first optional result is to have the workstation user verify that a memory dump file has been created correctly. The second optional result is to have the workstation user create a text file from the memory dump file to send to support personnel.

The proposed solution is to create a memory dump file by having the workstation user access System Properties in the Control Panel, select the "Write debugging information to:" recovery option, and specify a path and filename. Have the user copy the DUMPCHK.EXE, DUMPFLOP.EXE, IMAGEHLP.DLL, and KDEXTX86.DLL files from the Windows NT Workstation compact disc to a folder on the local hard drive. Have the user recreate the condition that caused the STOP error, and run the DUMPCHK and DUMPFLOP utilities.

What does the solution provide?

▶ **Correct Answer: B**

A. **Incorrect:** See the explanation for answer B.

B. **Correct:** Selecting the "Write debugging information to" Recovery option when a STOP error is generated creates a memory dump file. This file contains adequate debugging information to allow an analysis of the STOP error. Copying the listed files from the Windows NT Workstation CD allows the workstation user to use the utilities for processing memory dump files. The DUMPCHK utility is used to verify that the memory dump file has been created correctly. However, the DUMPFLOP utility cannot be used to create a text file from the memory dump file to send to support personnel. The DUMPFLOP utility is used to write a memory dump file in segments to floppy disks.

C. **Incorrect:** See the explanation for answer B.

D. **Incorrect:** See the explanation for answer B.

70-073.07.07.004

You are experiencing Kernel STOP errors on your Windows NT Workstation computer. You had previously configured your machine to write a memory dump file each time this occurs.

Which DUMPEXAM command should you use to obtain an analysis of virtual memory usage on your system at the time of the memory dump?

A. !VM

B. !MEMUSAGE

C. !LOCKS

D. !PROCESS

70-073.07.07.004

You are experiencing Kernel STOP errors on your Windows NT Workstation computer. You had previously configured your machine to write a memory dump file each time this occurs.

Which DUMPEXAM command should you use to obtain an analysis of virtual memory usage on your system at the timc of the memory dump?

▶ **Correct Answer: A**

A. **Correct:** The !VM command displays the current virtual memory usage of the system.

B. **Incorrect:** The !MEMUSAGE command displays the current memory usage of the system.

C. **Incorrect:** The !LOCKS command displays all locks held on resources by threads and is used to determine the nonexecuting thread that is locking a resource needed by an executing thread. The !LOCKS command is not used to obtain an analysis of conventional and virtual memory usage.

D. **Incorrect:** The !PROCESS command displays information on the process currently running. The !PROCESS command is not used to obtain an analysis of conventional and virtual memory usage.

Further Reading

 The *Microsoft Windows NT Workstation 4.0 Resource Kit* Chapter 39 provides detailed information on creating a memory dump file and using the DUMPEXAM, DUMPFLOP, and DUMPCHK utilities.

The Microsoft Certified Professional Program

The Microsoft Certified Professional (MCP) program is designed to comprehensively assess and maintain software-related skills. Microsoft has developed several certifications to provide industry recognition of a candidate's knowledge and proficiency with Microsoft products and technologies. This appendix provides suggestions to help you prepare for an MCP exam, and describes the process for taking the exam. The appendix also contains an overview of the benefits associated with certification, and gives you an example of the exam track you might take for MCSE certification.

Preparing for an MCP Exam

This section contains tips and information to help you prepare for a Microsoft Certified Professional certification exam. Besides study and test-taking tips, this section provides information on how and where to register, test fees, and what to expect upon arrival at the testing center.

Studying for an Exam

The best way to prepare for a Microsoft Certified Professional exam is to study, learn, and master the technology or operating system on which you will be tested. The Readiness Review can help complete your understanding of the software or technology by assessing your practical knowledge and helping you focus on additional areas of study. For example, if you are pursuing the Microsoft Certified Systems Engineer (MCSE) certification, you must learn and use the tested Microsoft operating system. You can then use the Readiness Review to understand the skills that test your knowledge of the operating system, perform suggested practices with the operating system, and ascertain additional areas where you should focus your study by using the electronic assessment.

▶   **To prepare for any certification exam**

1. Identify the objectives for the exam.

   The Readiness Review lists and describes the objectives you will be tested on during the exam.

2. Assess your current mastery of those objectives.

   The Readiness Review electronic assessment tool is a great way to test your grasp of the objectives.

3. Practice the job skills for the objectives you have not mastered and read more information about the subjects tested in each of these objectives.

   You can take the electronic assessment multiple times until you feel comfortable with the subject material.

Your Practical Experience

MCP exams test the specific skills needed on the job. Since in the real world you are rarely called upon to recite a list of facts, the exams go beyond testing your knowledge of a product or terminology. Instead, you are asked to *apply* your knowledge to a situation, analyze a technical problem, and decide on the best solution. Your hands-on experience with the software and technology will greatly enhance your performance on the exam.

Test Registration and Fees

You can schedule your exam up to six weeks in advance, or as late as one working day before the exam date. Sylvan Prometric and Virtual University Enterprises (VUE) administer all the Microsoft Certified Professional exams. To take an exam at an authorized Prometric Testing Center, in the United States call Sylvan at 800-755-EXAM (3926). To register online, or for more registration information, visit Sylvan's Web site at http://www.slspro.com. For information about taking exams at a VUE testing center, visit the VUE information page at http://www.vue.com, or call 888-837-8616 in the United States. When you register, you will need the following information:

- Unique identification number (This is usually your Social Security or Social Insurance number. The testing center also assigns an identification number, which provides another way to distinguish your identity and test records.)

- Mailing address and phone number

- E-mail address

- Organization or company name

- Method of payment (Payment must be made in advance, usually with a credit card or check.)

Testing fees vary from country to country, but in the United States and many other countries the exams cost approximately $100 (U.S.). Contact the testing vendor for exact pricing. Prices are subject to change, and in some countries, additional taxes may be applied.

When you schedule the exam, you will be provided with instructions regarding the appointment, cancellation procedures, identification requirements, and information about the testing center location.

Taking an Exam

If this is your first Microsoft certification exam, you may find the following information helpful upon arrival at the testing center.

Arriving at Testing Center

When you arrive at the testing center, you will be asked to sign a log book, and show two forms of identification, including one photo identification (such as a driver's license or company security identification). Before you may take the exam, you will be asked to sign a Non-Disclosure Agreement and a Testing Center Regulations form, which explains the rules you will be expected to comply with during the test. Upon leaving the exam room at the end of the test, you will again sign the log book.

Exam Details

Before you begin the exam, the test administrator will provide detailed instructions about how to complete the exam, and how to use the testing computer or software. Because the exams are timed, if you have any questions, ask the exam administrator before the exam begins. Consider arriving 10 to 15 minutes early so you will have time to relax and ask questions before the exam begins. Some exams may include additional materials or exhibits (such as diagrams). If any exhibits are required for your exam, the test administrator will provide you with them before you begin the exam and collect them from you at the end of the exam.

The exams are all closed book. You may not use a laptop computer or have any notes or printed material with you during the exam session. You will be provided with a set amount of blank paper for use during the exam. All paper will be collected from you at the end of the exam.

The Exam Tutorial

The test administrator will show you to your test computer and will handle any preparations necessary to start the testing tool and display the exam on the computer. Before you begin your exam, you can take the exam tutorial which is designed to familiarize you with computer-administered tests by offering questions similar to those on the exam. Taking the tutorial does not affect your allotted time for the exam.

Exam Length and Available Time

The number of questions on each exam varies, as does the amount of time allotted for each exam. Generally, certification exams consist of 50 to 70 questions and take approximately 90 minutes to complete. Specific information about the number of exam questions and available time will be provided to you when you register.

Tips for Taking the Exam

Since the testing software lets you move forward and backward through the exam, answer the easy questions first. Then go back and spend the remaining time on the harder questions.

When answering the multiple-choice questions, eliminate the obviously incorrect answers first. There are no trick questions on the test, so the correct answer will always be among the list of possible answers.

Answer all the questions before you quit the exam. An unanswered question is scored as an incorrect answer. If you are unsure of the answer, make an educated guess.

Your Rights as a Test Taker

As an exam candidate, you are entitled to the best support and environment possible for your exam. In particular, you are entitled to a quiet, uncluttered test environment and knowledgeable and professional test administrators. You should not hesitate to ask the administrator any questions before the exam begins, and you should also be given time to take the online testing tutorial. Before leaving, you should be given the opportunity to submit comments about the testing center, staff, or about the test itself.

Getting Your Exam Results

After you have completed an exam, you will immediately receive your score online and be given a printed Examination Score Report which also breaks down the results by section. Passing scores on the different certification exams vary. You do not need to send these scores to Microsoft. The test center automatically forwards them to Microsoft within five working days, and if you pass the exam, Microsoft sends a confirmation to you within two to four weeks.

If you do not pass a certification exam, you may call the testing vendor to schedule a time to retake the exam. Before re-examination, you should review the appropriate sections of the Readiness Review, and focus additional study on the topic areas where your exam results could be improved. Please note that you must pay the full registration fee again each time you retake an exam.

About the Exams

Microsoft Certified Professional exams follow recognized standards for validity and reliability. They are developed by technical experts who receive input from job-function and technology experts.

How MCP Exams Are Developed

To ensure the validity and reliability of the certification exams, Microsoft adheres to a rigorous exam-development process that includes an analysis of the tasks performed in specific job functions. Microsoft then translates the job tasks into a comprehensive set of objectives which measure knowledge, problem-solving abilities, and skill level. The objectives are prioritized and then reviewed by technical experts to create the certification exam questions. (These objectives are also the basis for developing the Readiness Review series.) Technical and job function experts review the exam objectives and questions several times before releasing the final exam.

Computer-Adaptive Testing

Microsoft is developing more effective ways to determine who meets the criteria for certification by introducing innovative testing technologies. One of these testing technologies is computer-adaptive testing (CAT). This testing method is currently available on a few certification exams, and may not be available for the exam you are currently studying. When taking this exam, all test takers start with an easy-to-moderate question. Those who answer the question correctly get a more difficult follow-up question. If that question is answered correctly, the difficulty of subsequent questions also increases. Conversely, if the second question is answered incorrectly, the following questions will be easier. This process continues until the testing system determines the test taker's ability.

With this system, everyone may answer the same percentage of questions correctly, but because the high-ability people can answer more difficult questions correctly, they will receive a higher score. To learn more about computer adaptive testing and other testing innovations visit http://www.microsoft.com/mcp.

If You Have a Concern about the Exam Content

Microsoft Certified Professional exams are developed by technical and testing experts, with input and participation from job-function and technology experts. Microsoft ensures that the exams adhere to recognized standards for validity and reliability. Candidates generally consider them to be relevant and fair. If you feel that an exam question is inappropriate or if you believe the correct answer shown to be incorrect, write or call Microsoft at the e-mail address or phone number listed for the Microsoft Certified Professional Program in the "References" section of this appendix.

Although Microsoft and the exam administrators are unable to respond to individual questions and issues raised by candidates, all input from candidates is thoroughly researched and taken into consideration during development of subsequent versions of the exams. Microsoft is committed to ensuring the quality of these exams, and your input is a valuable resource.

Overview of the MCP Program

Becoming a Microsoft Certified Professional is the best way to show employers, clients, and colleagues that you have the knowledge and skills required by the industry. Microsoft's certification program is one of the industry's most comprehensive programs for assessing and maintaining software-related skills, and the MCP designation is recognized by technical managers worldwide as a mark of competence.

Certification Programs

Microsoft offers a variety of certifications so you can choose the one that meets your job needs and career goals. The MCP program focuses on measuring a candidate's ability to perform a specific job function, such as one performed by a systems engineer or a Solution Developer. Successful completion of the certification requirements indicates your expertise in the field. Microsoft certifications include:

- Microsoft Certified Systems Engineer (MCSE)
- Microsoft Certified Systems Engineer + Internet (MCSE + I)
- Microsoft Certified Professional (MCP)
- Microsoft Certified Professional + Internet (MCP + I)
- Microsoft Certified Professional + Site Building
- Microsoft Certified Solution Developer (MCSD)

Microsoft Certified Systems Engineer (MCSE)

Microsoft Certified Systems Engineers have a high level of expertise with Microsoft Windows NT and the Microsoft BackOffice integrated family of server software, and can plan, implement, maintain, and support information systems with these products.

MCSEs are required to pass four operating system exams and two elective exams. The Networking Essentials exam earns core credit toward this certification.

MCSE Exam Requirements
You can select a Microsoft Windows NT 3.51 or Microsoft Windows NT 4.0 track for the MCSE certification. From within the track you have selected, you must pass four core operating system exams, and then pass two elective exams. Visit the Microsoft Certified Professional Web site for details about current exam requirements, exam alternatives, and retired exams. This roadmap outlines the path an MCSE candidate would pursue for Windows NT 4.0.

Microsoft Windows NT 4.0 Core Exams
You must pass four core exams and two elective exams. You may choose between Windows 95, Windows NT Workstation 4.0, or Windows 98 for one of the core exams. The core exams are as follows:

Exam 70-067: Implementing and Supporting Microsoft Windows NT Server 4.0

Exam 70-068: Implementing and Supporting Microsoft Windows NT Server 4.0 in the Enterprise

Exam 70-064: Implementing and Supporting Microsoft Windows 95, or exam 70-073: Microsoft Windows NT Workstation 4.0, or exam 70-098: Implementing and Supporting Microsoft Windows 98

Exam 70-058: Networking Essentials

MCSE Electives
The elective exams you choose are the same for all Windows NT tracks. You must choose two exams from the following list.

Exam 70-013: Implementing and Supporting Microsoft SNA Server 3.0, or exam 70-085: Implementing and Supporting Microsoft SNA Server 4.0 (If both SNA Server exams are passed, only one qualifies as an MCSE elective.)

Exam 70-018: Implementing and Supporting Microsoft Systems Management Server 1.2, or exam 70-086: Implementing and Supporting Microsoft Systems Management Server 2.0 (If both SMS exams are passed, only one qualifies as an MCSE elective.)

Exam 70-021: Microsoft SQL Server 4.2 Database Implementation, or exam 70-027: Implementing a Database Design on Microsoft SQL Server 6.5, or exam 70-029: Implementing a Database Design on Microsoft SQL Server 7.0 (If more than one SQL Server exam is passed, only one qualifies as an MCSE elective. Also note that exam 70-021 is scheduled to be retired in 1999.)

Exam 70-022: Microsoft SQL Server 4.2 Database Administration for Microsoft Windows NT, exam 70-026: System Administration for Microsoft SQL Server 6.5, or exam 70-028: System Administration for Microsoft SQL Server 7.0 (If more than one exam is passed from this group, only one would qualify as an MCSE elective. Also note that exam 70-022 is scheduled to be retired in 1999.)

Exam 70-053: Internetworking Microsoft TCP/IP on Microsoft Windows NT (3.5-3.51), or exam 70-059: Internetworking with Microsoft TCP/IP on Microsoft Windows NT 4.0 (If both exams are passed, only one would qualify as an MCSE elective.)

Exam 70-056: Implementing and Supporting Web Sites Using Microsoft Site Server 3.0

Exam 70-076: Implementing and Supporting Microsoft Exchange Server 5, or exam 70-081: Implementing and Supporting Microsoft Exchange Server 5.5 (If more than one of these exams is passed, only one would qualify as an MCSE elective.)

Exam 70-077: Implementing and Supporting Microsoft Internet Information Server 3.0 and Microsoft Index Server 1.1, or exam 70-087: Implementing and Supporting Microsoft Internet Information Server 4.0 (If both exams are passed, only one would qualify as an MCSE elective.)

Exam 70-078: Implementing and Supporting Microsoft Proxy Server 1.0, or exam 70-088: Implementing and Supporting Microsoft Proxy Server 2.0 (If both exams are passed, only one would qualify as an MCSE elective.)

Exam 70-079: Implementing and Supporting Microsoft Internet Explorer 4.0 by Using the Internet Explorer Administration Kit

Note that certification requirements may change. In addition, some retired certification exams may qualify for credit towards current certification programs. For the latest details on core and elective exams, go to http://www.microsoft.com/mcp and review the appropriate certification.

Novell, Banyan, and Sun Exemptions

The Microsoft Certified Professional program grants credit for the networking exam requirement for candidates who are certified as Novell CNEs, Master CNEs, or CNIs, Banyan CBSs or CBEs, or Sun Certified Network Administrators for Solaris 2.5 or 2.6. Go to the Microsoft Certified Professional Web site at http://www.microsoft.com/mcp for current information and details.

Other Certification Programs

In addition to the MCSE certification, Microsoft has created other certification programs that focus on specific job functions and career goals.

Microsoft Certified Systems Engineer + Internet (MCSE + I)

An individual with the MCSE + Internet credential is qualified to enhance, deploy and manage sophisticated intranet and Internet solutions that include a browser, proxy server, host servers, database, and messaging and commerce components.

Microsoft Certified Systems Engineers with a specialty in the Internet are required to pass seven operating system exams and two elective exams.

Microsoft Certified Professional (MCP)

Microsoft Certified Professionals have demonstrated in-depth knowledge of at least one Microsoft product. An MCP has passed a minimum of one Microsoft operating system exam, and may pass additional Microsoft Certified Professional exams to further qualify his or her skills in a particular area of specialization. A Microsoft Certified Professional has extensive knowledge about specific products but has not completed a job-function certification. The MCP credential provides a solid background for other Microsoft certifications.

Microsoft Certified Professional + Internet (MCP + I)

A person receiving the Microsoft Certified Professional + Internet certification is qualified to plan security, install and configure server products, manage server resources, extend servers to run CGI scripts or ISAPI scripts, monitor and analyze performance, and troubleshoot problems.

Microsoft Certified Professional + Site Building

Microsoft has recently created a certification designed for Web site developers. Individuals with the Microsoft Certified Professional + Site Building credential are qualified to plan, build, maintain, and manage Web sites using Microsoft technologies and products. The credential is appropriate for people who manage sophisticated, interactive Web sites that include database connectivity, multimedia, and searchable content. Microsoft Certified Professionals with a specialty in site building are required to pass two exams that measure technical proficiency and expertise.

Microsoft Certified Solution Developer (MCSD)

The Microsoft Certified Solution Developer credential is the premium certification for professionals who design and develop custom business solutions with Microsoft development tools, technologies, and platforms. The MCSD certification exams test the candidate's ability to build Web-based, distributed, and commerce applications by using Microsoft's products, such as Microsoft SQL Server, Microsoft Visual Studio, and Microsoft Transaction Server.

Certification Benefits

Obtaining Microsoft certification has many advantages. Industry professionals recognize Microsoft Certified Professionals for their knowledge and proficiency with Microsoft products and technologies. Microsoft helps to establish the program's recognition by promoting the expertise of MCPs within the industry. By becoming a Microsoft Certified Professional, you will join a worldwide community of technical professionals who have validated their expertise with Microsoft products.

In addition, you will have access to technical and product information directly from Microsoft through a secured area of the MCP Web Site. You will be invited to

Microsoft conferences, technical training sessions, and special events. MCPs also receive *Microsoft Certified Professional Magazine,* a career and professional development magazine.

Your organization will receive benefits when you obtain your certification. Research shows that Microsoft certification provides organizations with increased customer satisfaction and decreased support costs through improved service, increased productivity, and greater technical self-sufficiency. It also gives companies a reliable benchmark for hiring, promoting, and career planning.

Skills 2000 Program

Microsoft launched the Skills 2000 initiative to address the gap between the number of open jobs in the computing industry and the lack of skilled professionals to fill them. The program, launched in 1997, builds upon the success of Microsoft's training and certification programs to reach a broader segment of the work force. Many of today's computing professionals consider the current skills gap to be their primary business challenge.

Skills 2000 aims to significantly reduce the skills gap by reaching out to individuals currently in the computing work force, as well as those interested in developing a career in information technology. The program focuses on finding and placing skilled professionals in the job market today with Microsoft Solution Provider organizations. Microsoft will also facilitate internships between MSPs and students developing IT skills. In addition, Skills 2000 targets academic instructors at high schools, colleges and universities by offering free technical training to teachers and professors who are educating the work force of tomorrow.

For more information about the Skills 2000 initiative, visit the Skills 2000 site at http://www.microsoft.com/skills2000. This site includes information about starting a career in Information Technology (IT), IT-related articles, and a career aptitude tool.

Volunteer Technical Contributors

To volunteer for participation in one or more of the exam development phases, please sign up using the Technical Contributors online form on the MCP Web site: http://www.microsoft.com/mcp/examinfo/certsd.htm.

References

To find out more about Microsoft certification materials and programs, to register with an exam administrator, or to get other useful resources, check the following references. For Microsoft references outside the United States or Canada, contact your local Microsoft office.

Microsoft Certified Professional Program

To find information about Microsoft certification exams and information to help you prepare for any specific exam, go to http://www.microsoft.com/mcp, send e-mail to mcp@msprograms.com, or call 800-636-7544.

The MCP online magazine provides information for and about Microsoft Certified Professionals. The magazine is also a good source for exam tips. You can view the online magazine at http://www.mcpmag.com.

Microsoft Developer Network (MSDN)

The MSDN subscription center is your official source for software development kits, device driver kits, operating systems, and information about developing applications for Microsoft Windows and Windows NT. You can visit MSDN at http://www.microsoft.com/msdn or call 800-759-5474.

Microsoft Press

Microsoft Press offers comprehensive learning and training resources to help you get the most from Microsoft technology. For information about books published by Microsoft Press, go to http://mspress.microsoft.com, or call 800-MSPRESS.

Microsoft Press ResourceLink

Microsoft Press ResourceLink is an online information resource for IT professionals who deploy, manage, or support Microsoft products and technologies. ResourceLink gives you access to the latest technical updates, tools, and utilities from Microsoft, and is the most complete source of technical information about Microsoft technologies available anywhere. You can reach ResourceLink at http//mspress.microsoft.com/reslink.

Microsoft TechNet IT Home

Microsoft TechNet IT Home is a resource designed for IT professionals. You can find information on current IT topics, resources, and reference material at http://www.microsoft.com/ithome.

Microsoft Training and Certification Web Site

You can find lists of various study aids for the certification exams at http://www.microsoft.com/train_cert.

Self Test Software

Self Test Software provides the Readiness Review online assessment. For an additional fee, Self Test Software will provide test questions for this exam and other certification exams. For further information go to http://www.stsware.com/microsts.htm.

Sylvan Prometric Testing Centers

To register to take a Microsoft Certified Professional exam at any of the Sylvan Prometric testing centers around the world, go online at http://www.slspro.com. In the United States, you can call 800-755-EXAM.

Virtual University Enterprises (VUE)

You can register for a certification exam with VUE by using online registration, registering in person at a VUE testing center, or by calling 888-837-8616 in the United States. Visit http://www.vue.com/ms for testing sites, available examinations, and other registration numbers.

Glossary

A

access token An object that uniquely identifies a user who has logged on. An access token is attached to all of the user's processes and contains the user's security ID (SID), the SIDs of any groups to which the user belongs, any permissions that the user owns, the default owner of any objects that the user's processes create, and the default access control list to be applied to any objects that the user's processes create.

Advanced RISC Computer Specifications (ARC) pathname Used to describe the location of the boot partition of each instance of Windows NT installed on the computer.

answer file A script you create to run an unattended installation. The file can provide answers during text-mode setup that a user would otherwise be prompted for during the GUI-mode setup. (GUI stands for *graphical user interface*.)

application-termination message Messages warning you that the kernel is about to terminate either a process or a thread.

automated installation A way of installing Windows NT Workstation on a computer from the server automatically, without logging on to the computer.

B

backup domain controller (BDC) In a Windows NT Server domain, a computer running Windows NT Server that receives a copy of the domain's directory database, which contains all account and security policy information for the domain. The copy is synchronized periodically and automatically with the master copy on the primary domain controller. BDCs also authenticate user logons and can be promoted to function as PDCs as needed. Multiple BDCs can exist on a domain.

base priority levels Range from 0–31 and determine the status of a process or thread in relation to others.

bindings Connections that establish a communication channel between network cards, protocols, and services installed on a computer.

bottleneck A condition in which the limitations in one component prevent the whole system from operating faster. The device with the lowest maximum throughput is the most likely to become a bottleneck if it is in demand.

bus-mastering DMA The disk controller manages the I/O bus and uses the DMA controller to manage DMA operation.

C

cache A special memory subsystem that stores the contents of frequently accessed RAM locations and the addresses where these data items are stored.

callback A logon option for Dial-Up Networking that configures the server to disconnect and call the client back following authentication to reduce telephone charges and increase security.

clear-text passwords Passwords that are not scrambled, thus making them more susceptible to deciphering.

client A computer that accesses shared network resources provided by another computer, called a *server*.

Client Services for NetWare (CSNW) Software included with Windows NT Workstation, enables computers running Windows NT Workstation to make direct connections to file and printer resources at NetWare servers running NetWare 2.*x* or later.

computer name A unique name of up to 15 uppercase characters that identifies a computer to the network. The name cannot be the same as any other computer or domain name in the network.

Control Panel A graphic interface for configuring hardware and software for Windows NT Workstation.

Control Panel applications Applications that allow you to control configurations for a computer that are used regardless of which user is logged on to the computer.

control set Data required to control startup for Windows NT.

CONVERT utility Allows you to convert a FAT or HPFS partition to NTFS. This is a one-way process; there is no way to convert an NTFS partition to FAT or HPFS.

Creator Owner group Includes the user that created or took ownership of a resource. If a member of the Administrators group takes ownership of a resource, the new owner is the Administrators group. The Creater Owner group can be used to manage access to files and folders on NTFS volumes.

D

data link control (DLC) A protocol provided with Windows NT, primarily for accessing IBM mainframe computers rather than general networking on Windows NT. DLC is also used to connect printers that are connected directly to a LAN rather than to a specific computer.

default configuration The configuration saved when you shut down the computer.

default gateway In TCP/IP, the intermediate network device (router) on the local network that has knowledge of the network IDs of the other networks on the Internet. This is so it can forward the packets to the other gateways until the packet is eventually delivered to a gateway connected to the specified destination.

default printer The printer that is used if you choose the Print command without first specifying which printer you want to use with an application. You can have only one default printer; it should be the printer you use most often.

despooling The process of reading a spool file and sending the contents to a print device.

device driver A program that enables a specific piece of hardware (device) to communicate with Windows NT. Although a device may be installed on your system, Windows NT cannot recognize the device until you have installed and configured the appropriate driver.

Dial-Up Networking Provides low-speed connections and used by clients connecting to a RAS server or Internet service provider (ISP).

difference file A file used in the SYSDIFF utility that includes all the binary files, as well as the initialization file settings and registry settings, for the applications to be preinstalled.

direct memory access (DMA) Memory access that does not involve the microprocessor and is frequently used for data transfer directly between memory and an "intelligent" peripheral device, such as a disk drive.

disk controller A special-purpose chip and associated circuitry that directs and controls reading from and writing to a computer's disk drive. A disk controller handles such tasks as positioning the read/write head, mediating between the drive and the microprocessor, and controlling the transfer of information to and from memory. Disk controllers are used with floppy disk drives and hard disks and can either be built into the system or be part of a card that plugs into an expansion slot.

Distributed Component Object Model (DCOM) A tool (also known as *Networked OLE [object linking and embedding]*) used to integrate client/server applications across multiple computers using reusable and replaceable objects.

domain A collection of computers, defined by the administrator of a Windows NT Server network, that share a common directory database. A domain provides access to the centralized user accounts and group accounts maintained by the domain administrator. Each domain has a unique name.

Domain Name System (DNS) A TCP/IP protocol naming convention consisting of two parts: a host name and a domain name.

domain user account Contains information that defines a user to the domain. A user can log on to the domain and gain access to domain resources from any computer on the network using a single user account and password.

dual-boot computer A computer that can boot two different operating systems, with the choice of operating system to be made during system startup.

DUMPCHK utility Verifies that a memory dump file has been created correctly.

DUMPEXAM utility Examines a memory dump file, extracts information from it, and writes the information to a text file.

DUMPFLOP utility Writes a memory dump file to floppy disks.

Dynamic Host Configuration Protocol (DHCP) A protocol that offers dynamic configuration of IP addresses and related information.

E

emergency repair process The process of returning a computer running Windows NT to the state of the last emergency repair update using the original installation disks and the emergency repair disk.

emergency repair disk A disk that can (together with the original installation disks) repair missing or corrupt Windows NT files and restore the Registry.

encryption The process of making information indecipherable to protect it from unauthorized viewing or use, especially during transmission or when it is stored on a transportable magnetic medium.

environment variables Strings containing information such as a drive, path, or filename. These variables provide information that affects the behavior

of certain applications. For example, the TEMP environment variable specifies where applications can store temporary files.

event Any significant occurrence in the system or in an application that requires users to be notified or requires an entry added to a log.

Event Viewer Provides information about errors, warnings, and the successes or failures of tasks. This information is stored in one of three types of logs: system log, security log, or application log.

Everyone group Includes all local and remote users who have connected to the computer, including those who connect as Guest. You cannot control who becomes a member of the Everyone group; however, you can assign permissions and rights.

extended memory Memory beyond 1 megabyte in 80286, 80386, 80486, and Pentium computers.

F

fault tolerance Ensures data integrity when hardware failures occur.

FDISK utility An MS-DOS utility used to prepare a hard disk for an operating system, including the setup and deletion of system partitions.

File and Print Services for NetWare (FPNW) A Windows NT add-on utility that integrates NetWare clients into a Windows NT network and also allows them to access resources on computers running Windows NT Server.

file system In an operating system, the overall structure in which files are named, stored, and organized. NTFS and FAT are the two types of file systems supported by Windows NT.

File Transfer Protocol (FTP) Used to transfer files between local and remote systems on a TCP/IP network and will allow users on a company intranet to be able to transfer files to and from the Web site.

frame type Defines the way a network adapter card formats data to be sent over the network.

G

Gateway Service for NetWare (GSNW) Software included with Windows NT Workstation, enabling computers running Windows NT Server and using NWLink as a transport protocol to access files and printers at NetWare servers.

global groups Used to organize domain user accounts, typically by function or geographical location. Global groups can contain only user accounts from the domain where the global group is created. They cannot contain local groups or other global groups.

Gopher service A hierarchical system for finding and retrieving text files from Gopher servers on the Internet that will not allow users on a company intranet to navigate HTML documents.

group In User Manager or User Manager for Domains, an account containing other accounts, called *members*. The permissions and rights granted to a group are also provided to its members, making groups a convenient way to grant common capabilities to collections of user accounts. For Windows NT Workstation, groups are managed with User Manager.

GUI-mode setup In GUI mode, the user is presented with a graphical user interface and prompted for information used to customize the setup, such as which components to install. During GUI-mode setup, computer-specific information such as the computer name and username are supplied.

H

hardware profile Stores the configuration(s) for a set of devices and services.

hive A section of the Registry that appears as a file on your hard disk. The Registry subtree is divided into hives. A hive is a discrete body of keys, subkeys, and values that is rooted at the top of the Registry hierarchy.

HOSTS file A local text file that maps remote host names to IP addresses.

I

individual permissions Six NTFS permissions provided by Windows NT to specify the access that a user or group can have to the folder or file.

input/output (I/O) Read or write actions a computer performs. Reading is done with input devices such as the keyboard and the mouse, as well as disk files, while writing is usually done via the display and the printer for the user and via disk files or communications ports for the computer.

Integrated Services Digital Network (ISDN) line A type of telephone line used to enhance WAN speeds, ISDN lines provide two B channels for carrying voice and data at 64 kilobits per second and one D-channel for carrying information about the call at 16 kilobits a second. An ISDN line must be installed by the telephone company at both the server site and the remote site.

Internet Information Server (IIS) A network file and information server that supports multiple protocols. Primarily, Internet Information Server transmits information in Hypertext Markup Language (HTML) pages by using the Hypertext Transport Protocol (HTTP).

Internet Protocol (IP) address Used to identify a node on a network and to specify routing information. Each node on the network must be assigned a unique IP address, which is made up of the network ID, plus a unique host ID assigned by the network administrator. This address is represented in dotted decimal notation, with the decimal value of each octet separated by a period (for example, 138.57.7.27).

K

kernel STOP errors Errors that occur when Windows NT encounters hardware problems, inconsistencies within data necessary for its operation, or other similar errors and must stop. These errors are always displayed on a full character-mode screen rather than in a Windows-mode message box. Errors are also uniquely identified by a hexadecimal number and symbolic string.

key A folder that appears in the left pane of a Registry Editor window. A key can contain subkeys and value entries.

L

Last Known Good configuration The configuration that was saved when you last successfully logged on to the computer. Use the Last Known Good Configuration option if you change the Windows NT configuration and then have problems rebooting.

line printer daemon (LPD) A TCP/IP print service that receives print jobs from line printer remote (LPR) utilities running on client systems and submits them to the spooler.

Line Printer Remote (LPR) A protocol in the TCP/IP suite that provides the standard for transmitting TCP/IP print jobs between computers. A client running LPR can send a print job to a print spooler service on another computer running the LPD print spooler service.

LMHOSTS file A local text file that maps NetBIOS names to IP addresses.

local group account A collection of user accounts that can be granted permissions and rights only for its own workstation. However, it can contain user accounts from its own computer and (if the workstation participates in a domain) user accounts and global groups from both its own domain and from trusted domain. *See* trust relationship.

local user account Contains information that defines a user to the local computer. A user can log on to and access local resources. To access resources on another computer, the user must have a separate user account on the other computer.

M

Master Boot Record (MBR) The data structure that starts the process of booting a computer; contains the partition table for the disk and a small amount of executable code.

memory dump file A file that provides all error information to troubleshoot a kernel STOP error as if you were connected to the computer experiencing the problem.

mirror set A fully redundant or "shadow copy" of data. Mirror sets provide fault tolerance.

Multilink Protocol (MP) *see* PPP Multilink Protocol (MP)

N

NetBIOS Enhanced User Interface (NetBEUI) A small, efficient, and fast protocol designed for small LANs consisting of 20 to 200 workstations.

NetWare The Novell network operating system.

network adapter card An expansion card or other device used to connect a computer to a local area network (LAN).

network basic input/output system (NetBIOS) Windows NT networking naming convention, consisting of a single part. A NetBIOS name is created when server or workstation services initialize.

Novell Directory Services (NDS) A NetWare service that runs on NetWare servers. The service enables the location of resources on the network.

NTFS compression The NTFS file system supports automatic compression and decompression of files and folders. You can set compression attributes for a file or for a folder in which files are created.

NTFS permissions Permissions that are available only on a volume that has been formatted with the NT file system (NTFS). NTFS permissions provide a greater degree of security because they can be assigned to folders and to individual files.

NTLDR file A hidden, read-only system file that loads the operating system.

NT Virtual DOS Machine (NTVDM) A special Win32-based application that supports MS-DOS–based applications when launched on Windows NT Workstation computers.

NWLink A standard network protocol that supports routing and can support NetWare client/server applications. Provides computers running Windows NT and Windows NT Workstation with the ability to communicate with NetWare servers and clients.

P

page faults Occur when a program requests a page of code or data not in its working set (the portion of the physical memory used by a particular application). A hard page fault occurs when the requested page must be retrieved from disk. A soft page fault occurs when the requested page is found elsewhere in physical memory.

paging file A special file on a PC hard disk. With virtual memory under Windows NT, some of the program code and other information is kept in RAM while other information is temporarily swapped into virtual memory to the paging file. When that information is required again, Windows NT pulls it back into RAM and, if necessary, swaps other information to virtual memory.

parallel Handling more than one event at a time, with each event having its own portion of the system's resources.

path A sequence of directory (or folder) names that specifies the location of a directory, file, or folder within the directory tree. Each directory name and filename within the path (except the first) must be preceded by a backslash (\).

Peer Web Services (PWS) A collection of services that enable the user of a computer running Windows NT Workstation to publish a personal Web site from the desktop. The services include the World Wide Web (WWW) service, the File Transfer Protocol (FTP) service, and the Gopher service. PWS is optimized for use as a small-scale Web server suitable for exchanging information for a small department or individuals on the Internet.

permissions Rules that regulate which users can use a resource, such as a folder, file, or printer.

Phonebook entry A part of Dial-Up Networking that stores all of the settings needed to connect to a particular network.

Point-to-Point Protocol (PPP) A set of industry-standard framing and authentication protocols that is part of Windows NT RAS to ensure interoperability with third-party remote access software.

Point-to-Point Tunneling Protocol (PPTP) A new networking technology that supports multiprotocol virtual private networks (VPNs), enabling remote users to access corporate networks securely across the Internet by dialing into an Internet service provider (ISP) or by connecting directly to the Internet.

PostScript files Files that use the PostScript page-description language rules from Adobe Systems to create text and graphics.

PPP Multilink Protocol (MP) A protocol that provides the means to increase data transmission rates by allowing you to combine analog modem paths, ISDN paths, and mixed analog and digital communications links on both a client and the server computer.

preemptive multitasking A form of multitasking in which the operating system periodically interrupts the execution of a program and passes control of the system to another waiting program. Preemptive multitasking prevents any one program from monopolizing the system.

primary domain controller (PDC) In a Windows NT Server domain, the computer running Windows NT Server that authenticates domain logons and maintains the directory database for a domain. The PDC tracks changes made to accounts of all computers on a domain. It is the only computer to receive these changes directly. A domain has only one PDC.

print device In Microsoft networks, the actual hardware device that produces printed output.

print driver Software programs that enable applications to communicate fully and properly with print devices.

print job Source codes that contain both data and commands for print processing.

print monitor Controls the communication between a computer and a print device.

print server The computer that runs the printer software and receives and processes documents from clients.

print spooler A collection of dynamic-link libraries (DLLs) that receive, process, schedule, and distribute print jobs.

printer In Microsoft networks, a printer is the software interface between the operating system and print device. The printer determines how the document gets to the printing devices (for example, by means of a local port or to a remote print share) and other parameters of the printing process. A single printer can send print jobs to multiple print devices, and multiple printers can send jobs to a single print device.

printer permissions Printer permissions specify the type of access users or groups have to the printer. The printer permissions are No Access, Print, Manage Documents, and Full Control.

printer priority Printer priorities allow you to determine which documents print before others. Priorities range from 1–99, with 1 being the lowest priority (prints last) and 99 the highest (prints first).

By setting up two or more printers for the same print device, and then selecting the appropriate printer, documents can print based on time-sensitivity.

process When a program runs, a Windows NT process is created. A process is an object type that consists of an executable program, a set of virtual memory addresses, and one or more threads.

protocol Language a computer uses to communicate over a network. Computers must use the same protocol to communicate with each other.

public-switched telephone network (PSTN) A regular telephone line with worldwide availability.

R

redundant array of inexpensive disks (RAID) A method used to standardize and categorize fault-tolerant disk systems. Six levels (0 through 5) gauge various mixes of performance, reliability, and cost. Microsoft Windows NT Workstation includes only RAID level 0. Windows NT Server includes RAID levels 0, 1, and 5.

Registry A database repository for information about a computer's configuration. It is organized in a hierarchical structure and comprises subtrees and their hives, keys, and value entries.

Registry Editor A tool for viewing and editing the Registry. There are Registry Editors installed automatically with Windows NT, REGEDT32.EXE and REGEDIT.EXE.

Remote Access Service (RAS) A service that provides remote networking to telecommuters, mobile workers, and system administrators who monitor and manage servers at multiple branch offices. Users with RAS on a Windows NT–based computer can dial in to remotely access their networks for services such as file and printer sharing, electronic mail, scheduling, and SQL (structured query language) database access.

roaming mandatory user profile A preconfigured user profile that cannot be changed by the user. One mandatory profile can be assigned to many users, allowing an administrator to change multiple desktop environments at one time.

roaming personal user profile A user profile that can be changed by the user. The file is updated to include any changes made by the user when the user logs off. When the same user logs it again, the profile is loaded as it was last saved.

roaming user profile Provides a user with the same working environment, no matter which Windows NT–based computer the user logs on to. Roaming user profiles are stored centrally on a network server rather than on a local computer. There are two types of roaming user profiles: roaming mandatory user profiles and roaming personal user profiles.

router In the Windows NT environment, a router helps LANs and WANs achieve interoperability and connectivity and can link LANs that have different network topologies. Routers match packet headers to a LAN segment and choose the best path for the packet, optimizing network performance.

S

scsi() syntax Used in the BOOT.INI file to indicate that Windows NT needs to load a SCSI device driver and to use that driver to access the boot partition.

security identifier (SID) A unique number that identifies a logged-on user to the security system. SIDs can identify one user or a group of users.

serial Information transferred one bit at a time.

server-based installation A streamlined method of installation for multiple computers, achieved by copying Windows NT source files from the Windows NT compact disc to a shared folder created on the distribution server, and by connecting to the network share from the client computer and running the Setup program (WINNT or WINNT32).

service A process that performs a specific system function and often provides an application programming interface (API) for other processes to call.

Setup boot disks A series of three disks that contain a minimal version of Windows NT, under which the initial Windows NT Setup process runs.

share To make resources, such as directories and printers, available to others.

share permissions Used to restrict a shared resource's availability over the network to only certain users. You can assign share permissions to users, groups, or both.

shared directory A directory that network users can connect to.

shared resource Any device, data, or program that is used by more than one other device or program. For Windows NT, shared resources refer to any resource that is made available to network users, such as directories, files, printers, and named pipes. Also refers to a resource on a server that is available to network users.

Simple Network Management Protocol (SNMP) Used to monitor and report on the activity of network devices, including hubs, routers, printers, workstations and computers.

Small Computer System Interface (SCSI) A high-speed, parallel interface used for connecting microcomputers to peripheral devices such as hard disks, scanners, printers, and CD-ROM drives, and to other computers and local area networks.

spool file A file on disk that holds the contents of a print job.

spooling The process of writing the contents of a print job to a file on disk, called a *spool file*.

standard permissions Combinations of individual NTFS permissions that allow you to assign multiple NTFS permissions at one time.

stripe set Refers to the saving of data across identical partitions on different drives. Stripe sets do not provide fault tolerance.

subkey A key within a key. Subkeys are analogous to subdirectories in the Registry hierarchy.

subnet A portion of a network, which may be a physically independent network segment, that shares a network address with other portions of the network and is distinguished by a subnet number. A subnet is to a network what a network is to an internet.

subnet mask A 32-bit value that allows the recipient of IP packets to distinguish the network ID portion of the IP address from the host ID.

subtree During directory replication, this is the export subdirectory and all of its subdirectories.

system partition A portion of a physical disk that has the hardware-specific files needed to load Windows NT.

T

template user profile A user account that serves as a model for a profile.

text-mode setup In text-mode setup, all files required for installation are copied from the temporary directory into the installation directory on the hard disk of the target computer. After text mode setup is complete, GUI mode begins.

thread The smallest object within a process that runs program instructions.

throughput A measure of the data transfer rate through a typically complex communications system or of the data processing rate in a computer system.

thunk In WOW, the process of translating 16-bit calls into 32-bit calls and vice versa.

Transmission Control Protocol/Internet Protocol (TCP/IP) A suite of networking protocols that provide communications across interconnected networks made up of computers with diverse hardware architectures and various operating systems, including the Internet. TCP/IP includes standards for how computers communicate and conventions for connecting networks and routing traffic.

trap messages Messages generated by the SNMP agent program to notify an SNMP management console of changes such as system startup, shutdown, or password violation.

triple-boot computer A computer that can boot three different operating systems, with the choice of operating system to be made during system startup.

trust relationship A link between domains that enables pass-through authentication, in which a trusting domain honors the logon authentications of a trusted domain.

U

unattended installation A way of installing Windows NT Workstation on a computer from the server automatically, without logging on to the computer.

Uniform Resource Locator (URL) An address that uniquely identifies the location of a computer, directory, or file on the Internet.

Uninterruptible Power Supply (UPS) A battery-operated power supply connected to a computer to keep the system running during a power failure.

uniqueness database file In an unattended installation, UDFs work along with the answer file to provide replacements for sections of the answer file or supply additional sections. These replacement or additional sections are necessary when information (such as the computer name) must be unique to each computer.

uniqueness IDs Items specified and mapped to sections in the UDF. If a uniqueness ID is specified, values specified in the sections associated with that uniqueness ID override the values in sections in the answer file that have the same section names. A UDF can have multiple uniqueness IDs, each specifying a slightly different configuration. For example, you can have a uniqueness ID that specifies a computer name for each computer in your organization and have all those uniqueness IDs contained in one UDF.

universal naming convention (UNC) name A full Windows NT name of a resource on a network, conforming to the *SERVER_NAME\SHARE_NAME* syntax where *SERVER NAME* is the server's name, and *SHARE NAME* is the name of the shared resource.

user profile Contains all user-definable settings for the work environment of a computer running Windows NT Workstation, including Display, Regional, Mouse, Sounds settings, Network connections, and Printer connections.

user rights Rules that regulate which users can perform certain tasks on the system, such as creating a user account, logging on to the local computer, or shutting down a server.

V

volume set A combination of partitions on multiple physical disks that appear as one logical drive. Volume sets do not provide fault tolerance.

W

warning message Messages advising you to take an action that enables the kernel to keep running the process or thread. Or, messages warning you that although the process or thread continues to run, the results may not be correct.

wide area network (WAN) A communications network that connects geographically separated areas.

Win16 on Win32 (WOW) Allows Win16-based applications to run in a Win32 environment.

Windows Internet Naming Service (WINS) A name resolution service that resolves Windows networking computer names to IP addresses in a routed environment.

WINNT command Used to install Windows NT Workstation on a computer running a 16-bit Windows operating system, such as MS-DOS, Windows 3.1, Windows for Workgroups 3.1, or Windows 95.

WINNT32 command Used to upgrade from an earlier version of Windows NT Workstation.

workgroup A collection of computers that are grouped for viewing purposes. A workgroup is often referred to as a *peer-to-peer network* because all computers share files and printers as equals, or *peers*.

working set The portion of physical memory that a running program can use, as assigned by the operating system. When a process needs code or data that is not in its working set, a page fault occurs, and the Virtual Memory Manager adds the new pages to the working set. When memory is plentiful, more pages are added and working sets are larger. When memory is scarce, fewer pages are added and working sets are smaller.

World Wide Web service Based on HTTP protocol, which allows you to link to and navigate Web documents and applications.

Index

S

http://mspress.microsoft.com/reslink/

Look beyond the kits!

If you deploy, manage, or support Microsoft® products and technologies, here's a hot link to the hottest IT resources available—http://mspress.microsoft.com/reslink/. Microsoft Press® ResourceLink is an essential online information resource for IT professionals—the most complete source of technical information about Microsoft technologies available anywhere. Tap into ResourceLink for direct access to the latest technical updates, tools, and utilities—straight from Microsoft—and help maximize the productivity of your IT investment.

For a **complimentary 30-day trial CD** packed with Microsoft Press IT products, order via our Web site at http://mspress.microsoft.com/reslink/.

Microsoft Press

Real world training.
Real world productivity.

Gain work-ready expertise—and prepare for the Microsoft Certified Professional (MCP) exams—with self-paced training kits from Microsoft Press. Built with Microsoft Official Curriculum, these kits provide modular, self-paced lessons and hands-on labs to help you plan, manage, and optimize Microsoft Windows and BackOffice® technologies. Build real-world systems skills and increase your productivity with MCP training kits from Microsoft Press!

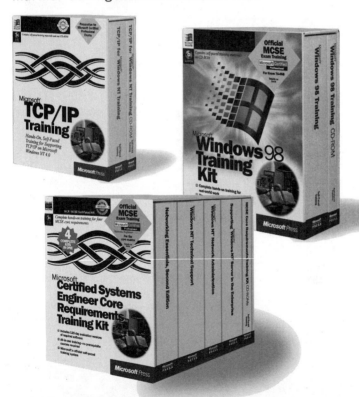

Microsoft® Windows NT® Server 4.0 Enterprise Technologies Training, Deluxe Multimedia Edition
ISBN 1-57231-829-5, U.S.A. $199.99, U.K. £187.99 [V.A.T. included], Canada $289.99

Networking Essentials, Second Edition
ISBN 1-57231-527-X, U.S.A. $99.99, U.K. £93.99 [V.A.T. included], Canada $140.99

Microsoft TCP/IP Training
ISBN 1-57231-623-3, U.S.A. $99.99, U.K. £92.99 [V.A.T. included], Canada $140.99

Microsoft Certified Systems Engineer Core Requirements Training Kit
ISBN 1-57231-905-4, U.S.A. $299.99, U.K. £249.99 [V.A.T. included], Canada $434.99

Microsoft Certified Professional + Internet Training Kit
ISBN 1-57231-906-2, U.S.A. $299.99, U.K. £249.99 [V.A.T. included], Canada $434.99

Microsoft SNA Server Training Kit
ISBN 1-57231-932-1, U.S.A. $149.99, U.K. £140.99 [V.A.T. included], Canada $217.99

Microsoft Windows® 98 Training Kit
ISBN 1-57231-730-2, U.S.A. $99.99, U.K. £93.99 [V.A.T. included], Canada $144.99

Microsoft Press® products are available worldwide wherever quality computer books are sold. For more information, contact your book or computer retailer, software reseller, or local Microsoft Sales Office, or visit our Web site at mspress.microsoft.com. To locate your nearest source for Microsoft Press products, or to order directly, call 1-800-MSPRESS in the U.S. (in Canada, call 1-800-268-2222).

Prices and availability dates are subject to change.

Microsoft®_Press_

Inside *info.*
On-the-job *results.*

Like the technologies they support, the solutions packed into these best selling Resource Kits come straight from the source—Microsoft. These powerhouse references deliver thousands of insider tips and strategies, plus exclusive tools, utilities, and accessory software on CD-ROM—all designed to help maximize your productivity with Microsoft Windows and BackOffice systems.

Microsoft® Windows® 98 Resource Kit
ISBN 1-57231-644-6, U.S.A. $69.99, U.K. £64.99 [V.A.T. included], Canada $100.99

Microsoft Internet Explorer Resource Kit
ISBN 1-57231-842-2, U.S.A. $49.99, U.K. £46.99 [V.A.T. included], Canada $71.99

Microsoft BackOffice® Resource Kit, Second Edition
ISBN 1-57231-632-2, U.S.A. $199.99, U.K. £187.99 [V.A.T. included], Canada $289.99

Microsoft Windows NT® Server 4.0 Resource Kit
ISBN 1-57231-344-7, U.S.A. $149.95, U.K. £140.99 [V.A.T. included], Canada $199.95

Microsoft Windows NT Workstation 4.0 Resource Kit
ISBN 1-57231-343-9, U.S.A. $69.95, U.K. £64.99 [V.A.T. included], Canada $94.95

Microsoft Internet Information Server Resource Kit
ISBN 1-57231-638-1, U.S.A. $49.99, U.K. £46.99 [V.A.T. included], Canada $71.99

Microsoft *Press*

Microsoft Press has titles to help everyone— from new users to seasoned developers—

Step by Step Series
Self-paced tutorials for
classroom instruction or
individualized study

Starts Here™ Series
Interactive instruction
on CD-ROM that helps
students learn by doing

Field Guide Series
Concise, task-oriented
A–Z references for
quick, easy answers—
anywhere

Official Series
Timely books on a wide
variety of Internet topics
geared for advanced
users

All User Training   All User Reference

Quick Course® Series
Fast, to-the-point
instruction for new users

At a Glance Series
Quick visual guides for
task-oriented instruction

Running Series
A comprehensive
curriculum alternative to
standard documentation
books

start faster
and go farther!

The wide selection of books and CD-ROMs published by Microsoft Press contain something for every level of user and every area of interest, from just-in-time online training tools to development tools for professional programmers. Look for them at your bookstore or computer store today!

Professional Select Editions Series
Advanced titles geared for the system administrator or technical support career path

Microsoft® Certified Professional Training
The Microsoft Official Curriculum for certification exams

Best Practices Series
Candid accounts of the new movement in software development

Microsoft Programming Series
The foundations of software development

Professional   Developers

Microsoft Press® Interactive
Integrated multimedia courseware for all levels

Strategic Technology Series
Easy-to-read overviews for decision makers

Microsoft Professional Editions
Technical information straight from the source

Solution Developer Series
Comprehensive titles for intermediate to advanced developers

Microsoft Press

mspress.microsoft.com

mspress.microsoft.com

Microsoft Press Online is your road map to the best available print and multimedia materials—resources that will help you maximize the effectiveness of Microsoft® software products. Our goal is making it easy and convenient for you to find exactly the Microsoft Press® book or interactive product you need, as well as bringing you the latest in training and certification materials from Microsoft Press.

Where do you want to go today?®

MICROSOFT LICENSE AGREEMENT

(Book Companion CD)

IMPORTANT—READ CAREFULLY: This Microsoft End-User License Agreement ("EULA") is a legal agreement between you (either an individual or an entity) and Microsoft Corporation for the Microsoft product identified above, which includes computer software and may include associated media, printed materials, and "on-line" or electronic documentation ("SOFTWARE PRODUCT"). Any component included within the SOFTWARE PRODUCT that is accompanied by a separate End-User License Agreement shall be governed by such agreement and not the terms set forth below. By installing, copying, or otherwise using the SOFTWARE PRODUCT, you agree to be bound by the terms of this EULA. If you do not agree to the terms of this EULA, you are not authorized to install, copy, or otherwise use the SOFTWARE PRODUCT; you may, however, return the SOFTWARE PRODUCT, along with all printed materials and other items that form a part of the Microsoft product that includes the SOFTWARE PRODUCT, to the place you obtained them for a full refund.

SOFTWARE PRODUCT LICENSE

The SOFTWARE PRODUCT is protected by United States copyright laws and international copyright treaties, as well as other intellectual property laws and treaties. The SOFTWARE PRODUCT is licensed, not sold.

1. GRANT OF LICENSE. This EULA grants you the following rights:

  a. Software Product. You may install and use one copy of the SOFTWARE PRODUCT on a single computer. The primary user of the computer on which the SOFTWARE PRODUCT is installed may make a second copy for his or her exclusive use on a portable computer.

  b. Storage/Network Use. You may also store or install a copy of the SOFTWARE PRODUCT on a storage device, such as a network server, used only to install or run the SOFTWARE PRODUCT on your other computers over an internal network; however, you must acquire and dedicate a license for each separate computer on which the SOFTWARE PRODUCT is installed or run from the storage device. A license for the SOFTWARE PRODUCT may not be shared or used concurrently on different computers.

  c. License Pak. If you have acquired this EULA in a Microsoft License Pak, you may make the number of additional copies of the computer software portion of the SOFTWARE PRODUCT authorized on the printed copy of this EULA, and you may use each copy in the manner specified above. You are also entitled to make a corresponding number of secondary copies for portable computer use as specified above.

  d. Sample Code. Solely with respect to portions, if any, of the SOFTWARE PRODUCT that are identified within the SOFTWARE PRODUCT as sample code (the "SAMPLE CODE"):

    i. Use and Modification. Microsoft grants you the right to use and modify the source code version of the SAMPLE CODE, *provided* you comply with subsection (d)(iii) below. You may not distribute the SAMPLE CODE, or any modified version of the SAMPLE CODE, in source code form.

    ii. Redistributable Files. Provided you comply with subsection (d)(iii) below, Microsoft grants you a nonexclusive, royalty-free right to reproduce and distribute the object code version of the SAMPLE CODE and of any modified SAMPLE CODE, other than SAMPLE CODE (or any modified version thereof) designated as not redistributable in the Readme file that forms a part of the SOFTWARE PRODUCT (the "Non-Redistributable Sample Code"). All SAMPLE CODE other than the Non-Redistributable Sample Code is collectively referred to as the "REDISTRIBUTABLES."

    iii. Redistribution Requirements. If you redistribute the REDISTRIBUTABLES, you agree to: (i) distribute the REDISTRIBUTABLES in object code form only in conjunction with and as a part of your software application product; (ii) not use Microsoft's name, logo, or trademarks to market your software application product; (iii) include a valid copyright notice on your software application product; (iv) indemnify, hold harmless, and defend Microsoft from and against any claims or lawsuits, including attorney's fees, that arise or result from the use or distribution of your software application product; and (v) not permit further distribution of the REDISTRIBUTABLES by your end user. Contact Microsoft for the applicable royalties due and other licensing terms for all other uses and/or distribution of the REDISTRIBUTABLES.

2. DESCRIPTION OF OTHER RIGHTS AND LIMITATIONS.

- **Limitations on Reverse Engineering, Decompilation, and Disassembly.** You may not reverse engineer, decompile, or disassemble the SOFTWARE PRODUCT, except and only to the extent that such activity is expressly permitted by applicable law notwithstanding this limitation.

- **Separation of Components.** The SOFTWARE PRODUCT is licensed as a single product. Its component parts may not be separated for use on more than one computer.

- **Rental.** You may not rent, lease, or lend the SOFTWARE PRODUCT.

- **Support Services.** Microsoft may, but is not obligated to, provide you with support services related to the SOFTWARE PRODUCT ("Support Services"). Use of Support Services is governed by the Microsoft policies and programs described in the user manual, in "on-line" documentation, and/or in other Microsoft-provided materials. Any supplemental software code provided to you as part of the Support Services shall be considered part of the SOFTWARE PRODUCT and subject to the terms and conditions of this EULA. With respect to technical information you provide to Microsoft as part of the Support Services, Microsoft may use such information for its business purposes, including for product support and development. Microsoft will not utilize such technical information in a form that personally identifies you.

- **Software Transfer.** You may permanently transfer all of your rights under this EULA, provided you retain no copies, you transfer all of the SOFTWARE PRODUCT (including all component parts, the media and printed materials, any upgrades, this EULA, and, if applicable, the Certificate of Authenticity), **and** the recipient agrees to the terms of this EULA.

- **Termination.** Without prejudice to any other rights, Microsoft may terminate this EULA if you fail to comply with the terms and conditions of this EULA. In such event, you must destroy all copies of the SOFTWARE PRODUCT and all of its component parts.

3. **COPYRIGHT.** All title and copyrights in and to the SOFTWARE PRODUCT (including but not limited to any images, photographs, animations, video, audio, music, text, SAMPLE CODE, REDISTRIBUTABLES, and "applets" incorporated into the SOFTWARE PRODUCT) and any copies of the SOFTWARE PRODUCT are owned by Microsoft or its suppliers. The SOFTWARE PRODUCT is protected by copyright laws and international treaty provisions. Therefore, you must treat the SOFTWARE PRODUCT like any other copyrighted material **except** that you may install the SOFTWARE PRODUCT on a single computer provided you keep the original solely for backup or archival purposes. You may not copy the printed materials accompanying the SOFTWARE PRODUCT.

4. **U.S. GOVERNMENT RESTRICTED RIGHTS.** The SOFTWARE PRODUCT and documentation are provided with RESTRICTED RIGHTS. Use, duplication, or disclosure by the Government is subject to restrictions as set forth in subparagraph (c)(1)(ii) of the Rights in Technical Data and Computer Software clause at DFARS 252.227-7013 or subparagraphs (c)(1) and (2) of the Commercial Computer Software—Restricted Rights at 48 CFR 52.227-19, as applicable. Manufacturer is Microsoft Corporation/One Microsoft Way/Redmond, WA 98052-6399.

5. **EXPORT RESTRICTIONS.** You agree that you will not export or re-export the SOFTWARE PRODUCT, any part thereof, or any process or service that is the direct product of the SOFTWARE PRODUCT (the foregoing collectively referred to as the "Restricted Components"), to any country, person, entity, or end user subject to U.S. export restrictions. You specifically agree not to export or re-export any of the Restricted Components (i) to any country to which the U.S. has embargoed or restricted the export of goods or services, which currently include, but are not necessarily limited to, Cuba, Iran, Iraq, Libya, North Korea, Sudan, and Syria, or to any national of any such country, wherever located, who intends to transmit or transport the Restricted Components back to such country; (ii) to any end user who you know or have reason to know will utilize the Restricted Components in the design, development, or production of nuclear, chemical, or biological weapons; or (iii) to any end user who has been prohibited from participating in U.S. export transactions by any federal agency of the U.S. government. You warrant and represent that neither the BXA nor any other U.S. federal agency has suspended, revoked, or denied your export privileges.

DISCLAIMER OF WARRANTY

NO WARRANTIES OR CONDITIONS. MICROSOFT EXPRESSLY DISCLAIMS ANY WARRANTY OR CONDITION FOR THE SOFTWARE PRODUCT. THE SOFTWARE PRODUCT AND ANY RELATED DOCUMENTATION IS PROVIDED "AS IS" WITHOUT WARRANTY OR CONDITION OF ANY KIND, EITHER EXPRESS OR IMPLIED, INCLUDING, WITHOUT LIMITATION, THE IMPLIED WARRANTIES OF MERCHANTABILITY, FITNESS FOR A PARTICULAR PURPOSE, OR NONINFRINGEMENT. THE ENTIRE RISK ARISING OUT OF USE OR PERFORMANCE OF THE SOFTWARE PRODUCT REMAINS WITH YOU.

LIMITATION OF LIABILITY. TO THE MAXIMUM EXTENT PERMITTED BY APPLICABLE LAW, IN NO EVENT SHALL MICROSOFT OR ITS SUPPLIERS BE LIABLE FOR ANY SPECIAL, INCIDENTAL, INDIRECT, OR CONSEQUENTIAL DAMAGES WHATSOEVER (INCLUDING, WITHOUT LIMITATION, DAMAGES FOR LOSS OF BUSINESS PROFITS, BUSINESS INTERRUPTION, LOSS OF BUSINESS INFORMATION, OR ANY OTHER PECUNIARY LOSS) ARISING OUT OF THE USE OF OR INABILITY TO USE THE SOFTWARE PRODUCT OR THE PROVISION OF OR FAILURE TO PROVIDE SUPPORT SERVICES, EVEN IF MICROSOFT HAS BEEN ADVISED OF THE POSSIBILITY OF SUCH DAMAGES. IN ANY CASE, MICROSOFT'S ENTIRE LIABILITY UNDER ANY PROVISION OF THIS EULA SHALL BE LIMITED TO THE GREATER OF THE AMOUNT ACTUALLY PAID BY YOU FOR THE SOFTWARE PRODUCT OR US$5.00; PROVIDED, HOWEVER, IF YOU HAVE ENTERED INTO A MICROSOFT SUPPORT SERVICES AGREEMENT, MICROSOFT'S ENTIRE LIABILITY REGARDING SUPPORT SERVICES SHALL BE GOVERNED BY THE TERMS OF THAT AGREEMENT. BECAUSE SOME STATES AND JURISDICTIONS DO NOT ALLOW THE EXCLUSION OR LIMITATION OF LIABILITY, THE ABOVE LIMITATION MAY NOT APPLY TO YOU.

MISCELLANEOUS

This EULA is governed by the laws of the State of Washington USA, except and only to the extent that applicable law mandates governing law of a different jurisdiction.

Should you have any questions concerning this EULA, or if you desire to contact Microsoft for any reason, please contact the Microsoft subsidiary serving your country, or write: Microsoft Sales Information Center/One Microsoft Way/Redmond, WA 98052-6399.

Register Today!

Return this
*MCSE Readiness Review—Exam 70-073:
Microsoft® Windows NT® Workstation 4.0*
registration card today

Microsoft®*Press*

mspress.microsoft.com

OWNER REGISTRATION CARD   0-7356-0537-8

MCSE READINESS REVIEW—EXAM 70-073: MICROSOFT® WINDOWS NT® WORKSTATION 4.0

_____   _____   _____
FIRST NAME   MIDDLE INITIAL   LAST NAME

_____
INSTITUTION OR COMPANY NAME

_____
ADDRESS

_____

_____   _____   _____
CITY   STATE   ZIP

_____   ( )_____
E-MAIL ADDRESS   PHONE NUMBER

U.S. and Canada addresses only. Fill in information above and mail postage-free.
Please mail only the bottom half of this page.

start faster **go** farther

For information about Microsoft Press®

products, visit our Web site at

mspress.microsoft.com

Microsoft Press